The Archive
of Loss

Maura Finkelstein

The Archive of Loss

LIVELY RUINATION
IN MILL LAND MUMBAI

Duke University Press   *Durham & London*   2019

Designed by Courtney Leigh Baker and typeset in
Minion Pro and Courier by Tseng Information Systems, Inc.

Library of Congress Cataloging-in-Publication Data Names:
Finkelstein, Maura, author.
Title: The archive of loss : lively ruination in
mill land Mumbai / Maura Finkelstein.
Description: Durham : Duke University Press, 2019. |
Includes bibliographical references and index.
Identifiers: LCCN 2018044274 (print)
LCCN 2018056887 (ebook)
ISBN 9781478004608 (ebook)
ISBN 9781478003687 (hardcover)
ISBN 9781478003984 (pbk.)
Subjects: LCSH: Textile industry—India—Mumbai—History.
| Textile workers—Housing—India—Mumbai. |
Architecture, Domestic—India—Mumbai. |
Tenement Houses—India—Mumbai.
Classification: LCC HD7287.6.I42 (ebook) |
LCC HD7287.6.I42 M86 2019 (print) |
DDC 338.4/767700954792—dc 23
LC record available at https://lccn.loc.gov/2018044274

COVER ART: Digbijayee Khatua, *Locating Past and Present.*
Detail. 2015. 60 × 66 inches. Courtesy of the artist.

Contents

Acknowledgments

This book is the product of a decade of learning to stumble with grace. Of learning to see, of learning to pay attention. Of practicing patience and being quiet enough to hear the whispers. Such an undertaking was certainly not tackled alone. I am grateful to all those who have helped me to learn these lessons.

I was lucky enough to grow up as a scholar in a supportive and brilliant family: at Stanford University and the University of California, Berkeley, I was lucky enough to find mentorship from Paulla Ebron, Lawrence Cohen, Thomas Blom Hansen, Barbara Voss, and Sylvia Yanagisako. I also found a home among the support, engagement, and care of Tania Ahmed, Lalaie Ameeriar, Nikhil Anand, Jonathan Shapiro Anjaria, Ulka Shapiro Anjaria, Hannah Appel, Elif Babül, Melanie Abrams Chandra, Vikram Chandra, William Elison, Anastasia Kayatios, Tomas Matza, Ramah McKay, Ana Minian, Robert Samet, Max Strassfeld, Rania K. Sweis, Zohar Weiman-Kelman, and Austin Zeiderman.

My research in India was supported by the American Institute of Indian Studies and the Stanford University anthropology department. Follow-up research on the book was funded by Muhlenberg College, both through the Provost's Office and through Faculty Development Grants. Kaveri Dadhich was friend, partner, research assistant, and interpreter — once in the city, I would only have wandered in circles without you.

In Bombay I was lucky enough to find a community that fed my heart and made the city into a second home over the past decade. Vikram Doctor, Kaveri Dadhich, PK Das, Sabina Gulati, Alok Gupta, Anurag Kanoria, Finn Lewis, Shalini Mahajan, Meena Menon, Chayanika Shah, and Simran Singh: thank you for opening up your worlds to me. In particular, Kabi Sherman and Neera Adarkar became my closest friends and greatest source of inspiration. Their love for and knowledge of Bombay infused my own encounters, and their generosity and wisdom helped me find my footing and learn how to see what was not immediately obvious to my naive and untrained eyes.

I am a writer before I am anything else. My writing teachers, Faith Adiele, Steve Almond, Samantha Dunn, Pam Houston, and Cheryl Strayed, reminded me that my voice is as important as my research. That the structure of language is just as important as the theory that structures my arguments. Renee Gladman's world of Ravicka helped me remember these lessons and reminded me of why and how I think about space, of material structures, of the feeling of being in a built world. Thank you for writing and drawing worlds that activated mine. Thank you to Sharmistha Ray, who turned my mapping-words into the stunning visual maps that appear in this book—it has been thrilling to think/see with you.

At Muhlenberg College I have found friendship, inspiration, and support with an incredible group of colleagues: thank you to Aggie Ebrahimi Bazaz, Irene Chien, Beth Corzo-Duchardt, Veronica Corzo-Duchardt (guilt by association!), Dawn Lonsinger, Roberta Meek, Ranajoy Ray-Chaudhuri, Robin Riley-Casey, Sahar Sadeghi, Danielle Porter Sanchez, and Frederick Charles Staidum Jr. (missed but still held close after your migration). I extend my awe and appreciation to the students of my fall 2017 ethnographic methods seminar, who read my draft introduction and generously told me it was "the clearest you've ever been": Samantha Brown, Michaela Feinberg, Kalie Jamieson, Brock Juliano, Rachel Koerwer, and Emma Shavrick. Thank you to Janine Chi for helping me carve out space to write among a culture of busyness and Ben Carter and Casey Miller for tolerating my disappearances with compassion and good humor. Thank you to Lora Taub-Pervizpour for collaboration, embodied feminist politics, radical pedagogy, and general badass-ness: I am eternally grateful for your mentorship and friendship.

This book came into being through years of generous thoughts, feedback, and questions from numerous friends and colleagues. In particular, thank you to Naisargi Dave, Paulla Ebron, Thomas Blom Hansen, Jennifer Harford Vargas, Mythri Jegathesan Naveeda Khan, William Mazzarella, Marcia Morgan, Shakthi Nataraj, Ramnarayan Rawat, Christopher Roebuck, Harris Solomon, Mathangi Subramanian, Sharika Thiranagama, and Barbara Voss: your fingerprints are all over this book. Thank you for helping me to think and to write, and for carefully handling/pushing at the delicate edges of my obsessions. It continues to be an honor to share space and thoughts with you.

Audiences at the annual conferences of the American Anthropological Association and the American Ethnological Society; the annual conference on South Asia in Madison, Wisconsin; the Center for the Advanced Study of India at the University of Pennsylvania; and the "Inhabiting the Past" workshop at the University of Chicago provided critical space and feedback while I worked through my understanding of the ethnographic archive. Portions of chapter 1 appeared in "Landscapes of Invisibility: Anachronistic Subjects and Allochronous Spaces in Mill Land Mumbai," *City and Society* 27, no. 3 (2015): 250–271. Versions and portions of chapter 3 appeared in "The Chronotope of the Chawls: A Ghost Story in Three Acts," in *Galleries of Life: The Chawls of Mumbai*, ed. Neera Adarkar (Delhi: ImprintOne, 2011), 49–57, and "Ghosts in the Gallery: The Vitality of Anachronism in a Mumbai Chawl," *Anthropological Quarterly* 91, no. 3 (2018): 936–966. I am grateful to the editors, reviewers, and readers at Duke University Press for helping this manuscript take shape. In particular, a thousand thank-yous to Elizabeth Ault, who saw a book in the chaos of my thoughts years before I could ever imagine such a thing coming to be in the world. Thank you for your support, your encouragement, your patience, and your feedback. My endless appreciation to the two anonymous readers whose care and critique helped this manuscript become the book I wanted, I *had*, to write: I can't imagine two more engaged and generous readers.

A lifetime of gratitude to Brinda Adhikari, who helped me find India, and to Gautam and Rita Adhikari, who helped me find Bombay and its mill lands. My family—Esther, Nat, Mike, Hilary, Zach, and Maia Finkelstein—provided the numerous means of support necessary to connect to curiosity, explore the world, wander, and always find a home base waiting and welcoming. Without you I wouldn't have had a foundation from which to throw myself into the precarity of academia. Thank you for holding space for me and for providing support to me while I floundered through the emotional insecurities of graduate school and the material insecurities of contingency. Thank you for being my anchor in these unruly seas and for tolerating me (and still loving me) when my language began to sound a bit too much like the pretentious thesaurus that made a home in my brain.

Finally, I dedicate this book to the Dhanraj workforce, past, present and future. In particular, to the workers I call Sushila, Manda, Raj, Sudarshan, and Kishan: thank you for showing me how you have made a home in the world. I am forever grateful for your friendship, for your stories, and for your sense of humor in the shadows of a rapidly changing and increasingly alienating future. You have taught me so much about what it means to inhabit a world, a life, a shifting landscape that—even among the falling rocks and treacherous footing—still provides some solid ground. This book and the last decade of my life are only possible because of you.

A Note on *Intimate Geographies*

India, the country of my birth, has been a long-standing obsession of mine. Even though the greater portion of my life has been spent outside of its borders, it has never ceased to be a figment of fantasy, a place of epic proportions beyond facts. I had the privilege of returning to the country—living in Calcutta briefly, and then Bombay—between 2006 and 2017. It was a time that yielded a much sought after intimacy with a culture, with a place. For a self-proclaimed nomad, the time spent there meant a great deal to me. As an artist, it is the firmament upon which I stand.

The four hand-drawn illustrations in this book were specially commissioned by Maura Finkelstein. I am grateful to her for giving me free rein to interpret the four maps of India, the states of Uttar Pradesh/Bihar and Maharashtra, and the city of Bombay. Central Bombay, where much of the author's research takes place, was also the location of my most recent solo exhibition. I worked within the compound of the old textile mill central to this monograph, in one of the magnificent crumbling rooms, to produce many of the works. I can still smell the mold and visualize the old, crackling walls.

These drawings are an assimilation of my lived experience. Although I referenced nineteenth-century anatomical illustrations, I fancy the resulting marks as resembling a form of hieroglyphics. I wanted to internalize what India means to me and, undoubtedly, what it means to all those who labor for love in forgotten spaces. These are maps that reimagine political maps as the body turned inside out.

The personal is political—if you will.

—Sharmistha Ray   *New York*   April 2018

The Archive
of Industrial Debris

Memory is not an instrument for surveying the past but its theater. It is the medium of past experience [*Medium des Erlebten*], just as the earth is the medium in which dead cities lie buried. He who seeks to approach his own buried past must conduct himself like a man digging.—WALTER BENJAMIN, "Excavation and Memory," 1932 (in *Selected Writings*, 2005)

What is a ruin, after all? It is a human construction abandoned to nature, and one of the allures of ruins in the city is that of wilderness: a place full of the promise of the unknown with all its epiphanies and dangers. Cities are built by men (and to a lesser extent, women), but they decay by nature, from earthquakes and hurricanes to the incremental processes of rot, erosion, rust, the microbial breakdown of concrete, stone, wood, and brick, the return of plants and animals making their own complex order that further dismantles the simple order of men.—REBECCA SOLNIT, *A Field Guide to Getting Lost*, 2005

I have been digging: both through memory and through ruins. This digging is a practice of time travel, and it moves me between two overlapping habitations of the present. When I stand at the gate of Dhanraj Spinning and Weaving, Ltd., one of the last privately owned textile mills operating in Mumbai, I feel an eerie sense of disconnect. Along Ambedkar Road, under the flyover (overpass) construction, thick with the ringing and honking of traffic, I am in the urban present. Here, the air is heavy with smog, and the streets smell of exhaust and frying oil from the *dhabas* (roadside restau-

FIGURE I.1. The gate to Dhanraj Spinning and Weaving, Ltd.

rants) and chai stalls. People rush by on their way to work. Others move slowly as they carry heavy burdens on tired legs. A double-decker bus swings by and slows down; masses of people jump off and leap on. There is ongoing motion and a sense of urgency on the street.

But as I cross through the gate of Dhanraj, the world begins to shift. Chandan, the elderly North Indian security guard, smiles at me with recognition and waves me across this threshold between worlds. I walk down a dirt lane flanked by tall, crumbling stone walls. Vines push through the gaps that reveal a barren field to one side and a mill chimney to the other. It is quiet on this side of the gate. The traffic is muffled, and the airy corridor carries a cool breeze. This is one of the few places in the city where I walk alone on a road, save an occasional truck that rumbles through and reminds me that I am in a bustling city. I hear birds and, in the distance, the ducks that live by the small pond behind the main compound. When I draw near to the mill building, even the sun cannot penetrate the shady pathway, and I move into shadows. The canteen beside the entrance is serving chai, and several men I know sit on the wood benches by the door, resting their sweaty backs. They nod at me and I wave back: Raj, Dilip, Bhalchand, and

FIGURE I.2. The Dhanraj ducks on the lane inside the mill compound.

Sudarshan. It's almost time for their shift to start: a shift at a functional textile mill in a city without functioning textile mills. They put down their cups and join me as we head up to the second floor, where the machines live. I can smell cool dirt and damp wood and old stone. I can hear the rumbling of machines above me and I climb the stairs in semidarkness. The noise draws me closer and closer as it becomes louder and louder . . .

I know this place now, but it took years before I encountered Dhanraj. I was not looking for enlivened spaces or for spaces of productivity: I was only looking for spaces of abandoned ruination, and those stories of abandoned ruination were everywhere. Down the road from Dhanraj, off the main thoroughfare of Ambedkar Road, sits the Dr. Bhau Daji Lad Mumbai City Museum, Mumbai's oldest museum. Built in 1872, it is a museum of the city: a grand colonial structure now dedicated to the history, culture, and art of Mumbai. Early into my fieldwork, in December 2008, Partners for Urban Knowledge, Action and Research (PUKAR, a word that also means "to call out") opens an exhibit at the City Museum entitled *Girangaon—Kal, Aaj Aur Kal* (*Yesterday, Today and Tomorrow*).[1] Part of the project involves providing cameras for the children of former

FIGURE I.3. The Dr. Bhau Daji Lad Mumbai City Museum.
Photograph by Kabi Sherman.

textile mill workers — "Barefoot Researchers" — and asking them to document the central city neighborhoods they grew up in. The first time I wander through the second-floor exhibit, traces of the British Raj all around me, I marvel at the stories and pictures of loss and absence: the former industrial city, the mill land that once was, the *chawls* (tenement buildings) being torn down. The only way this exhibit can see the mill lands is as abandoned and already dead.

I walk through this exhibit feeling confused and disoriented. I was just in Dhanraj a few hours before. I was just with the workers while they ran the old machines. I just watched as they spun thread out of raw cotton. Only yesterday I sat with Manda in her chawl unit down the road and sipped chai while she told me her stories. Yet, the exhibit does not account for these pockets of productivity and vitality still scattered throughout the central city. These spaces are of the same city and of the same time: How can I reconcile the narratives displayed in the museum space and the experiences of Dhanraj workers down the street? Inside this exhibit I lose all sense of time.[2]

There is no doubt that Central Mumbai is currently undergoing de-industrialization and massive redevelopment. These are not new urban phenomena; however, while industrial decline is undoubtedly occurring at a rapid rate, low-level production continues, even as the contributions and concerns of these laborers are largely unseen by most urban residents. This book, then, emerges from an ethnographic puzzle: when I arrive in Mumbai I am told that there are no mills operating or workers working in the low-lying industrial buildings scattered through Central Mumbai's mill land neighborhoods. However, once I find Dhanraj, I also encounter a small and unrecognized community of mill workers who continue to work within Mumbai's semiformal industrial sector. The mill lands are characterized as completely abandoned because spaces like the PUKAR exhibit display only death and absence. Because of the seamlessness of these narrative spaces, the remaining mills are omitted from the many discussions and accounts of the city. This book asks what it means to be an active worker in an industry that is understood to be defunct. How do Dhanraj workers understand their identities as industrial workers in a "postindustrial" landscape? And what is achieved by denying the presence and continuing productivity of the lively ruin of Dhanraj?

The workers of Dhanraj answer these questions for me every day. Manda tells me how it feels to stand on her feet all day for years, winding thread the city believes is no longer produced in Mumbai. Sushila lays out her aches and pains, the accumulations of a lifetime of industrial bodily breakdown. Raj explains the mysterious negotiations between mill owners and union representatives—secretive meetings to determine the future of a city in flux. Sudarshan shows me how he balances mill work during the day and taxi driving at night—precarious, informal labor supplementing the once steady, now disappearing, future he bought into four decades ago. Kishan reveals how ethnicity-based tension, infusing city identity and politics, operates on the micro level of the mill. Through their storytelling, my Dhanraj informants remind me (and perhaps themselves) of the liveliness existing within spaces of perceived ruination.

Where do these stories live? I argue throughout this book that the mill land neighborhoods of Central Mumbai are an ethnographic archive of the city: a semipublic space of documents, artifacts, and stories, held by the workers inhabiting these still-breathing but slowly decaying spaces.[3] An enlivened archival space that is "more fractious than cumulative, more a space of catachresis than catharsis" (Arondekar 2009, 171). I am not the first ethnographer to invoke a concept usually reserved for historical work.[4] In utilizing "the archive," however, I am not attempting to organize and understand paper documents that sit outside a structured and curated space. Instead, I am seeking to expand the form of the archive in order to access an orientation of knowledge that has been disappeared or overlooked. Or, to borrow from the historian Antoinette Burton, I understand "archive" to be both discourse and reality, and I follow her call to read archives "ethnographically" (2003, 27). In following such a call, I push against it, as well: before I can read archives ethnographically, I must construct them ethnographically.

When the archive becomes a form of methodology, contemporary trends and phenomena emerge through alternative prisms. Central Mumbai may appear as a city in transition—the industrial making way for the postindustrial. However, through the ethnographic archive, the temporality of lively ruins pushes me to consider how the industrial still remains in the postindustrial. This is not a story of infrastructural shift; this is instead a story of embodied time and place. When we encounter global cities only through structural trends, we miss the liveliness of living *in* the global city. This book is an intervention and a challenge to this zoomed-out urban narrative: the challenge is to become lost in the city, lost in the experience of loss, and lost in the lives lived despite trends and expectations. It is an intervention made by swapping out the lens currently used in writing urban anthropology and instead beginning from the space of the ethnographic archive.

And so this book is an ethnographic archive of loss and life in the mill land neighborhoods of Mumbai: an exploration of lively ruination and anachronistic vitality. In archiving loss, this project emerges from both histories *of* loss and histories that *are* lost.[5] Through this "archive of loss," I call for the soothsaying potentiality of the archive, located in its absences or losses. In this way, I am not simply looking to fill gaps or produce a lost whole but instead emphasize the power of loss as generative and critical. At the same time, I am also invested in making certain people and places and stories more visible than others. These two moves are not necessarily contradictory when I operate within the analytic of the archive. I do not attempt to replace one story with another. I simply acknowledge the existence of multiple stories and reveal the power that positions them in uneven ways.[6]

Throughout this book I will act as an ethnographer-archivist, taking you, the reader, through the archives I have chosen. Like *Girangaon—Kal,*

Aaj Aur Kal, these archives are curated through interpretation.[7] They are incomplete—limited by my placement, my perspective, my positionality. The archive holds power through these limitations. There is no way to know what has been lost and there is no way to know what was never there. The archive is a realm of secrets, and only some of these secrets can be told.[8] But among these accessible secrets are stories of vitality, of survival, of presence: of life lived within and around the lively ruins of mill land Mumbai.

The Museum of Mill Land Mumbai: Notes on Narrative

I could not persuade her that a place does not merely exist, that it has to be invented in one's imagination.—AMITAV GHOSH, *The Shadow Lines*, 1988

This book begins with the claim that official histories and master narratives, like *Girangaon—Kal, Aaj Aur Kal*, are straightforward and simplistic. This does not (necessarily) make them wrong, but it does make them intentional and strategic. Their goal is to produce stories that are easily circulated and seamlessly consumed. In claiming that visible histories of mill land Mumbai are akin to a museum, I argue that spaces like Dhanraj, then, are reflective of the archive—messy and chaotic lives and documents and records and spaces that contradict, expand, and interrupt the narrative of the museum. Throughout this ethnography I use the space of Dhanraj as both a challenge to and an expansion of the official museum history. The archive is a disruption. But these spaces of disruption are often unseen, and this lack of visibility allows museum stories to blanket the entrances to spaces where archives might be encountered. This ethnography is an exploration of these unseen histories of mill land Mumbai: the archives of a museum of loss.

But the basement archives lack the power of response if they are not first entered through the museum. And so here I present the standard (abridged) history of mill land development and the current crisis facing Dhanraj, as told through the framing of a museum. It tells several visible stories: these stories are the ones I interpret as "official," "accepted," and "understood." I am not—in any way—attempting to *rewrite* this master narrative. It is important, it is well thought out, it helps us understand critical phenomena across the landscapes of our lives. But this is not the only way of seeing, engaging with, and understanding these landscapes, and this master narrative is incapable of illuminating the lively ruination of unseen, overlooked spaces. Museum narratives are necessarily simple. They are

FIGURE I.4. Sharmistha Ray, *Intimate Geographies (Mapping India)*, 11-¾ × 12-¾ inches, porous point black ink pen on Fabriano paper, 2018.

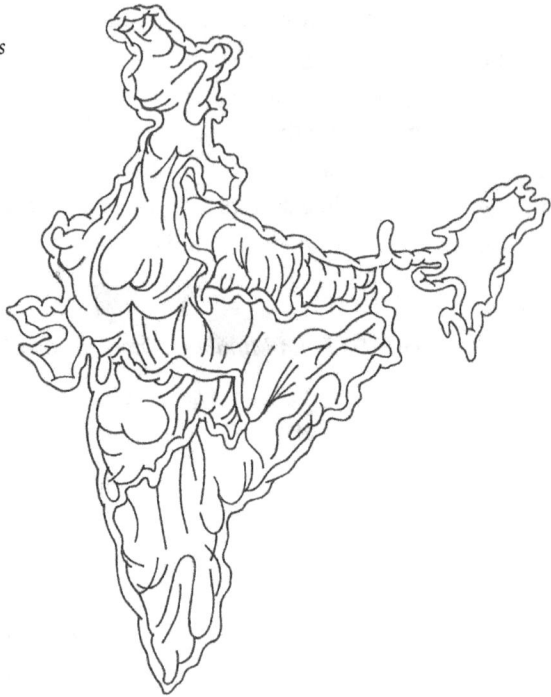

clear. They are accessible. But the archives tell additional stories: the ones that would muddy the museum. The ones that would throw the gallery exhibit into chaos and confusion. The ones that challenge not only the materials of the museum but also the very foundation of museum constructions.

For an outsider with an untrained eye, walking through the mill lands of Mumbai is an exercise in confusion: How do I *see* this area, seemingly so chaotic and unplanned? Spatially, Central Mumbai's neighborhoods stand beneath the shadows of the city's numerous flyovers and are barely visible from the highway. Because of this, it is possible to drive between downtown and the northern suburbs without ever seeing the mills, except for an occasional chimney jutting above the low-lying industrial mill compounds. In thinking about this cloistered spatiality, mapping the mill lands must also become an intentional and embodied engagement in place-making. Sharmistha Ray's maps, *Intimate Geographies*, are one such remapping exercise. This book is also a practice of remapping: remapping histories, remapping experience, remapping space. A practice of remapping that which is no longer visible.

FIGURE I.5.
Sharmistha Ray,
*Intimate Geographies
(Mapping Bombay)*,
11-¾ × 12-¾ inches,
porous point black
ink pen on Fabriano
paper, 2018.

But the industry once had global visibility: the first textile mill, the Bombay Spinning Mill, was set up in 1854 in response to Britain's demand for cotton textiles.[9] Wealthy Indian merchant families, who made fortunes trading with the British, were able to acquire mills on low-cost land leases (ranging from 100 to 999 years) from the colonial government, transforming the city from a trade hub into a major manufacturing center. By the 1930s, half the city's population was economically dependent on the industry, which continued to grow (Surve 2011).

By the early 1960s, the city had fifty-eight cotton textile mills employing more than 600,000 workers. But increasing international cotton production (primarily from Japanese-controlled, China-based mills) led to a decline in the demand placed on the Indian market. Throughout the late 1960s and 1970s, the city's mill owners cut jobs and wages to keep up with this newly unstable market, and the textile industry found itself in crisis.[10] This resulted in a massive, industry-wide strike from 1982 to 1983, known as the Great Textile Strike. Most mills never recovered from the economic devastation of those years.[11]

While the 1980s were known as a time of crisis, the 1990s became a decade of confusion. As much of the city's textile production came to a near standstill, the development laws lingering from colonial zoning legislation created a situation of stagnation. As it turned out, the mill land was "locked" and unavailable for any other manufacturing activities and future development. This situation grew into an urban planning dilemma for the city. First, the mill lands occupied six hundred conjoined acres in the middle of the city. This extensive patch of underutilized land created an obstacle for development in the heart of Mumbai. Second, the lack of access to the mill lands produced exorbitant property values in the city that discouraged investment and development. Third, development in Mumbai was limited by the city's location on a peninsula. Because of this, new businesses and other developments needed to be built to the north of the locked land. A lawyer representing the Bombay Environmental Action Group (BEAG) put the consequences of these factors into perspective for me:

> What was unusual [about the industry] was that you had your prime economic activity within the heart of a city—so clearly not suitable from a planning perspective, but because cities in India are not planned in any organized way (they instead grow organically) you have these mill lands. And that's probably what gives them the kind of significance—even today, one hundred years later—is because of their location. We're not talking about industries on the periphery of a city, which is now being developed commercially. We're talking about industries in the heart of a city. And we're not talking about one plot or two plots. We're talking about six hundred acres of mill lands. . . . When Bombay grew as a city in the twentieth century, it grew around this industrial activity.

Eventually, these factors burdened Mumbai's development such that the government of India changed its position and acknowledged the need to free up the locked land, but how to unlock the land for development was controversial and involved two rounds of litigation.

The sale of mill land was and still is enmeshed in social and political controversy. Issues of lost labor, worker rights, environmental conservation, and the desire for open space complicated the ways in which development can (and will) take place. This crisis was first addressed among the various structural adjustment changes occurring across India in 1991.[12] Emerging from these changes were the Development Control Rules (DCRs), specifically DCR-58, commonly known as the "one-third plan." The original rule (DCR-58) stated that two-thirds of the land area must be turned over to the state (one-third for open space and one-third for low-income housing). The remaining one-third could be retained by owners and developers and used as they saw fit. However, both the government-controlled National Textile Corporation mills and private mill owners argued that this formula, when properly employed, applied only to *unused* land, free from industrial structures. This interpretation implied that, if any of the mill land was presently built upon, that land would be excluded from the formula and retained by the owner. Under this interpretation, the land available for open space and low-income housing was insignificant because mills were typically low-lying structures occupying a substantial part of the land area in question. To put it simply, open space essentially didn't exist in the congested mill lands. If this formula were applied only to those few pockets of open land, there would be no real public purpose that could be served, either for green space or for public housing. The next decade resulted in several major court cases and virtually no substantial development.

In 2001, following several rounds of litigation, the city government finally amended the rule: DCR-58 became DCR-58 (I), which stated: "Only land that is vacant on mill properties — that is with no built-up structure — would be divided by the one-third formula." Following this alteration, mill owners could retain the majority of their land, as the area claimed by the city and former workers was limited to 6 to 10 percent, as opposed to two-thirds, of the mill land. This defeat was doubly devastating for the petitioners in favor of the one-third formula, as the plan was believed to be the salvation for a city often understood as dangerously overcrowded and completely lacking in open space. At a roundtable organized for World Health Day, Pankaj Joshi of the Urban Development and Research Institute explained: "Only 6 percent of the total land in the city [of Mumbai] is made up of open public spaces. Out of this, 45 percent is partially or completely encroached upon. A citizen of Mumbai gets 1.95 square meters of open space against the international standard of 11 square meters per person." In one of the most congested areas of the world, the one-third plan had the potential to alleviate the density, pollution, and infrastructural strain placed on the central city. And yet private interests got in the way.

A lawyer representing the BEAG explained to me:

I think what really brought the matter to life for us was knowing what could have been, had the result been the other way. And we knew it firsthand because we met with them [the planners], we saw their blueprints, we saw their reports. And if those blue prints of potential urban planning of the mill lands had been put into effect and implemented, it really would have made a difference to that part of Bombay, which is otherwise extremely congested, very chaotic, and—because it's in such a strategic location—could have really provided solutions to infrastructure problems that Bombay, as a city, faces. Transportation issues, but also most importantly, parks and green space. And that is the potential that the mill lands had for the city. And therefore, having had an insight, when we lost, we knew that it was not just losing a legal argument, but also a potential would be lost for all times to come.

This sense of colossal loss was shared unanimously by those engaged in defending the one-third plan, whether from the perspective of environmental concerns, working-class housing issues, or the loss of architectural heritage. In many ways, this ruling was seen as the beginning of the end for the possible creation of a more sustainable city.

By 2003, a combination of rising real estate costs and the supposed stability of DCR-58 (I) placed mill owners in a prime position to sell their land for enormous profits. However, a decade of court cases and ambiguous legal interpretations resulted in dramatic uncertainty as to the actual status of the land and the risk involved in selling, renovating, razing, and rebuilding mill lands.[13] This ambiguity stalled the activity of some landowners hoping to turn major profits in the wake of industry's decline.

For Dhanraj, this story is particularly complicated.[14] The owners of Dhanraj, the Lal family, entered into a partnership with the development company Mahindra Lifespaces in 1995.[15] However, Mahindra then outwardly claimed that its dedication to transparency and hyperlegality did not allow it to engage in extralegal business, which was common in the mill land district. This led to Mahindra stalling development of the compound and Dhanraj attempting to extricate itself from any legal partnership in court. At the end of my long-term fieldwork, in 2012, the company was locked in a court battle with Dhanraj; as a result, no development could proceed until all the workers retired and were paid sizable settlements.[16] This situation resulted in a skeleton workforce running a seemingly decayed and unproductive mill. From the bustling sidewalk running along Ambedkar Road, Dhanraj looks like just another boarded-up, abandoned mill, awaiting the development plans of Mahindra Lifespaces.

An Archive of Lively Ruination: Notes on Time

People are collecting found objects snatched off the literal or metaphorical side of the road. Things that have dropped out of the loop or have been left sagging somewhere are dragged home as if they are literal residues of past dreaming practices.

The snatching practice mixes a longing for a real world (or something) with the consumer's little dream of spying a gem or tripping over a bargain. And in the mix, all kinds of other things are happening, too.—KATHLEEN STEWART, *Ordinary Affects*, 2007

According to the museum narrative, Dhanraj industrial production is no more. But Dhanraj industrial production is *not* over, even if the museum narrative has convinced the city that it is. Walking through the gate to the mill compound is like crossing over into another time: life in the mill moves slowly in dimly lit spaces, seemingly unaware of the fast pace and bright lights of the city around it. But the mill is not a relic from the past: while Dhanraj may invoke a sense of pastness, this orientation toward ruin forecloses our ability to engage it as a lively and vital space of modernity.[17] This is a crisis of temporality: at the gate of Dhanraj, diverse planes of time and space merge in a single moment and place, shaping the meaning of work and life that unfolds within the mill compound. This ruinous space is an allegory for our present moment, which appears industrial and post-industrial, simultaneously—an alternative "now," in contrast to shifting economies and skylines outside the compound gate.[18]

I can *see* this collision of alternative times.

If I choose to pay attention. . . .

So how does an ethnographer-archivist pay attention? From the street, Dhanraj appears to be nothing more than a semi-abandoned textile mill, in the process of demolition and redevelopment. But once inside its walls, I find myself in a crucible of temporal reimagining. This mill, in its ruination, is an uncanny space and—if we (you as my reader, me as your ethnographer-archivist) listen—it has much to tell us about the present and the future. Dhanraj is an uncanny ruin because it is both a (seeming) leftover of modernity and its counterpart (a production *of* modernity)—the mill is a collision of multiple modernities.[19] Throughout this ethnography, I show how Dhanraj is a lens through which to challenge, reimagine, and alter how the present moment we *think* we find ourselves in speaks to the future. But in order to take such a thought experiment seriously, we must reimagine how we can see the world. It is difficult to see zombified economic and social spaces such as Dhanraj because they defy our expectations of progress, of time, of modernity. They lie outside what we think we know of the world.

Economic history is usually narrated by eras: industrial capitalism and postindustrial capitalism, liberalism and the age of the neoliberal.[20] One gives way to another, and the world changes through acts of assigning labels as a practice of movement. But does this temporal progression actually map onto the materiality of the everyday? There is a disconnect between the naming of time and the mapping of time-names onto the material, enlivened world. This practice makes it very difficult to see (and then to narrate, to make sense of) anachronistic spaces like Dhanraj.

As both a place and an idea, Dhanraj is *present*: I have been there, I return often as a reminder. It is and continues to be *real*. But it is also dying: an ongoing and incomplete process of decay and transformation.

There is a double anachronism here:

Dhanraj is alive, but it will die soon.
Also Dhanraj is already dead.

Therefore, Dhanraj is a sort of death that is deeply alive: a space of alternative life, a life outside of language. What do we do with this zombified place, both alive and undead? Both decaying and vital, ruinous and lively? A location where the past becomes alive because it *is* still alive? Instead of thinking about liveliness as generative, I propose a form of lively ruination and anachronistic vitality. Life exists on multiple planes, and in the mill lands, life and loss envelop each other in a nonlinear form. Therefore, Dhanraj is a dialectical space of life and loss; I thus employ a wider lens through which to grapple with this world I find myself in because while I write this ethnography in the time of the "postindustrial," I simultaneously attend to what this means for people still living industrial lives.

I propose Dhanraj provides a nonlinear timeline of decay: while deindustrial narratives show that the global collapse of industrial production has already happened, attention paid to spaces of local-level industrial production (like Dhanraj) reveals a discordant collision of time and production. Narratives of collapse and practices of local-level production collide in spaces where the aftershocks of peak industrialization are still playing out on a local scale. Recently there has been a surge in the field of "ruin studies," particularly in anthropology, archaeology, history, and cultural studies. My work is indebted to this conversation, as the materiality of decay and abandonment is central to my framing of Mumbai's mill lands (Edensor 2005; DeSilvey 2006; Stoler 2008; Yablon 2009; Bennett 2010; Hell and Schönle 2010; Gabrys 2013; Gordillo 2014). Even as this scholarship provides a platform from which my work takes off, this book engages with the spaces of ruins in very different ways, since my ruins are still *alive*. They have not yet been abandoned, even if they are overlooked. And they have much to tell us if we focus both on their ongoing vitality and on what it means to live within this process of collapse. By taking Dhanraj seriously as a lively ruin, I theorize how this decay occurs, what it looks like as a process, and what messianic messages for the future are embedded in its rubble. Ruins are both remainders and reminders (Boym 2008a): my goal as an ethnographer-archivist is to trace and interpret the stories these ruins are trying to tell.[21]

Methodologically, this ethnography is driven by an engagement with attention: social practices (such as the writing of history; the reporting of news; the development of infrastructure and the identities placed upon spaces through naming) can temporally displace communities, rendering them "out of time." Displacement from the current moment leads to a social inability to *see* those who have been temporally displaced. Once spaces and communities are erased from our social vision, we must relearn how to see what exists but has been rendered invisible. Through this method of attention, a series of interconnected questions emerge: What does it mean to inhabit a dying space? What does it mean to inhabit a dying way of life? Dhanraj keeps shrinking, and yet it also remains alive. It is dying as it is living. It is decaying, and yet it does not disintegrate. What does it mean to attend to these processes of decay, and what might be learned about potential practices of regeneration in doing so? How do I slow down my conceptions and experiences of the passage of time in order to inhabit the worlds of my informants? These processes and practices reveal alternative modernities, but they also demand a willingness to engage elegiac practices: Dhanraj workers are mourning a dying city, a dying way of life. And they are also mourning themselves, their communities, their bodies. These spaces of lively ruination are speaking: What meanings emerge through listening?

While these questions emerge from the specific ethnographic space of Dhanraj, they also speak to a state of global crisis: the crisis of modernity and labor.[22] The space of Dhanraj offers up answers to such a current crisis, but in unexpected ways. The liveliness of ruins draws attention to patterns of decay and regeneration inaccessible through standard economic projections. But this vitality must first be seen before it can teach lessons of justice and imagination.

This form of seeing, I find, is very difficult to do.

In the Darkroom of Fieldwork: Notes on Methodology

The past is hidden outside the realm of our intelligence and beyond its reach, in some material object (in the sensation that this material object would give us) which we do not suspect. It depends on chance whether we encounter this object before we die, or do not encounter it. —MARCEL PROUST, *Swann's Way*, (1913) 2002

The lively ruins of Central Mumbai are palimpsests, and much gets concealed through this layering. History and memory are embedded in this industrial debris, dwelling alongside future prophecies. Ethnography offers the opportunity to encounter both this past and this future, while theory (through the philosophy embedded in *all* literature) offers up tools for analysis. In Renee Gladman's uncanny novel, *Event Factory*, an unnamed linguist-traveler arrives in the fictional city-state of "Ravicka." The traveler, a linguist competent in the language but still unable to truly communicate, attempts to move through a space that is at once foreign, at once familiar. This is a story of failure: her failure to record, to understand, to inhabit. The failure of fluency. But this is also a story about the potentials that emerge from and sit alongside this failure.

Halfway through the novel, the unnamed linguist-traveler discovers something critical about her new location, and yet is unable to articulate and access, through language, her discovery. She explains: "Most of us believed that in that duration I had been exposed to the truth about Ravicka, yet, perhaps for some reason innate to being an outsider, I had not recognized it" (Gladman 2010, 88). For years I have been writing about the misrecognition of Central Mumbai's textile industry, obsessed as I was and am with the fact that—even as the industry persists—the city denies this reality.

Or, to be more generous, that there is a misrecognition of presence for absence.

And yet for years I also never really paused to consider, with any great detail or care, the consistent continuation of my *own* misrecognition, so deeply rooted in the ethnographic encounter. In *Mimesis and Alterity*, Michael Taussig proposes that writing—particularly ethnographic writing—may be a form of magic, harnessed through the "sensuous sense of the real, mimetically at one with what it attempts to represent" (1993, 16). What if the magic Taussig writes of is not of re-creating the power of the original in the copy but of seeing the negative before it becomes a photograph?

There is a photograph of Central Mumbai that I took in the winter of 2009: I managed to talk my way onto the roof of a nearby apartment building, providing myself the first bird's-eye view of the area by which I felt enveloped for so long. With my digital camera in hand, I attempted to capture the feeling of a shifting perspective, of seeing from above what I had only ever seen from below, from within. I tried to capture with my camera's eye what appeared to me as visual markers of presence. I saw the mill, I saw low-lying industrial buildings: other mills and nearby chawls. I saw emerging skyscrapers in the distance, alongside cranes enabling their emergence above and beyond the urban skyline. I saw quite a number of trees, not so surprising even considering the lack of greenery throughout the city, as most mills had a water source of some sort. I knew Dhanraj had a small human-made lake populated by geese, even if I couldn't see it from my perch. I saw smog. I saw roads. I thought about all the things I couldn't see. I thought about shadows. I thought about cities beneath other cities. Burial sites and subterranean life and what it means to be invisible. These are the photographic negatives of the city's gallery of memory. Everything present but unseen (fig. 1.6).

When I utilize the digital there are no negatives, there are no darkrooms. I can immediately look at this digital image appearing on my camera or phone and assume that this representation is "real." That it is a fluent translation of the skyline. Without negatives, where are my ghostly images? Where are the traces that haunt the photograph? In this particular image I miss all that is absent, all that is unseen. All that is no longer there or was never there or is hidden and waiting to appear.

After wandering for many days, Gladman's unnamed linguist-traveler finds herself atop an elevated plane, looking down on the city of Ravicka. She finds that she cannot see anything: no people, no houses. None of the elusive skyscrapers she searches for, in hopes of discovering where the

FIGURE I.6. The photographic negative of the city's gallery of memory.

"real" city lies. She reflects: "Local life is inscrutable if you are too far out of it, or above it in the way I was. And this, I acknowledged, had become my new problem. My wanderings began to lead me repeatedly to the same predicament: standing in relation to something I could not see. But, I reasoned from that elevated place, my time here had proved that what one 'couldn't see' was not always what was there" (Gladman 2010, 108).

What does it mean to stand in relation to something we cannot see? I read in Gladman's allegory a sense of the world aligned with what I know to be this ethnographic crisis: I have, for too long, been attempting to tell a story that does not take account of all the absences and ashes and shadows and ghosts that make up the photographic negatives of a life.[23] While we can tell some stories through the social life of the structures that contain us, just as important are the stories that cannot be encased in steel and stone, that cannot be articulated and translated. That elude our attempts at ethnographic fluency and are always emerging horizons of "maybe not there."

It has been years since I worked with film, watching ghostly images emerge from the dark, taking over with first their shadows, then their lines and forms. Now I have only this digital photograph, no negatives to return to. But somehow the frame has shifted: maybe the digital photograph has become the negative, the city skyline has become the photograph. Over time I return to this image, I push myself to see things emerge from the shadows of misrecognition, previously unnoticed or misunderstood. I find that the way I see these images changes over time. Some previously unseen traces emerge now, but were not noticeable then. But then I might have seen things that I no longer notice now. The unseen traces, these "ghostly matters," are both what is missing and what must be addressed.[24] I am looking for my particular ghostly matters, both in photographs that only "sort of" capture the landscape and in words that only "sort of" capture a life.

And so this book is an experiment with time and word-images: ephemeral ethnographic matter that disrupts the time-world I first create and then believe to be natural, real. My methodology places at its center a continual (but never complete) search for the meanings (always shifting) in the negatives of ethnography. To understand how "what one 'couldn't see' was not always what was there." Perhaps this is the continual return to the darkroom of fieldwork, of revisiting the process of chemical exposure in an attempt to access shapes emerging through contact with light. And then a set of questions emerge from these shadows: What do our anthropological darkrooms look like? Where are our ethnographic archives? Where do we go to draw meaning from recorded words and sentences and conversations made from speech words and sentences and conversations, rooted in place but disrupted through our note taking, our recording, our interpretations? Our misrecognition of (ethnographic) competence for (anthropological) fluency. Nancy Scheper-Hughes (1992) has suggested that an ethnographer must be the "clerk of the records," but what do we do when we realize we do not (and cannot) possess all the files? What if we are not in search of a complete collection at all?

Ethnographic note taking (like the notes of this introduction) follows the process of developing film in a dark room—a frame encloses a space, the negatives capture shadows and light, and the photograph makes sense of what can be processed. Similarly, our field notes are not simply a collection of observations. They are also the suggestions of ghostly matter, lingering at the edges of language and sight. When I look back through my files of field notes, how do I remember what that ephemeral matter looks like? Sounds like? Feels like? How do I account for what it means to stand in relation to something I cannot see?

From this question two interconnected threads of engagement emerge: First, the question of material. What do I use, both theoretically and ethnographically, to account for the lively ruin of the mill? Second, the question of method: What methodology can account for the ghostly matter of lives lived among the debris of lively ruination? Throughout this book I show how affective traces provide my material and the theoretical form of the archive provides my methodology. The archive, then, is also the darkroom, littered with all the negatives left over after the photographs are developed and hung in the museum. Or overlooked in corners, yet to become photographs. Or lost or destroyed or torn or buried. I have been collecting some of these negatives: traces of places, of bodies, of events, of time. These traces stand in the shadows of more solid photographic narratives, but that does not diminish their power of prophecy.

At least half my files are ghostly. They are maybe not there, or perhaps I haven't yet encountered them, or possibly I did already and I either knew it or I didn't know it but it doesn't matter because they have disappeared.[25]

For now, I am haunted by ghosts: they are trying to tell me what is missing.

Missing from the city and from the photograph.

Missing from stories of structure, of interests, of history.

Missing in the shadows of photographic negatives and in the pauses between spoken words.

There is power and promise in the incompleteness of this archive, with and among the ghosts of "maybe not there."

Why Infrastructure Tells Us Nothing of What It Means to Feel in the World: Notes on Alternate Urbanisms

The paved road is a story and a poem. —RENEE GLADMAN, *The Ravickians*, 2011

The cityscape of Central Mumbai appears to be a construction site: cranes jut out and over a once low-lying landscape, writing the prologue of a new city. Skyscrapers emerge from holes in the ground that were once sprawling mill compounds, buried beneath the tree line. This transformation evokes a story of infrastructural shift—architects, planners, developers, and engineers have stories to tell about this fluctuating cityscape, but they are not the only ones. The stories I hear in Dhanraj are not ones of "infrastructural expertise," but they are stories of expertise, all the same. My mill

FIGURE 1.7. The cityscape of Central Mumbai.

worker informants "feel" the changing atmosphere and shifting landscape of Mumbai. However, this "feeling" is not (just) the sensations of the body in a phenomenological sense, but instead echoes, resonances, ephemeral sensations that come and go and tell us just as much (if not more) about time and space as they do about bodily sensations.[26] Therefore, this tension in scale—in terms of how the story of a city can be "told"—can be read as a battle between affect and structure.[27] I am invested in the "affectsphere" of Central Mumbai's mill lands, which encompasses the emerging worlds that cut across hegemonic temporal and spatial frames.[28]

The affectsphere undermines hegemonic infrastructure. In constructing the affectsphere of Central Mumbai, I challenge traditional engagements with infrastructure, present in recent urban scholarship. By examining the tensions between my informants and the city of Mumbai, I present this ethnography as an intervention in the growing subfield of "infrastructure studies" within the anthropology of capitalism and neoliberalism.[29] My work is indebted to these engagements, which have generated new openings through which we approach ethnographies of urban space, capital accumulation, and uneven systems of power. Much of this work focuses on how systems, resources, and technologies help us understand the construction and habitation of space. While I would consider my work in conversation with this, I draw attention to the ways in which "infrastructure studies" often decenters the experiences of our informants.[30] Instead, this book is invested in how my informants *experience* infrastructure and ruination. We cannot understand one without the other.

Throughout this book, ethnographic stories of mill work and chawl habitation are at once deeply structural *and* deeply sensorial: indeed, I argue that the collection of ephemera through the methodology of the archive destabilizes our understanding of knowledge, of history, and of truth and, instead, allows new forms of knowing to emerge. This pushes at deeper issues that recent work on systems and structures seems to avoid in terms of what ethnography can do and what our anthropological approach can bring to a *sense* of the world. I argue — ethnographically — throughout this text that there is a creativity and sense of imagination in lived experiences that activates and unleashes the ambience of everyday urban life.

Brian Larkin frames infrastructure as a way in which to "generate the ambient environment of everyday life" (2013, 328). I am invested in this ambience: I choose not to explore in detail how development is working (or not working) in Mumbai.[31] Instead, I focus on what it feels like to live in the shadows of this development. My informants tell me stories of the fear, anxiety, and sadness in watching industrial buildings give way to glass and steel skyscrapers. I argue that feelings about and engagements with infrastructure are just as critical as an exploration of how these buildings come to be. To suggest that systems and structures must somehow be explained before they can be experienced threatens the foundation of ethnography's promise: the potential to understand the world in ways it has never been understood before by engaging the impressions, experiences, and affects of our informants as forms of critical expertise.

Keller Easterling has described infrastructure as the "operating system" of the city (2014, 12). As a person absolutely *convinced* that my computer runs on magic, I find that my ignorance of its operating system rarely gets in the way of my ability to engage it in a day-to-day manner (after all, there are magicians to fix it when it breaks down). Similarly, I see structure and affect as inextricably linked: to *feel* infrastructure may not be to "know" it (in the sense of engineering), but in focusing on affect, my work challenges this framing of expertise and draws urban anthropology away from city planning and back to ethnography. As an ethnographer-archivist, I search for ways to capture how my informants experience the lively ruins in which they live. What does Sudarshan *see* when he drives his taxi through the transforming mill lands? How does Sushila *feel* when she stands on her aching feet all day? What does Manda *say* to the looming skyscrapers when she walks through her Lower Parel neighborhood? What does Raj *hear* in the dark, deafening space of the mill? While I cannot fully access the experiences of my informants (nor can I adequately translate that limited access through language), I argue that returning to experience-as-aspiration is critical nonetheless.[32] "Knowing" the legal loopholes of mill land development, the economic benefits of industrial fire, or the future trends of city planning cannot allow one to answer these questions of mill worker experience. And it is this issue of archiving Central Mumbai's affectsphere that drives my ethnography.

The collision of affect and infrastructure transforms Central Mumbai into a haunted city. Work on temporality and memory has opened up critical avenues for exploring the politicization of heritage and the impact of spatial histories on the construction and reconstruction of identities.[33] Central Mumbai—as a site of memory production and consumption—reveals how the past is still present; ghosts inhabit the everyday spaces of the living; and topographies of space can be re-understood in ways that challenge established trends of urban transformation. The historian Gillian Tindall writes: "In Bombay . . . the past continues not only to be but also thrive, coexisting chaotically but apparently profitably with more recent developments" (1982, 2). This past, at least as it is framed within the former textile mill districts, becomes—in the words of Denis Byrne—a "signature of loss in the landscape" of Central Mumbai (2007, 59).

So as I stand in the Dr. Bhau Daji Lad Mumbai City Museum on that December afternoon in 2008, I am struck by the stories being told.[34] The museum exhibit I stand within is thoughtfully and intentionally curated: it is "both a place and a practice" (Taylor 2003, 66). Yet, I am less interested in what is included—my attention turns to what is discarded, relegated to the museum archives.

The remainders. The outliers.

The files and folders and boxes that do not fit within the exhibit as planned: the negatives of the museum photographs.

As I walk through PUKAR's exhibit of loss, I think about these basement archives, still present and yet also somehow not visible. Accessible yet overlooked: "orphaned collections" awaiting attention (B. Voss 2012). I have always been more interested in these hidden, subterranean spaces.

Spaces like Dhanraj: archives of loss.

Mapping the Archive of Loss: Notes on Form

Here we have a man whose job it is to pick up the day's rubbish in the capital. He collects and catalogues everything that the great city has cast off, everything it has lost, and discarded, and broken, he goes though the archives of debauchery, and the jumbled array of refuse. He makes a selection, an intelligent choice; like a miser hoarding treasure, he collects the garbage that will become objects of utility or pleasure when refurbished by Industrial magic.—CHARLES BAUDELAIRE, "Du Vin et du haschisch," *Oeuvres*, vol. 1, in Walter Benjamin, *The Arcades Project*, 1999

This book is a collection of five archives—the archive of the mill, of the worker, of the chawl, of the great textile strike, of industrial fire. In drawing on the concept of "the archive," my book pushes against the notion that "the archive" is a place, a location.[35] Or *just* a place, a location. There are archival places here, yes. But the archive is also about time, events, and bodies. I theorize the archive beyond boundedness, and in doing so, I reveal how conceptions of time transform *ideas* into places, just as maps, names, borders, and boundaries transform spaces into places.[36] Events and bodies can be archives, just like spatial locations.

I draw on the archive-optic as a tool through which memory, nostalgia, and experience—often understood as linkages to the past—can be temporally reframed as future-focused. Here I am influenced by William Mazzarella's (2017) framing of "the mimetic archive": the conscious and unconscious ways we access collective experiences across space and time. This framing of the mimetic archive challenges a superficial rendering of nostalgia and complicates ways of engaging the past in the present moment, like echoes in a shared chamber of memory and experience. Instead of returning to the memory archive as (just) a space of storage, I instead understand the ethnographic archive as a repository of resonances, available as resources through which the contemporary moment can be understood. The past has much to tell us about the present and future, as the process of interpretation (conducted by both ethnographer and informant) is filtered through the immediacy of the now.[37] Throughout these archival spaces I search out resonances: echoes of intertwined history, experience, and expectation.[38] These resonances are archives of emotion, experience, feeling, memory, connection: residue that ties together "unseen things" (Lepselter 2016).[39]

I offer this book as an accidental archive, divided into five smaller archive-chapters. Like the rubbish of Baudelaire's ragpicker, my archival collection is composed of material that has been cast off but, similarly, has been refurbished with industrial magic. These archives lie buried beneath three layers: first, the Mumbai mill lands as mythological creations; second, the mill lands as temporal ruptures in the history of Mumbai; and third, Dhanraj mill workers as anachronistic subjects. In uncovering these layers, I make visible the promises and possibilities present in spaces of lively ruination. Each archive takes as its central question the traces of industrial production and livelihood still present in Central Mumbai and, in doing so, foregrounds unruly and contradictory ethnographic material.

Chapter 1, "The Archive of the Mill," is centered on "nonrecognition" (Hansen 2012) as archival material and practices of "unseeing" (Miéville 2009) as the mode through which such nonrecognition comes to be. I argue that—through the circulation of narratives of industrial finality—nonrecognition turns the liveliness of Dhanraj into an absent place, and this resulting mythology of absence and finality renders current mill workers "unvisible." This unvisibility is an active way of "unseeing" and "unhearing" inconvenient urban lives. By replacing "invisible" with "unvisible" and "misrecognition" with "nonrecognition," I argue that what we cannot see and hear is a form of practice enforced by infrastructure, not an accident naturally occurring in space and time.

Chapter 2, "The Archive of the Worker," is an archive of bodily pain and considers the discontinuities and continuities between scales of experience. Through narratives of embodiment (pain, illness, exhaustion, injury), this chapter pushes beyond a phenomenological sense of the body and instead considers how these narratives of bodily pain reveal the decay of an industrial cyborg body: older bodies, fused and infused with industrial possibility, are becoming both unusable and unwanted. This archive explores the meaning of inhabiting broken and decaying bodies, no longer modern and productive but once central and vital for the health of both the local and the global economy. In doing so, it asks how bodies are understood to be both "in" time and "of" time.

Chapter 3, "The Archive of the Chawl," is an archive of "queer time." Beyond the space of Dhanraj, this archive engages mill worker chawls as additional spaces of vital ruination. These structures, framed as dangerously uninhabitable in popular urban imagination, are lively places of history, memory, and possibility. However, they are also places that do not engage with accepted and assumed forms of temporal progression: they defy the nuclear family, they defy capitalist productivity, and they defy the laws of development through complicated zoning and ownership laws. Therefore, the queerness of this "chawl time" resists the forward march of "modernity" and instead allows for a mode of living "elliptically" (Berlant 2012) as a form of temporal resistance.

Chapter 4, "The Archive of the Strike," is an archive of "untruths": through memories of the Great Textile Strike of 1982–1983, this archive reveals how the "fictions" told by Dhanraj workers have much to tell about what it means to live precariously in a space of ruination. Through "untrue" stories, I engage the notion of an impossible subject and explore the crisis of an impossible story: what do anthropologists do with informant testimonies we know to be factually incorrect? How do we collect, interpret, and use informant lies, manipulations, and untruths as critical archival material? I argue that, through Theodor Adorno's negative dialectic, untruths in Dhanraj reveal a crisis of identity for minority (North Indian) workers, who have been cast as "other," both in the city and in the mill. Through a negative dialectic, "untruth" and "nonidentity" resist this othering and create an alternative being-in-the-world.

Chapter 5, "The Archive of the Fire," expands the notion of untruth to understand how and why Dhanraj workers circulate rumors in the wake of the 2009 industrial fire. This chapter-archive shows how—through rumor—workers make sense of the continued survival and vitality of a mill that lives on and functions through decades of decline and death. This ongoing regeneration of Dhanraj as zombified mill draws attention to the survival of spaces, economies, and individuals commonly understood to disappear through shifting socioeconomic eras.

The book's epilogue, "The Archive of Futures Lost," concludes with a return to Dhanraj in December 2016 through January 2017. A majority of the land has been sold to an international development company, but the mill, still operating with a skeletal workforce of fifty, occupies a small home on the edge of the retained property. While bulldozers clear the sold land and make way for luxury high-rises, Dhanraj workers continue to spin cotton thread. When the union contracts of local workers expire, the mill will eventually shift to Silvassa, an industrial hub three hours north of Mumbai. However, the next few years will involve the continuation of industrial production in Mumbai, unseen and unacknowledged by the city at large. In this way, the five archives of loss come together as spokes on a wheel that allow for the economic center vampirically to survive off the blood of downwardly mobile unvisible industrial labor. I end the book with a call to think seriously about how we frame narratives about urban futures and how these narratives impact the lives of the remainders of past urban moments. In doing so, I make an argument for the messianic potentiality of lively ruination. This will only be possible if we can learn to see what still remains.

1

The Archive
of the Mill

If I tell you that the city toward which my journey tends is discontinuous in space and time, now scattered, now more condensed, you must not believe the search for it can stop.

Perhaps while we speak, it is rising, scattered, within the confines of your empire; you can hunt for it, but only in the way I have said. —ITALO CALVINO, *Invisible Cities*, 1972

We are all philosophers here where I am, and we debate among many things the question of where it is that we live. On that issue I am a liberal. I live in the interstice yes, but I live in both the city and the city. —CHINA MIÉVILLE, *The City and the City*, 2009

Arrivals: Walking through Ruins

I am lost before I find Dhanraj.

My first encounter with the mill lands occurs in 2006. I am in Mumbai for the first time and think—in my naïveté—I should wander around. See the city. Get a sense of the place. I get off the train at Lower Parel station and start walking, but I find myself going in circles. Have I seen this mill gate before? Is this the same market? Is that the same vegetable stand? I don't yet know the city, and I definitely don't know the central neighborhoods, home to a once prominent, now dying industry. I *think* I know how to walk in a city, but I haven't before attempted to walk in Mumbai. I *think* I know how to pay attention to the urban landscape, but I haven't yet learned how to see things I have been taught not to see.

I am lost in the city.

My second encounter with the mill lands occurs in 2007. I am with Nitan, a young Marxist union organizer (and "Barefoot Researcher" in his own right). The first time we walk through the city together we meet in Dadar, a half mile north of Dhanraj and the City Museum. We walk past King's Circle, under the railway station, and toward Prabhadevi.

"Did you know," he asks, "that Bombay's independence movement began with the mill workers in the chawls?" Curious for his story, I tell him no. He continues:

> It was the workers, of course: the textile mill workers. Everything that makes this country Indian is because of them. It was trade unions that brought the city's working-class consciousness. People say that Calcutta is the center of Marxist India, but it's here, too, in the mills, in the chawls. People forget, especially now. All this development, and the city forgets. These people that you see here, they aren't even the workers. So many of the workers have left; they've gone back to their families in the villages. All these people came later: from Bihar, from Bengal. And so no one remembers that it was the workers who fought the British, the workers who organized the Nationalist movement. This city is built on the back of Marxists, but that history is gone. There's a new history now.

I am lost in the story.

My third encounter with the mill lands occurs in 2008. I stumble upon Dhanraj and keep stumbling once inside its gates. The compound feels unreal to me, the workers seem translucent. I don't know how to reconcile what I think I am seeing with what I have been told I should be seeing.

I am lost in the ruins.

This ethnography is an attempt to find my footing through three layers of loss, while also retracing my steps to the place before I was lost. In doing so, I am moving through a tangled veil of history and possibility, unraveling what I have been told so that I can more clearly view what I am seeing. What I might be seeing. I find that my earliest guides are also my most powerful gatekeepers. Nitan's recounted history corresponds to various stories I read and hear regarding the critical role of mill workers in the establishment of India's independence. When hearing about my research, most people I encounter outside of Dhanraj tell a similar version of this story. The history of textile production is central to ordinary urbanites' identification with Mumbai, and the shifting visibility of laborers looms large in public memory of the city's past. But the strongest thread connecting the histories I encounter—whether from individuals like Nitan, the "Barefoot Researchers" of PUKAR, academic texts invested in the mill lands, or media reports on the fate of these neighborhoods—is one of absence: lost jobs; dispersed workers; razed and redeveloped mills; decrepit and decaying (if not already redeveloped) chawls.

I believe I am walking through graveyards.

When I find Dhanraj, this story begins to shift. I am surprised to find this operational space in 2008, and I am even more surprised to know it remains operational in 2018. Before I find Dhanraj, the mill lands are shown to me as abandoned ruins: I am led through their decaying structures, entertained in their redeveloped compounds, and encouraged to understand the time of urban industrial productivity as a past epoch long gone. However, Dhanraj—in addition to several other mills—continues to employ workers and produce cotton thread. What does such a reality have to say to the seeming postindustrial present, which frames spaces like Dhanraj as sites of ruin and Mumbai mill workers as impossible subjects?

Through my time at Dhanraj I find that the experience of being a "textile worker" is not merely a way to describe one's position in the economy. It is also a means to describe one's social status, sense of self, and contribution to the city. Indeed, the category "textile worker" was once associated with progress, modernity, and economic stability. A maintenance worker named Raj explains to me the pride that was felt in the city at the height of textile manufacturing: "At that time, everyone wanted their daughter to marry a mill worker." Today, these meanings associated with mill work have shifted: this is no longer the space of the future. There is no longer hope here. Yet these spaces, still, remain: an anachronistic vitality in the center of the city, hiding in plain sight. But even people like Nitan— engaged activists invested in the mill lands—cannot or do not see the liveliness of the ruins we walk through.

I find that practices of seeing and unseeing in the mill lands result in a refusal to engage the liveliness of ruination and the critical possibilities they hold about our futures. By framing Dhanraj as an "archive," I dig through the ruins of industry generally understood as abandoned. I am not looking to recuperate a lost whole: this is not a project of recovery or

FIGURE 1.1.
Raw cotton being
processed inside
Dhanraj.

restoration. It is instead an attempt to locate and engage remainders that
cannot be seen through the frame dictated by the city. This archive of the
mill is an archive of "nonrecognition" (Hansen 2012): throughout these
pages I contrast the experiences of Dhanraj workers with the mythologies
of the mill lands spread throughout the city. These two forms of storytelling (that of Dhanraj worker experience and that of mill land mythology)
are porous in the space of Dhanraj: it is very hard to separate one from the
other. However, in attempting to do so, this chapter-archive uncovers a
trail of industrial breadcrumbs that vitalizes the abandoned stories of mill
land Mumbai through the presence and productivity of Dhanraj workers.
In the process, I reframe the mill compound as a site of lively ruination.

Within the archive of the mill, I make an argument for "nonrecognition" (Hansen 2012) as my archival material and "unvisibility" (Miéville
2009) as a way of seeing/unseeing this material in the archive. In doing so,

I explore the space of Dhanraj as a vibrant economic and social place, in terms of both lingering textile production and unregulated non-textile-related activity. From the space of the factory floor, I consider how Dhanraj workers understand their lived, ongoing experience at the mill, even as larger narratives of history, media accounts, and urban infrastructure challenge their existence: they are not *misrecognized* (as I initially thought) but *nonrecognized*. Similarly, they are not *invisible*: they are *unvisible*. I reframe these passive terms as active words: there is work being done in the mill lands of Mumbai; this way of not recognizing and not seeing is far from accidental. While I initially bought into these stories of absence, the continuing presence of my informants helps me reframe the way I engage their worlds.

"Nonrecognition" and "unvisibility" can be understood as frames through which we understand both the power of the urban gaze and the organization of the mill itself: within Dhanraj there are unvisible economies and visible economies. The former allow for the latter. And yet by seeing the visible economies, we must "unsee" the "unvisible" economies. This practice of nonrecognition allows me to expand my frame to include not just the employed workers at Dhanraj but also unemployed former textile workers, now active in the activist space of the Girni Kamgar Sangharsh Samiti (GKSS). The GKSS, originally a textile worker union that emerged during the strike of the 1980s, has evolved into a social organization invested in reparations for mill workers no longer employed by the industry. By considering both Dhanraj workers and GKSS members, I push the frame of the archive to think alongside practices of "nonrecognition" through a distinction between "unvisible" workers (at Dhanraj) and "visible" workers (in the GKSS). In thinking through this dichotomy, I argue that the circulation of mill land mythology results in "unseeing" employed workers by privileging both the presence of unemployed workers and the narrative of deindustrialization in the mill lands.

FIGURE 1.2. The mill ruins in transition. This structure is shifting from part of the mill compound to a building utilized by the lifestyle store.

An Archive of Unvisible Workers

The forensics principle: that every action or contact leaves a trace.
—CAROLINE BERGVALL, *Drift*, 2014

Early into my fieldwork in late 2008, while visiting the office of several labor lawyers, a particularly jaded activist-advocate named Dipti tells me: "Dhanraj? Come on. That's a *fake* mill. They aren't making anything!" Throughout much of my fieldwork I am haunted by her comment. I know that Dhanraj is not officially shut and that the mill employs a real work-force. However, I learn that its reputation for engaging in dubious deals, combined with the prevailing deindustrialization discourse, results in the assumption that the mill is a scam. As my fieldwork progresses, the following story unfolds before me: Dhanraj is caught up in a messy and complicated economic landscape that results in locked-down industrial land and an unviable textile industry. Within this larger web of dependency and limitations exist both industrial workers (who provide legal legitimacy) and extralegal industries (which provide viable income). These extralegal industries include both unregulated sweatshops and a pseudolegal "lifestyle store," owned and operated by the mill owner's son, Arvind Lal. The lifestyle store sells expensive antiques and art to an elite group of consumers and constructs and restores much of its inventory in former mill spaces, now converted into artist workshops. Over the course of my fieldwork, Arvind becomes a helpful informant and a friend and provides the necessary access for my fieldwork at Dhanraj.

While the textile industry has not been economically productive or sustainable for decades, the unvisible presence of workers and the veneer of production enable the extremes of an unregulated industry (these sweatshops and lifestyle store) to exist and thrive. In this way, it makes sense that Dipti characterizes Dhanraj as "fake," since the logic of the market demands that a productive space is one that is producing a desirable product: How do we make sense of a textile mill that does *not* produce textiles? This logic, however, dismisses several hundred workers who continue to spin real cotton from very old, creaky machinery. What is gained by writing these productive spaces out of the city's contemporary history? Does this unacknowledged work result in more than just a paycheck for the workers at Dhanraj? Some of these questions can be answered on Dhanraj's factory floor, where workers are caught between an attachment to a form of labor that gives them identity and meaning and a history of deindustrialization and nonrecognition that renders them unvisible and anachronistic.

The morning shift usually begins at 7:00 AM, and I meet the workers on the shop floor, watching them work and then joining the group for rest and conversation during their breaks. When I first arrive in the mornings, the two remaining women on the Dhanraj workforce, Sushila and Manda, are already walking up and down the row of machinery, winding thread onto mechanical bobbins and beaming at me with toothless smiles. I shout my hellos to them over the din and ponder the impossibility of conversation above the sound of the machinery. But the women tell me they are used to the noise. They have learned to speak loudly when the machines are on.

The light is dim and the temperature much higher than outside. Cotton particles fly through the air, carried by the exhaust of machinery. They stick to my body and make me furry. I am planted on a table near the window and told to relax. There is a tea break in an hour. Sushila and Manda don't seem to be bothered by the heat and the noise and the flying cotton particles: I watch as they walk up and down the aisles of machinery to wind thread, movements embedded deep inside their bodies. When the thread is moved off of the top cones on the machines, new cones are placed in the

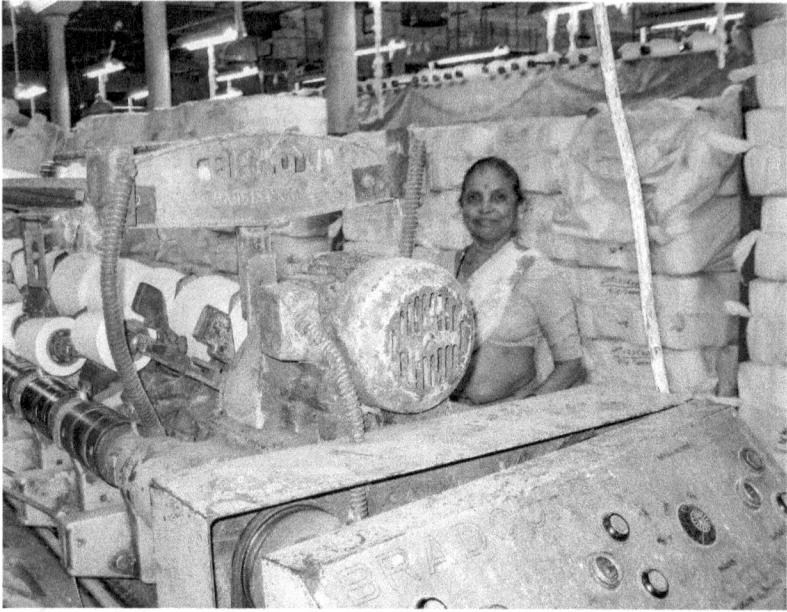

FIGURE 1.3. Manda posing with her winding machine.

middle section. A man named Dilip comes through with glue to affix the new cones. As they work, Manda and Sushila catch my eye, smile, and return to their winding. It is unusual for them to have an audience; however, they seem to welcome the opportunity to be observed, to show off their work, to occasionally teach me something about their routinized actions. Throughout my fieldwork Manda often tells her neighbors, "This woman is writing a book about us so that people will know we are here."

As the weeks and months progress, I find a rhythm in the mill, among the workers and the heat and the dust and the noise. When I arrive in the morning, I walk through the main room, lined with rows of machinery, to the back of the building, through a small breezeway, and sit by the window while work is carried out. Sometimes I read, sometimes I write field notes, sometimes I wander around and watch the workers, sometimes I chat and gossip with my research assistant, Kaveri, and sometimes I stare out into space: out the crumbling window, across the empty lot filled with two decades of litter, and into the trees that separate the compound from Ambedkar Road. As I sit on the wooden bench, littered with burlap bags and newspapers for padding, I can hear music and chatter and the clanking of machinery coming

FIGURE 1.4. A view of the vacant lot.

from the shoe factory to my right and the bag factory to my left. For the most part, these worlds remain separate. Additionally, the upper level of the mill building has been converted into rented storage godowns.[1] There, young male (mostly Muslim) workers, carrying large, unremarkable parcels up and down the stairs, often clog the hallways. None of the mill or shop workers interact with these young men, and I am advised to keep my distance.

However, I am not immediately told the same about the sweatshop workers. Early in my fieldwork, in December 2008, a young Maharashtrian woman named Anuja comes out of the shoe factory and asks me if I want to come in and see what she is doing. Eager to punctuate my boredom, I happily follow her inside, where a group of other young women, likely in their early twenties, sit around cutting machines and high-powered sewing machines used for making and piecing together rubber shoe soles. These will be sent to another small urban factory, where the rest of the shoe will be attached. The women never make a full product. I wonder aloud what they think when they encounter men's business shoes in the local market stalls: "Did I help make this shoe?" But they laugh at my question and shake their heads no, asking instead if I want tea.

Anuja takes me across the hall to the bag factory. Again, this space is staffed entirely by young women, save the male manager, who I guess to be in his late twenties or early thirties. Unlike in the shoe factory, where the women show me the machinery, demonstrate how it works, and let me help cut and sew several shoe soles, here the manager explains the process but doesn't have the women demonstrate. Unlike across the hall, here the bags are being pieced together with parts assembled elsewhere and sent in for the last stage of assembly. The shipment for the day hasn't yet arrived.

Our tea arrives, and Anuja sits down next to me while the manager explains: "We only take these spaces on lease for eleven months. After that time we have to find a new space. The owner doesn't want us to be here for a year or then we would no longer be temporary." These forms of informal spaces, I am told, exist throughout the Central Mumbai mill lands. Old mills, warehouses, factories: now many of the empty spaces are rented out as mobile factories, or sweatshops, where (mostly) young (mostly) female workers help assemble common market items.

The layers of visibility and unvisibility are almost uncanny at Dhanraj. The incredible visibility of Arvind's store and the hyperinvisibility of the sweatshops reveal how legitimacy is funneled through narratives of expectation relatively detached from legality and extralegality. Workers at Dhanraj believe Arvind's lifestyle store is actually an illegal project. A maintenance worker named Raj tells me that no permits were ever garnered for its opening, as the owners argued that it was, in fact, the mill's "showroom."[2] Since I began fieldwork in 2008, the store has expanded to four times its original size, and business is booming.[3]

And yet . . . the shoe and bag sweatshops are just two of the many informal factories that support the economy of Central Mumbai. The mill owner, Mr. Lal, refuses to talk to me about these economies operating on the mill premise, saying: "This is not a textile activity. This is not of interest to you." But I find these operations are of great interest to the workers. Raj tells me that the godowns and sweatshops are rented out for approximately thirty-five lakh rupees per month.[4] When speaking of money, the workers tell me that the mill is really quite useless for the owner: after paying taxes to the Brihanmumbai Municipal Corporation, Mumbai city's civic body, and other billed expenses, there isn't much money being made.

The workers know this, and their insecurity is apparent: the real money-makers, after the lifestyle store, are the shoe and bag factories and the storage godowns on the third floor. Everyone working in these informal spaces is friendly, but I learn to keep my distance: after I have tea with Anuja and the women at the bag factory, Manda asks me not to do so again.

The workers, in addition to mill land activists I speak with over the years, tell me that, without the front of the mill, these unregulated industries cannot continue to exist. Similarly, both the union representatives and Arvind inform me that the lifestyle store's existence is entirely reliant upon the happiness of the union—"Keep the mill open and functioning, and you can sell most of the land, retaining a small section to grow this emerging business." In 2013, Dhanraj and Mahindra sell five acres of the plot to Peninsula Developers for 650 crore rupees (approximately US$95 million). The two corporations split the sale fifty-fifty, releasing Dhanraj from its contract with Mahindra. When I return to the compound in the winter of 2015–2016, the five acres of purchased land are being cleared for development. Arvind tells me he doesn't know what the developers plan to do with their new acquisition, and he doesn't seem interested or invested in his eventual neighbors.

But while the future of the adjacent five acres is uncertain, the lifestyle store is growing exponentially, both within the Byculla compound and as satellite stores in Colaba and Vikhroli. Its website explains: "At the Byculla premises, while the staccato rhythm of looms fusing warp with weft are only a distant memory, the chimney—that proud sentinel and iconic symbol of a veritable era—still stands tall, now serving as a unmistakable landmark, helping our visitors locate us from miles away." This location is complicated, both spatially and logistically. On its website, the store is both described and defended, as its location can be a deterrent for desirable customers:

> While it is generally believed that being successful in retail largely depends on being at the right place, we think otherwise. We believe there are buyers out there, who like us, value aesthetics, craftsmanship and quality, and are willing to go the extra mile. So even though conventional market wisdom dictated a concrete-glass-steel mall, we opened our doors in 2007 within the charming precincts of one of Mumbai's oldest textile mills—established in 1839. We take pride in having revived the Mill's legacy, reflected in the Store's branding....

In a space-starved city, the Store stands out as a one-of-its-kind. Spread over more than 50,000 square feet, it is a cluster of large, high-ceilinged spaces that retains most of its original character and feel. Trailing the facade are ancient banyans and luxurious bougainvillea. Adjoining the Store at the far end is a freshwater pond.

The air changes from the time you drive through the gates, just off one of Mumbai's main arterial roads, and step onto the covered entrance porch. The . . . experience is not about making a quick sale. In fact, we encourage our customers to browse at their own pace, and linger for as long as they like, often over a cup of coffee.

Over the course of my two years in Mumbai, in addition to yearly visits from 2011 to 2018, the store expands from one to five buildings, spread throughout the mill compound. This expansion follows the downscaling of mill work, machinery, and workers. As of the writing of this in 2018, just enough mill activity is present to please the single union, the Rashtriya Mill Mazdoor Sangh (RMMS), allowing for the retail store to pull in the real money. The possibilities for Arvind's empire, it seems, are limited only by his imagination.

An Archive of Nonrecognition

I am invisible, understand, simply because people refuse to see me. Like the bodiless heads you see sometimes in circus sideshows, it is as though I have been surrounded by mirrors of hard, distorting glass. When they approach me they see only my surroundings, themselves, or figments of their imagination—indeed, everything and anything except me.—RALPH ELLISON, *Invisible Man*, (1952) 1995

It would be easy to see the textile mill as "the past" and the lifestyle store as "the future." Even now, I find it difficult to remove myself from this temporal framing of presence and productivity. But I also often feel as though I am asking the wrong questions: I push myself instead toward a discovery of what is remembered and what is forgotten, locating dates and places and watching them transform immediately into something else. My fieldwork experience often feels to be one of failure: an inability to access and understand a time and place I believe exists but have been told otherwise. My need to chart a history—whether the history of work, of buildings, of events—limits me to moving along a linear plane that my informants refuse to follow. My challenge is to find a way to dwell in between these two locations, to find the ethnographic balance between my narrative construction and that of my informants. To accept the inevitability of this failure and reframe it as generative: to challenge what I think I recognize, what seems familiar, what I have always/already accepted as true.

As I walk through the PUKAR museum exhibit displaying the narratives of "Barefoot Researchers," I realize that I am being given a *postindustrial* narrative of the city: "The textile industry is over, let us gaze upon the ruins." However, my time in Dhanraj shows me a *still-industrial* city, even if that city is nominal and in decline. Between the space of PUKAR's photographs and the whining of Dhanraj's winding machines, I understand the mill land neighborhoods of Mumbai as both postindustrial *and* industrial: these still-industrial areas are neither invisible, as I first thought they were, nor misrecognized, as I later assumed, but instead "nonrecognized."[5] I take my definition of nonrecognition from Thomas Blom Hansen, who defines it as "a willed incomprehension derived from a lack of desire, intimacy, and respect" (2012, 97). Nonrecognition is not passive: it is instead an active process, cultivated through care and practice. Nonrecognition is political and it is practical. And it is far from accidental.

The state of mill worker nonrecognition results in conflicting senses of betrayal by and love for the city of Mumbai. Here I place the city itself—as a character—at the center of my ethnography. In writing of a relationship between the city and my informants, I do not merely draw on a rhetorical strategy of urban personification. Instead, the stories my informants tell me articulate a relationship with Mumbai, as an actor, that mirrors the language I assume would be directed toward individuals and institutions associated with power: mill owners, developers, government bureaucrats, and so forth.[6] Instead, I am shown how infrastructure *itself* has agency, at least when seen through the eyes of economically and politically disenfranchised communities: when Dhanraj workers speak of progress, they articulate how the new buildings and flyovers signal a modernity in which they are not included. While they *could* speak at length about the individuals and institutions barring them from this progress, they instead see the *materiality* of infrastructure—steel, glass, asphalt, concrete—as a message, and this message comes from "the city."[7]

This message is one of exclusion, but my informants simultaneously experience a conflicting desire: the desire to be recognized and included, even as such a desire seems to be an impossible one. There is, for workers, no alternative source of recognition.[8] Desire is an acknowledgment of loss: a yearning for that which is always/already absent. Mill worker desire is twofold: it is the desire for the life of a worker and the desire to be seen as a worker.[9] Dhanraj workers are in constant conversation with the city of Mumbai. As this conversation, articulated through a relationship with the city's changing infrastructure, becomes more and more dismissive, mill workers—once the backbone of the city—have come to inhabit anachronistic subjectivities.[10] This relationship of subject (mill workers)/power (Mumbai) constructs the subject as ambivalent in terms of its relationship *to* power, as subjects become attached to the structures of power that subordinate them.[11] The workers of Dhanraj are experiencing a social death as *workers*, and their ability to imagine eventual recognition becomes less and less possible every day.[12]

Returning to Hansen, this is an attachment to a dialectical nonrecognition: on the one hand, Dhanraj workers understand that Central Mumbai is becoming (and needs to become) postindustrial. A North Indian worker named Sudarshan often tells me: "Development is necessary, it is the duty of humanity." However, their attachments to an industrial way of life make this form of seeing very difficult. Sudarshan also tells me: "It is because of these buildings that we have lost our daily bread." These attachments are messy because, even as they are infused with pain, they are also infused with the desire for normalcy, the yearning for a dependable life, an optimism Lauren Berlant (2011) calls "cruel."

These attachments I hear articulated by Dhanraj workers do not make sense on many levels: a desire for work that, in turn, brings pain and suffering, as well as a relatively low social status (at least in the current moment); a desire to live in tenements generally understood to be cramped and dilapidated and otherwise uninhabitable. But these desires are connected to larger attachments to a way of life and a future that, in many ways, no longer exists. The anachronism of these workers is twofold: first, their mere existence is anachronistic, as the textile industry is no longer a material necessity in Mumbai. Not only is there no demand for the cotton thread produced in the few operational mills, but also—for the mills that are still, nonetheless, operating—their existence is dependent on legal loopholes, extralegal strategies, and the lack of liquid capital needed to cover the pensions of those still employed. The extralegal efforts of Dhanraj's owners occur *because* the industry is, and has been, obsolete. If the Lal family, who own the mill, were to listen to the public, visible market, the gates of the mill would have shut many years before. It is for these reasons, and *not* the rules of supply and demand, that my informants continue to clock in and experience the boredom and frustration of redundancy.

Second, the workers' actual desires and attachments are anachronistic because "the city" (being not only the material infrastructure but also the academics, activists, journalists, artists, and policy makers writing its past, present, and future) as their "Master" (in a Hegelian sense) does not acknowledge that they exist at all: they are nonrecognized by these narrative powers. The only acknowledged textile mill workers in Mumbai are those who—because they are unemployed and seeking reparations—have entered the activist sphere as they exited the sphere of current workers: those I will frame as "visible" workers. The irony here is that the only way to be recognized as a worker is to stop being a worker. In addition to being nonrecognized by the city, Dhanraj workers *also* fail to receive recognition from these activist workers and their interlocutors.[13] This double refusal of recognition places Dhanraj workers in an impossible position: not only has their work *not* freed them from the Master, but the fact that they work at all denies them recognition from subjects that would, in other circumstances, be their allies. In fact, it is through work that Dhanraj workers lose their own value.[14]

This contradiction permeates every interaction I have with Dhanraj mill workers. The fleeting nature of contemporary mill work, the imminent possibility of redevelopment, and the eventual displacement of chawl dwellers and mill workers constitute a constant reality in the everyday lives of my informants. However, alongside this stark eventuality, I still witness an attachment to forms of life constantly under threat and a hope for a recognition that will eventually lead to preservation, even though notions of this preservation are murky, at best. These forms of attachments are both bewildering in their optimism and banal in their sense of suffering. While, historically, textile workers (who are, by their very definition, migrant workers of some sort) draw their own legitimacy in Mumbai from their employment in the mills, my informants desire the legitimacy of urban citizenship—a recognition from the city based on the accumulation of their contribution (as well as that of generations preceding them) to the building of modern Mumbai.

Instead, the decline of industrial employment robs them of legitimacy, and the city—their Master—turns away from them as their relevance declines. It is this disavowal, I argue, that fuels the nostalgia for work permeating mill land Mumbai. If Dhanraj workers cannot access the recognition of citizenship on their own terms, they instead cleave to the one thing that brought them legitimacy in the past: their work. And so this archive is an archive of nonrecognized mill workers, who are unseen by the city, even as they remain at its center, occupying its lively ruins. But how has this non-recognition come to be? I argue that it is through learned practices of "un-visibility," which allow multiple cities to exist simultaneously: the industrial city sits alongside the postindustrial city, but the former has learned how to "unsee" and "unhear" the latter.

A Tale of Two Cities

This is the time of night
Where instead of seeing the city
The city sees me
—MAGED ZAHER, *The Consequence of My Body*, 2016

In China Miéville's fantasy police procedural novel, *The City and the City*, the dead body of a mysterious young woman turns up in an abandoned neighborhood in the city of Besźel. Except the city of Besźel is not actually *one* city, it is instead two "topolganger" cities: Besźel and Ul Qoma, both occupying the same space, at the same time.[15] Miéville tells us:

> Besźel's dark ages are very dark. Sometime between two thousand and seventeen hundred years ago the city was founded, here in this curl of coastline. There are still remains from those times in the heart of the town, when it was a port hiding a few kilometers up the river to shelter from the pirates of the shore. The city's founding came at the same time as another's, of course. The ruins are surrounded now or in some places incorporated, antique foundations, into the substance of the city. . . . It may or may not have been Besźel, that we built, back then, while others may have been building Ul Qoma on the same bones. Perhaps there was one thing back then that later schismed on the ruins, or perhaps our ancestral Besźel had not yet met and standoffishly entwined its neighbor. I am not a student of the Cleavage, but if I were I still would not know. (2009, 42)

Or perhaps this is the space of three cities, as the mysterious murdered woman turns out to be an American archaeologist named Mahalia Geary, who is investigating the possible existence of a third and mythological city, Orciny, rumored to exist *between* Besźel and Ul Qoma. As the plot unfolds, the reader learns that although the two (and perhaps three) cities occupy the same space, residents are taught to "unsee" and "unhear" the parallel city right before them.

Even so, while movement between the two cities is heavily regulated, it is not entirely impossible. To move between the two cities, travelers must pass through Copular Hall—a checkpoint that transforms one's ability to see and engage with space, an uncanny voyage through the looking glass: "But pass through Copular Hall and she or he might leave Besźel, and at the end of the hall come back to exactly (corporeally) where they had just been, but in another country, a tourist, a marveling visitor, to a street that shared the latitude-longitude of their own address, a street they had never visited before, whose architecture they had always unseen, to the Ul Qoman house sitting next to and a whole city away from their own building, unvisible there now they had come through, all the way across the Breach, back home" (2009, 70). I borrow Miéville's framing of "unvisible" in contrast to "invisible"—like nonrecognition, "unvisible" suggests agency and refusal: a practice of unseeing something until it no longer *can* be seen. Like Besźel and Ul Qoma, the industrial and postindustrial cities of Central Mumbai occupy the same space and time within the city. However, residents of each subcity learn to unsee and unhear each other until "unvisibility" becomes a state of being.

This tension is palpable within the Dhanraj compound. The textile operation of Dhanraj lies hidden within two extremes of visibility and unvisibility: the lifestyle store is hypervisible, yet dubious in its legal legitimacy. The sweatshops are completely unvisible and impermanent, yet widely acknowledged throughout the city. Yet neither operation can continue without the foundation of textile production continuing, unseen and unacknowledged, yet legally legitimate. In this way, the continuing unvisible labor of Dhanraj workers allows for the "real" production of the enclave to continue and shields both the lifestyle store and the sweatshops through this unvisible cover. This unvisible cover is similar to the duck-rabbit made famous by Wittgenstein: when looking directly at Dhanraj, one will likely "see that" as the lifestyle store and unregulated sweatshops. Like the residents of Besźel, Mumbai city residents "see" the lifestyle store and "know" that sweatshops operate throughout the mill lands. Dhanraj's mill operation, like the city of Ul Qoma, remains unseen. However, when looked at from a different angle, this unvisible cover becomes transparent, allowing for observers to "see (the space of Dhanraj) as" a much messier place of both postindustrial *and* industrial activity.

Additionally, Miéville's framing of alienated urban space provides a way of understanding how unvisible workers occupy the shadowy and semiproductive industrial spaces of the city (particularly as employed workers in Dhanraj) and how visible workers, now unemployed, are centrally located and visible as activists (particularly as members of the GKSS). When I begin preliminary fieldwork in Mumbai in 2006, most of my mill land fieldwork occurs around meetings of the GKSS, which was begun in 1989 as the Closed Mills Committee and fought for six years (until 1995) to reopen ten mills, still shut years after the failed 1982–1983 strike. While six of the mills are eventually reopened, in 1991 the Development Control Rules begin to change the stakes for mill land development: even if mills *are* pushed to reopen, many of them find alternative pathways toward nonindustrial development, and job opportunities dwindle. Because of this the Closed Mills Committee drastically alters the approach of its activism. With a membership of more than fifteen thousand workers, it is the major opposition to the single officially recognized labor union, the RMMS, which is affiliated with the ruling Congress Party.

Today the GKSS is primarily concerned with issues of housing and employment opportunities for former mill workers and schooling opportunities for their children. In addition, the GKSS often organizes in opposition to various development schemes throughout the area of Central Mumbai. When I attend its events, I can't locate any members or participants who are still employed in a textile mill. When I speak to Dhanraj workers, none have heard of or seem interested in the activity of the GKSS.

While Dhanraj workers are largely unvisible within the landscape of Mumbai, I watch the unemployed workers of the GKSS occupy a site of growing visibility in the city, whether through news media, narrative film, histories, or documentary film. Within all these forms of media, the out-of-work mill worker becomes a hypervisible sign of increasing inequality, informality, and injustice, as well as urban loss, redevelopment, and displacement.

It is unsurprising that Dhanraj workers have little to no knowledge of the GKSS activities, as their daily survival (in part) involves protecting themselves against the shock of the urban gaze, just as the GKSS (and the city at large) protect themselves from the reality of vitally anachronistic current workers.[16] The acknowledgment of "the other" requires the shock of a counternarrative, one that punctuates a daily and banal mythology of normalcy. Once again, Berlant helps draw such an experience away from the mythic realm and root it once again within the experiences of precariousness and survival. She frames "aspirational normalcy" as "a desire to feel normal and to feel normalcy as a ground of dependable life, a life that does not have to keep being reinvented" (Berlant 2007, 281). When understood through this lens, normalcy is something to be desired, particularly for those living outside of its frame. However, to *aspire* to normalcy, one must forge an attachment to forms of optimism and possibility that are inextricably linked to cruelty and compromise.[17]

What resonates here is how Berlant suggests that the attachment itself makes possible a (compromised) ability to live on and "to look forward to being in the world." I find this frame helpful in understanding how the workers at Dhanraj conceive of their tenuous employment status and abandonment by the public sphere, particularly after the strike of the early 1980s and the rise of GKSS activism. Over the course of my fieldwork, the workforce at Dhanraj shrinks from 150 to 104 to 97 to 62 to just around 50, and these lingering laborers hold on to jobs virtually eradicated during the strikes. Talk of retirement within the mill is generally filtered through the language of loss, and retrenched workers disappear into the ether of the city. My Dhanraj informants struggle to create a sense of normalcy within extraordinary conditions, all the while deflecting the realities I see as far too clear: the termination of employment signals the loss of social relations, the closing of the mill, and the final death of the industry. Employment at Dhanraj isn't merely a job, but to think of it in any other terms is too devastating to bear.

While the unvisibility of current workers is tenuously connected to collaborative activism through which the GKSS participates, I do not want to conflate the construction of mill land mythology and the elevation of a mythic subject with the work of the GKSS: members of the GKSS are *also* aspiring to normalcy, albeit in a very different way. These aspirations—for lost wages, housing, and education opportunities—are framed in terms of accessing a life in which city space once again becomes available to the urban poor. In doing so, this narrative of aspirational normalcy is predicated upon the myth that such spaces had once been livable but are recently rendered inaccessible. Regardless of historical and contemporary accessibility, the development of Central Mumbai is ensuring it becomes less and less democratic every day. However, GKSS agitations draw constant attention to a critical urban question: Who is the city *for*? Is urban access unlocked only through wealth and upward mobility?

Many residents of Mumbai live and work in obsolete economies. While India's new economy (including but not limited to energy, science and technology, and medical services) and the powerful narratives of globalization and technological infrastructures frame the country through newness and future possibilities, my time in Central Mumbai reveals how these new economies do not actually affect many city residents. Instead, many Mumbaikers work in older economies that are marginal to these newer economies. The narratives of development cannot eclipse the material reality of the city: old, decaying buildings, precarious informal economies, and waves of migrant laborers who transform the cityscape overnight through temporary residential and commercial structures. Semifunctional mills provide legitimacy for sweatshops, storage units, and other unregulated industries. These older, declining spaces may be sites of ruination, but these ruins are lively and vital. There is still so much life in these spaces of loss.

When the archive becomes a more visible city space, narratives of newness and development pale in comparison to the overwhelming materiality of the present and thriving antique city. So how do we learn to unsee people and places that inconvenience our museum narratives?

In some ways, the workers of Dhanraj benefit directly from both earlier and current agitations of the GKSS, as public protest not only reopens several mills in the 1980s and 1990s but also continues to draw attention to questions of housing for poorer communities. However, continued employment also ensures that Dhanraj workers cannot benefit directly in the current moment, as contemporary GKSS agitation has become predicated upon the argument that no mills continue to function. Dhanraj workers linger at the threshold of legibility, but their job security, ironically enough, leaves them insecure.

This job security (being contracts and pension plans) does not exist until the textile industry has already begun to decline in Mumbai, in the aftermath of the 1982–1983 strike, meaning that such protection for current workers has been unthinkable for those who haven't found mill land employment since the strikes. The early 1980s resulted in a visible rupture in mill employment practices. While the majority of workers employed before the strike were *badli* (temporary) workers with no job security, no tenure, and no entitlement to pensions, in the aftermath of the strikes, when the Congress-backed union, the RMMS, locked the remaining mill workers into permanent employment agreements with their employers, those rehired as mills reopened found themselves protected, regularized, and entitled to the benefits of tenured employment. However, those workers fortunate enough to secure one of the limited permanent jobs in the mills begin to simultaneously see the end of industry emerge before them: the paradox of permanent employment in an impermanent industry. As urban textile production becomes economically unviable, operational mills gradually seek opportunities to close down and redevelop, in order to keep up with a sense of progress and modernity that is coming to dominate a different narrative of postindustrial Mumbai.

While employed workers, like my informants at Dhanraj, are few in number and arguably irrelevant in the large-scale economic life of the city, I am still invested in their subjective experiences as they struggle to exist within the contemporary moment they are simultaneously being excluded from. While I *am* arguing that Dhanraj, as a space of vital ruination, has much to say about the future, I am *not* arguing that the textile industry is dynamic or in need of revitalization. Indeed, it is through the process of Dhanraj's death that urban futures may be predicted: redevelopment, the disappearance of the industrial city, the displacement of former mill workers . . . these are not process that can be reversed.[18] However, I do argue that the lives lived on the margins of progress and modernity can tell us a great deal about progress because they *too* are modern. If ethnography has anything to offer the world, it is a methodology that privileges "experience" as the nexus of our data. The practice of "unseeing" these marginalized communities does not make them disappear, it simply makes them unseen. There are two cities coexisting in Central Mumbai: the visible city of postindustrial modernity and the unvisible city of the anachronistic present. What can this unvisible archive of nonrecognition show us if we cross over its threshold?

Leakage in an Unvisible City

Not to find one's way around a city does not mean much. But to lose one's way in a city . . . requires some schooling. —WALTER BENJAMIN, *Berlin Childhood around 1900*, 2006

My days in Dhanraj involve slowly chipping away at inconvenient industrial debris, so present and yet so hard to recognize. I tell the workers I feel overwhelmed by the layered histories of the neighborhood: How do I *see* what is right before me? Sudarshan, a Dhanraj worker from the northern state of Uttar Pradesh, tells me he can help. He drives a taxi at night and is saving his extra money in hopes of buying his own chawl unit one day. There is a petrol station down the street from the mill with a friendly chai-wallah stationed on the corner. Dozens of taxi-wallahs park their *kali-peelis* ("black and yellow" non-air-conditioned Fiats and Ambassadors) there, and Sudarshan hangs out with a large congregation of North Indian taxi drivers after his shift at the mill. Some drivers park on the shady lane and sleep in their backseat; others squat with their glass cups of tea and packaged biscuits, sharing the neighborhood gossip. One hot day in March 2009, I meet Sudarshan, and he drives me through the mill lands, pointing out the changing urban skyline, the abandoned lots, and the new developments.

Sudarshan tracks those changes with a shadow of hopelessness, telling me: "Changes are only for the rich people. Because of our conditions, we have to leave this area and move out. It's a fact." He drives his taxi from 7:00 PM to midnight, after working at the mill from 7:00 AM to 2:00 PM and resting in the afternoon. He explains, "The rich people don't take taxis anymore . . . they have Meru."[19] He tells me the taxi rates are too low: petrol prices keep going up, but the pay he receives remains the same.

Taxi driving is not a vocation, Sudarshan tells me. With mill work, he arrives every day at Dhanraj, performs honorable manual labor, and receives a steady paycheck for his efforts. This is something respectable: this is *work*.[20] In fact, driving his taxi is a source of shame in many ways: the daily drudgery and toil, the impermanence and futility, are mere *labor* and exist simply for his own daily survival and the daily survival of his family. He makes nothing through driving: he leaves no traces on the city.

But even a "worker" struggles in a city becoming more and more economically impossible for nonelite residents: although his mill work is more respectable, it doesn't pay enough for him to support himself and his male family members (living in Mumbai), while also sending payments

FIGURE 1.5. The ruins of India United Mills No. 1, visited with Sudarshan as we drive through the mill lands.

home to his wife and daughters in the northern state of Uttar Pradesh. Driving the night shift reveals this: he is saving up for a flat of his own, which will increase his sense of respectability, and therefore his driving has noble elements. But he still sees driving as a form of lesser work, of labor. Retirement or retrenchment will take away his "real" source of income and destroy the buffer between him and drivers with no other vocation.

Sudarshan wants to show me the graveyard of the neighborhoods around Dhanraj. We meet up early, but it is already unbearably hot: the humidity from the city concentrates in the taxi, and more hot air blows in through the open windows. As he drives me through the textile neighborhoods that day, he pays careful attention to the remnants of industry: former mills, operational mills, and ghost mills now redeveloped as shopping malls or apartment complexes. I force myself to see not abandonment and absence but instead a still-ongoing process of lively ruination. As he speaks of the neighborhood's postmill progress, he articulates how the new buildings and flyovers signal a modernity in which he is not included. While he could speak at length about the individuals and in-stitutions barring him from this progress, he instead sees the *materiality* of infrastructure—steel, glass, asphalt, concrete—as a message, and this message comes from "the city." As we drive he explains: "These big new buildings are for the big people, not for us. It is difficult; it is a problem for us. It is because of these buildings that we have lost our daily bread. Rich people move into these big houses, they have money, they will move in here. But we used to work here. I feel a little heartache." I ask him to ex-plain why he says "we used to work here." Doesn't he work here still? He tells me he feels it is inevitable that he will lose his job and the mill will close. There are so few workers left, it is as though there are no mills at all. As we drive, we pass by Victoria Mills and he stops the car, pointing out the carefully executed, beautiful gate, now in disrepair. We continue on. As we pass by Crown Mills he continues: "Development is certainly good: it's a duty of humanity, so development is necessary for progress. It doesn't always benefit poor people, but it's not a problem. Poor people are not capable of development. Only rich people can afford development; poor people can't afford to participate. So they don't benefit. Workers get paid for the work they do: that's their due. Nothing else." Sudarshan tells me he accepts the inevitability of Dhanraj's closure, but with a heavy heart: he watches it come closer every day.

As we drive through the mill lands together, Sudarshan points out the few mills that are still operational: five mills controlled by the National Tex-tile Corporation (NTC) and one privately owned mill (Dhanraj). Through-out our tour I find that the operational mills, from the road, look like con-struction sites and abandoned compounds, with no outward indications that mill workers are employed behind the archaic gates. Without Sudar-shan's knowledge, I would never know that Central Mumbai still employs hundreds of unvisible textile workers in the lively ruins decaying beyond the mill gates.

Conclusions: What Does It Mean to Disappear When No One Can See You?

We tried to understand the crisis on a large scroll of paper that many of us carried through the city. . . . It was something unfurling, taking the place of events that were no longer occurring. —RENEE GLADMAN, *Ana Patova Crosses a Bridge*, 2013

Perhaps the visible worker cannot exist alongside the unvisible worker: after all, Miéville's protagonist eventually discovers that the two cities are actually just one. And once you know the secret, what's the fun in a magic trick? Over the past thirty years, the public face of remnant mills has been one of rapid disappearance: the industry largely exists in the past tense of history books, an uneven public imagination, and the built form of the city. The fields of urban studies and urban anthropology are far too often framed through the language of absence: Who has gone? Who has been displaced? What has disappeared? This language of loss and absence is powerful: these forms of interpretation contribute to an understanding of the shifting nature of cities through the places and people who used to exist but have now made way for new trends and demographics. Similarly, current trends in anthropology privilege a forward form of looking: forms of development and institutional ethnographies that unravel how government structures and bureaucratic institutions fuel a teleological conception of progress. While I do not dispute the importance of such engagements, I want to suggest that such a lens simultaneously renders those on the margins intelligible only as leftovers and archaic spaces: as cities redevelop, as markets restructure, and as communities are formed and reformed, the traces of such forward motion—those who are "left behind" or continue to struggle at the margins—become the unseen casualties of more convenient stories. This urban narrative demands a postindustrial identity, therefore making those outside such a story ghostly specters. It is very difficult to see that which has been made unvisible.

Therefore, Dhanraj workers and GKSS members occupy two very different temporospatial cities: one industrial, one postindustrial. I conceptualize these two spaces as a dialectical relation, one in which the two terms are both mutually imbricated and disjunctive. These conflicting embodied experiences bar solidarity *and* mutual recognition. When Datta Iswalkar, the long-term president of the GKSS, speaks with me about mill land activity, he begins with the argument of absence. When I ask him about spaces like Dhanraj, he tells me, "Mills still aren't really running now. At Dhanraj there are less than a hundred workers; at Bombay Dyeing, less than a hundred. Two, three . . . only for show. But otherwise all the mills are closed." Such a dismissal of these lingering mills makes sense; they do not seem to represent the current trends of Mumbai's development trajectory. Like the work of PUKAR and others attempting to characterize deindustrialization in Mumbai, I find the GKSS framing of deindustrialization as a definitive, homogeneous, and linear process. And although the GKSS's narrative accounts for a teleological temporality of industrialization, the lively ruination of Dhanraj and the continued presence of my informants disrupt this narrative and shed light on how such progression is neither linear nor seamless.[21]

Given the hypervisible developments in the center of the city, the decline of the industry is jarring and dramatic and lends itself to thoughts of finality. Yet machines still grumble from the mill compounds of Byculla, Lal Baug, and Parel. What allows this perceived silence, even as current workers remain existent and functional in several of the city's mills? While Dipti's earlier reading of Dhanraj as a "fake" mill acknowledges that Dhanraj workers, though "fake," do, indeed, exist, I find instead that many Mumbaikers assume that Central Mumbai's mills are closed and its workforce dispersed. Such an assumption is encouraged not only by historians, media coverage, and activists but also by city infrastructure that shadows the low-lying industrial buildings with high-rises and flyovers.

But living in the shadows is still living a life. These lives do not cease to exist simply because they are unseen.

The GKSS provides a network of support for former workers seeking financial reparations, housing, and education opportunities for their children. Through this network, members are kept aware of litigation on their behalf, development projects in the mill lands, and housing lotteries for which they are eligible. And such movements result in various forms of public agitation, which will be covered by the print media. Such is the space of visibility. In Dhanraj, however, unvisibility comes with varying degrees of vulnerability. Current workers not only are rarely given updates on union activity and negotiations but also are unaware of any planning involving the future of the mill and the likelihood of their own retention or retrenchment. Such precarity enforces a desperate cleaving onto worker identity; the ephemerality of future employment results in workers too terrified to advocate for themselves or ask questions of union leaders. Even as retaining a worker identity is an all-consuming topic in conversations at the mill, Dhanraj workers also feel too precarious to search for sources of support, whether through outside advocates or insider information.

Toward the end of my long-term fieldwork in 2010, several hundred GKSS-affiliated former workers gather at Azad Maidan (freedom park) in downtown Mumbai to protest the government's unwillingness to back pre-strike workers' dues. These dues are engaged specifically through housing, which is promised but as yet only given in small numbers to workers residing in decrepit chawls in the mill lands. This protest draws massive media attention and large-scale participation. Videos circulate on YouTube, and various Mumbai-focused listservs advertise the event. A couple of years later, in 2012, a similar protest draws more than a thousand people. The visibility of GKSS, it seems, is growing.

That same year, in 2012, the GKSS starts a Facebook page titled "Girangaon: City of Mills" on which are posted news articles and updates surrounding GKSS activity in Hindi, Marathi, and English. One of the first posts alerts readers to the city's development of two committees intended to supervise the allocation of housing to former mill workers. Several months later, I am alerted to a celebratory news update from GKSS vice president Meena Menon that reads: "On the 28th of June 2012, the Government of Maharashtra will conduct the lottery for the distribution of 6,948 tenements, the first phase of housing built for out-of-work textile mill workers" (2012a).

The GKSS not only is continuing its decades-long agitation for the rights of former workers but also, through a marriage between protest and new media, it is effecting change on a government level. This citywide visibility is something unimaginable to the workers in Dhanraj, whose daily grind at the mill continues on unseen, be it by the GKSS, the government, or mill land news media and their consumers. As Dhanraj workers watch their worker-based identity slip away, GKSS members strengthen their out-of-work identity through tactics of visibility. This visibility, in turn, enforces a citywide mythology of mill work as past tense and all mill workers as unemployed. The experience of employment has no place here.

The GKSS imagines a future in which the past is paid for, while the workers at Dhanraj imagine a future in which the present is paid for. Both groups are awaiting their dues, whether those dues are lost wages, pensions, or housing. And even as both groups experience themselves as vitally present, imagining a solid foothold in Central Mumbai's future feels fantastical: it seems, instead, that both groups imagine the future of the mill lands as a place in which they are not just unvisible but finally truly absent. Gaston Bachelard tells us: "The imagination separates us from the past as well as from reality; it faces the future. To the *function of reality*, wise in experience of the past, . . . should be added a *function of unreality*, which is equally positive. . . . If we cannot imagine, we cannot foresee" (1994, xxxiv). So who sees behind the walls that hide unvisible communities, buildings, and economies? Who imagines their futures? Who are the architects of their potential?

The gate at Dhanraj separates two worlds of workers: On one side is the "modern" city of Mumbai, home to the unemployed and visible workers of the GKSS. On the other side, within the walls of the mill, are the workers of Dhanraj Spinning and Weaving, Ltd., who inhabit a time of vitally anachronistic urban modernity and a space of lively ongoing ruination. These worlds exist in isolation from each other because the vitality of ruination is often mistaken for absence and emptiness. However, the lively space of Dhanraj and the continued presence of Dhanraj workers contain an alternative future: by attending to the process of decay inside the mill compound (instead of pronouncing it already dead), I am learning about the future of the world beyond the limits of my own imagination.

2

The Archive
of the Worker

The sphere is the interior, disclosed, shared realm inhabited by humans—in so far as they succeed in becoming humans. Because living means building spheres, both on a small and large scale, humans are the beings that establish globes and look out into horizons. Living in spheres means creating the dimension in which humans can be contained.—PETER SLOTERDIJK, *Bubbles: Spheres*, 2011

I am a time being. Do you know what a time being is? . . . A time being is someone who lives in time, and that means you, and me, and every one of us who is, or was, or ever will be.—RUTH OZEKI, *A Tale for the Time Being*, 2013

Arrivals: Tales of Time Beings

PART ONE: ONE DAY IN NOVEMBER 2008

"My legs ache from twenty years of standing," Manda tells me. It is early afternoon, the workers have congregated in the back of the building, and the machinery has been turned off for the next hour. This happens for several isolated hours throughout each shift: there simply isn't enough work to justify the electricity bill. Several workers are napping. Others drink chai, read newspapers, or complain about the poor quality of the raw cotton. In the corner beside the window, Manda, Sushila, and I sit on the floor, cooled by the breeze carried off the adjacent abandoned lot. The women massage their calves while we talk: their legs are knobby and sinewy and look incredibly strong.

"My legs ache from twenty years of standing," Manda tells me. I know that she is telling me something important. I write her words down. I circle them, removing them from other sentences. I note that these eight words will lead me to a destination I cannot yet see. I trust that I will find it.

I think again of Renee Gladman's unnamed linguist-traveler, who asks me: "Have you ever tried to spell something out that you have not heard exactly, in a language that, while you have mastered it, is not your own, using diacritics that are not your own?" (2010, 116).

"Yes," I tell her, as I read. "I do this every day. I am an ethnographer."

I have been coming to this textile mill for three weeks now. This textile mill in Mumbai I call "Dhanraj." A textile mill functioning in a city convinced there are no functioning textile mills. A "space on the side of the road," in the words of Kathleen Stewart. A cohort of employed workers working in a city convinced that there are no currently employed workers left working. Layers of unvisibility exist here in this space, underneath the emerging vertical city.[1] And yet unvisibility is simply a question of scale and perspective. We can all see each other in this space of the mill. Ghosts do not look like ghosts when you can see them full on.

And so there is nothing spectacular about these uncanny hauntings: sometimes the light filters through the cracks in the ceiling, and the dust and cotton particles appear like the shadows of bodies not here or once there, and the workforce has somehow doubled at the edges of my peripheral vision. Do bodies feel differently in this space, the way old ghosts become visible when the light is controlled mostly by darkness?

And yet still there is magic here: "ethnographic hypnosis," to borrow and adapt from Roland Barthes: I am here and also not here (1975, 347). I am in the story and I am writing the story. But who is telling the story?

"Tell me a story!" I ask, like an expectant, overly eager child. The women look at me strangely, blushing. They tell me they have no stories to tell. Nothing interesting ever happens here, they tell me. In "The Storyteller," Walter Benjamin writes, "More and more often there is embarrassment all around when the wish to hear a story is expressed. It is as if something that seems inalienable to us, the securest among our possessions, were taken from us: the ability to exchange experiences" (2007, 83). Perhaps aches and pains are like cotton particle ghosts, and the women think I will not believe them or I will choose not to see what maybe is not there.

"I want to hear everything," I say. And so, slowly, Manda tells me of her aches, Sushila tells me of her pains. I look around, and I immediately be-

FIGURE 2.1. Rows of cotton/ghosts.

lieve I understand why because, as an ethnographer, I am only three weeks old. The floor is lined with corrugated metal, a brutal surface to stand on. The women are wearing simple plastic chappals, footwear that provides no support. I take a metaphorical step back from where I am seated, survey the space. It is dark in the mill, light creeping in from the dirty windows, cracked to the gray, smog-filled sky. Weak light emanating from fluorescent lights encased by cobwebs. Dust and debris and pieces of cotton rolling along the floor like tumbleweed blown by the few fans, which do not seem to affect the temperature. And then there is the sound: when the machines are on, they roar at us, almost impossible to hear over. I notice how every muscle relaxes in my neck when they are turned off.

And so I look around me and believe I understand how such working conditions would break a body down. I'm not even standing and I feel broken. Broken and bored.

"My legs ache from twenty years of standing," Manda tells me. I know that she is telling me something important. I write the words down. I circle them, removing them from other sentences. I note that these eight words will lead me to the destination I cannot yet see. I trust that I will find it. But,

FIGURE 2.2. Sushila and Sudarshan working the winding machines.

you see, I do not understand the temporality of this story. I think Manda is telling me about the passage of time.

Gladman's unnamed linguist-traveler, on finding herself alone in Ravicka, realizes:

> Of course, I had not been on my own that long. The last time I saw Dar—if I counted back from the point of my stink, having yet come upon a body of water or a generous tap—was just over a week ago, and three days since my time with Ulchi. To say that, though—that I have not been on my own for very long—would mean that I have been following a linear path. That the event of sleeping on the grass led to my waking on the bench and the disconsolation of waking on the bench, in a serenely decimated city, led to Ulchi and his making of the map. This linearity could form only if there had been no events in between. I am saying that things happened that have not been reported, and it is in virtue of those missing things that I was here. Had I spoken of them, at this point in the story, I would be elsewhere. (2010, 81–82)

And then I realize that I, too, am sitting alone on a park bench in Ravicka, dirty and alone. What parts of the story have I not told? Which parts of the story did the storyteller omit from the telling?

PART TWO: ONE DAY IN APRIL 2011

"'My legs ache from twenty years of standing,' Manda told me two and a half years ago in November." I have returned to my notes, it seems. I have returned to Manda's eight words. I am looking at this now, six years later, reflecting on a conversation from two and a half years earlier. Where is the story in these words now? Benjamin tells us: "The value of information does not survive the moment in which it was new. It lives only at that moment; it has to surrender to it completely and explain itself to it without losing any time. A story is different. It does not expend itself. It preserves and concentrates its strength and is capable of releasing it even after a long time" (2007, 90). Eight words, one sentence. Building in strength in my imagination as the years pass. I think I am getting somewhere: OK, her body was and continues to be an archive of memory; this is not just the breakdown of muscle and bone. This is accumulated exhaustion. This is aching and paining as proof that work has happened and continues to happen. She is telling me this story because the aching and the paining make her real, and she has told me that not that many people see her because she is a worker and there are no workers left. This is a physical sensation in the unvisible present that connects Manda to the remembered past. She tells me this story because it is a reminder that she is not just a ghost, living here in the realm of the unreal. It took me two and a half years to come to this place. Am I getting somewhere? Am I getting close? Where do I want to be with this story now? This "theory of memory as haunting."[2]

PART THREE: ONE DAY IN MARCH 2017

"My legs ache from twenty years of standing," Manda told me in November eight and a half years ago. These eight simple words, this uncanny sentence, continually haunting me. Constantly returning to me in disfigured form, much like the persistence of vital industrial ruin I sit within. I am "glued to this representation," to once again return to Barthes, as "the Real knows only distances, the Symbolic knows only masks; the image" (or words, for me) "alone is close, only the image" (or words) "is '*true*'" (1975, 348). Manda's body was and continues to be a witness to her history, even as such "exposure" remains contained within the archive of her

FIGURE 2.3.
Ghostly Manda at
the machine.

body.[3] The past still remains, layered under the present moment and embedded under skin. Do I understand this now?

Maybe. When Manda told me, "My legs ache from twenty years of
standing," maybe she wasn't just explaining how her labor was embedded
in her bones and muscles, layered under her skin. Maybe she was also telling me how the past twenty years, like a noxious chemical, were inhaled
and absorbed into her body, changing it. Transforming her into an industrial cyborg of time, space, steel, and flesh.

Changing her into the negative of the city infrastructure I see outside
the dirty windows. Changing her into the ghostly image reflected by the
skyscrapers looming above us. Rendering her the negative of the photograph of the urban landscape, where "official" stories dwell. I am among
the unvisible opposites of the urban imaginary, emerging above and beyond the skyline.

We are underground. But only because the ground is moving upward, above us, as flyovers are built, moving the city skyward. We suddenly find ourselves below the road because the road is shifting. But we are not sinking.

I go back to my original notes.

I also wrote:

Manda is complaining about the raw material.
  Sushila is rubbing her feet.
  Sudarshan is taking a nap, Hindi-language newspaper spread over his face for darkness.
  Raj is laughing, talking to Govinda about something I cannot hear.
  Kishan is smirking. Or frowning. I don't know if he's happy or sad. I don't like Kishan.

I forgot—or perhaps I didn't know—that I could not remove these eight words from all the others. But I remember now, I know now: I am looking for traces. The workers in Dhanraj are filled with feelings and experiences that exist beyond the bounds of the body and remind me that the boundaries of this archive are more expansive than simply skin and bone.

We Are All Chimeras

A humanoid robot is like any other machine; it can fluctuate between being a benefit and a hazard very rapidly. As a benefit it's not our problem.—PHILLIP K. DICK, *Do Androids Dream of Electric Sheep?*, (1968) 2017

Over time I learn that a lifetime of labor transforms Dhanraj workers: industrial debris leaves traces on the body through exposure and experience. With this in mind, this chapter-archive explores how the experience of and exposure to degeneration and pain (through daily aches and injury, through embodied memory and practices of storytelling) are felt and understood by Dhanraj workers. This is not just the matter of feeling or inhabiting the body, but instead the pain and pleasure of *becoming* a worker-body.

Of becoming something new through breakdown.

Of becoming an industrial cyborg.

The matter of embodied labor is not just a question of how the environment and landscape transform the body or of how injury feels in the body, but also a question of how the act of work itself transforms the worker into something completely new.[4] This archive is carried in the body, under the skin, across the factory floor, and within the ancient machinery. The cyborg body is the archival space, and the files are experiences of pain, physical degeneration, and growing irrelevance.

These bodily archives, what Peter Sloterdijk (2011) calls "spheres," contain the universe of labor and life and love involved in working in a mill, living in a chawl, being of a family, a class, a caste, a city, a future, an anachronistic dead end. Over time I learn that being a worker at Dhanraj results in particular sensations within the body, whether that be exhaustion from a long day or pain from too much standing. This affective resonance leads to pleasure, pain, meaning, and loss. The body of the mill worker becomes an archive of physical sensation that develops over years of industrial labor and continues into a postproductivity moment of stagnation and disappearance. The mills might close, workers might be displaced, neighborhoods might be redeveloped . . . but the ghosts of industrial labor continue to haunt the bodily spheres of the workers I come to know through their aches, pains, coughs, and chronic exhaustion. The industrial cyborg remains, even after its usefulness is no longer.

I enter this chapter-archive with questions about experience and transformation: What does it mean to become a worker-body? What does it mean to become an out-of-work worker-body? How does such experience and transformation control the narrative of feelings for workers still employed by the textile industry? I find that memory is concentrated through injury and accessed through pain, allowing mill workers such as Manda and Sushila to inhabit the active experience of work, even as such work is overlooked as it disappears. These bodily experiences cannot be disconnected from the bodies of machinery, as a lifelong fusion of flesh and steel results in chimeric workers. These workers are industrial cyborgs, experiencing a process of decay that runs parallel to the ruination of both the mill and the industrial city.

Aging bodies, aging machines: there are no young textile workers at Dhanraj. Everyone is older: most are in their late fifties or early sixties, but they look much older to me. They look elderly. Their bodies are aging ahead of their years, and yet they remain strong, active, productive. But in thinking through the archival space of "the worker," I am compelled to push beyond the limits of aging as an experience suspended in forward-moving time. Scholarship on aging bodies (both in India and elsewhere) helps me to take seriously questions of embodied pain and attend to the material decay of the body.[5] However, I want to push past this bodily sense of breakdown along the lines of aging (in a temporal sense) and instead think worker bodies alongside processes of industrial decay: How does the work environment at Dhanraj become absorbed by Dhanraj workers and, in turn, transform these workers into cyborgs of industrial debris?[6] Here I deviate from the future-oriented bent of cyborg studies (as well as work on aging) and instead suggest that the industrial cyborgs of Dhanraj, while once the products of the industrial future, are no longer the result of rising technology. They are instead emerging among processes of ruination. This absorption of technology and environment is also an accumulation of passing time.

In drawing on "absorption" as both a process and a practice, I am influenced by Harris Solomon, who defines absorption as "the possibility for bodies, substances, and environments to mingle, draw attention to each other, and even shift definitional parameters in the process" (2016, 5). Dhanraj workers have absorbed the landscape, the machinery, and the sensations of the industrial assembly line. They have also absorbed a once-modern, now anachronistic time period through this process of porosity. However, nothing of this absorption remains future-oriented: both their bodies and these spaces are decaying. How can this timeline of decay be understood as "natural," now that the body has become mechanized?

In engaging the mechanized body, or the body-as-tool, my thinking is indebted to women-of-color feminist scholars engaging the history of enslavement, the commodification of women's bodies, and the fusing of body and tool as a cyborg construction. In particular, the historical scholarship of Leslie A. Schwalm (1997), Judith A. Carney (2001), and Jennifer L. Morgan (2004) reveals the ways in which forced, enslaved labor transformed African women into "hoeing machines" in the American antebellum South—any discussion of cyborg genealogies must begin here. While I am not comparing enslaved African women in the Americas to Mumbai-based working-class industrial laborers, I am rooting my understanding of cyborg workers to this legacy of theoretical thought.

Industrial work demands that bodies of flesh (workers) and bodies of steel (machines) work together as one. Haraway writes: "Through labor, we make ourselves individually and collectively in a constant interaction with all that has not yet been humanized. Neither our personal bodies nor our social bodies may be seen as natural, in the sense of existing outside the self-creating process called human labor" (1991, 10). An extensive body of literature has explored how the "naturalized" body (of agrarian rhythms, of seasons, of temporalities based on lightness and darkness) learns to be mechanized on the assembly line, particularly during the rise of industrial labor in Victorian England.[7] In drawing upon these debates, I choose not to wade into the waters of efficiency versus dehumanization but instead consider how—for Dhanraj workers—the mechanized labor they engage with day in and day out over decades is absorbed, transforming them into industrial cyborgs. What does this transformation *feel* like in the body?[8] How do workers *understand* the feeling of being efficient? Of being productive? Of breaking down? Of experiencing the buildup of aches and pains through the mechanized use of the body along the assembly line, such as slow walking, constant standing, and small, repetitive movements?[9]

This question of industrial absorption pushes me in two interconnected directions. First, what *is* the body of a worker? And second, what does the body of a worker *feel* like? In her critical and classic essay "A Cyborg Manifesto," Haraway writes: "By the twentieth century, our time, a mythic time, we are all chimeras, theorized and fabricated hybrids of machine and organism. In short, we are cyborgs. The cyborg is our ontology; it gives us our politics. The cyborg is a condensed image of both imagination and material reality, the two joined centers structuring any possibility of historical transformation" (1991, 292). We may all be cyborgs, but this hybridization looks and feels different, depending on the machinery we meld with and its orientation with time and futures. Industrial cyborgs are now archaic, no longer future oriented, and unavoidably breaking down. As I sit in Dhanraj, I watch bodies work with machines in ways that alter the chemical, material, and affective dimensions of what it means to be human. And later, I sit with Sushila in Vikhroli following her retrenchment.[10] I watch as her body struggles to reconstitute itself in the wake of this cyborg industrial labor: once both strengthened and weakened by the tolls of factory work, she now sits for hours and rarely travels beyond the confines of her apartment complex. The chimera she has become is being reclaimed by the body she was born into, and yet this struggle can only be unsuccessful: an industrial timeline has taken over her body, and a naturalized timeline is failing to reclaim it. Her aches and pains are evidence of this cyborg body: a body occupied and controlled by the passage of industrialized time and the residue of this industry. A lifetime of labor on Dhanraj's factory floor transforms bodies into elements of industrial machinery: What is left for these cyborg bodies now that industrial labor is receding? How do bodies experience the battle of two different timelines of ruination, playing out through the aging process?

The Daily Grind

Like going to sleep by contrasting a bed with a pavement, I sometimes find myself thinking that if the worst comes to the worst, I can always earn a living by my hands . . . : all you have in the end is your labour. — CAROLYN KAY STEEDMAN, *Landscape for a Good Woman*, 1987

Throughout my days at the mill, I begin to notice how time, labor, and sensation challenge my ability to understand what I am seeing: the stories of work told to me by workers seem to contradict the actual work I see being done.

Or *not* being done.

After the early morning rush, most of the shift involves sitting back by the window, resting, gossiping, napping. Manda tells me, "We were here before 7:00 AM, so we can rest now." I start to notice that conversations with workers always involve an explanation of how long and hard the work day is, how impossible the quota is to fill, how there is no time to rest under the burden of quotas. However, threads concerning the scarcity and low quality of the raw material weave themselves into these discussions, as we sit at the back by the window, *not* working. At first I wonder if I am being badly lied to, but later I sense the accumulation of a lifetime of labor, experienced in the present as I sit idly by. At the time of my fieldwork there is less work, but twenty years ago there was a constant flurry of activity. The accumulation of those days is written on the body.

"My legs ache from twenty years of standing," Manda tells me.

There is also an anxiety present in this talk of hard work. Sushila tells me stories of an early career haunted by the industry's instability, not only in the 1980s following the two-year strike but also in the 1970s and 1990s. Before Sushila was hired as a permanent worker in 1999, she worked as a *badli* (temporary) worker, showing up at the mill each morning in hopes there was extra work to be done that day. If the manager needed a substitute or extra labor, Sushila might find herself employed that day. She tells me:

I had to go every day for attendance but we only worked once in five days. The officer would tell us that there was no work and then we would leave. We would go at 7:00 AM to sign our name and we would work until 3:30 if there was work to do. Otherwise we would go home. We worked in the winding department—if there was a heavy workload, then we would get nice wages, but if there was less production, we would earn much less. We worked very hard: we only got a break at 11:00 AM for half an hour and then we were back to work. I enjoyed this work because I wanted money; I would pray that I would get more work and then I would earn more money.

After the textile strike, Dhanraj officially reopens in 1983, but production does not officially begin again until 1987. In 1991, the mill enters into an agreement with the union, the RMMS, but very few workers are rehired on a permanent basis. Those years are a terrifying memory of how insecure mill work can be. With this in mind, it makes sense that even in the present, speaking of mill work requires the language of high production. The memories of those grueling and backbreaking days exist in the present and help justify the remaining workers' presence at the mill. Perhaps, without the presence of this past experience, worker irrelevance will be all too apparent.

This specter of irrelevance emanates from citywide discourses concerning the future of the mill lands and bleed into the everyday interactions I share with workers. Mornings observing work in the mill and afternoons in the chawls move back and forth between conversations regarding the work done (and still being done) in the mill and the life lived (and still being lived) in the chawl. The temporal tensions present in this storytelling practice reveal how anxieties about the future impact not just how Dhanraj workers understand their present moment of employment, but also how they understand the experience of inhabiting a body built and broken down through a lifetime of industrial labor. Even as continuing employment exacerbates this breakdown, the fear of losing such employment is often far more terrifying.

Months before her retrenchment, Sushila tells me of her conflicting fears. Decades of mill work unquestionably break her body down—the endless standing, feet protected only by plastic chappals as she walks along an uneven ground of concrete and sheet metal. High, filthy windows cracked to the sky let in a thin stream of light, but it seems fresh air cannot infiltrate the darkened factory. Several fans attempt to ventilate the space but instead move the dusty, cotton-filled air from one side of the factory to the other. When the machines are turned on, the noise is deafening—the workers have no ear protection, just as their feet and legs and eyes remain vulnerable to the weight of their body, gravity, and dust. Nothing keeps them from breathing in the debris that fills the air. No water coolers exist in the mill space. Instead, workers are responsible for their own water, brought each day in reused soda bottles filled from their home taps.

Even so, Sushila tells me that her mill work keeps her young—the travel, the movement, the social interaction with non-kin. Before her retrenchment, Sushila is my first and closest contact at Dhanraj: a mother-like figure who pulls me into her Dhanraj circle and makes me feel at home. As I observe daily work on the factory floor, she constantly checks in with me, keeps me updated on her progress, and takes time to explain the ins and outs of the machines her body knows so well. After the morning work is done, I join her and the other workers in the back of the mill near a large window. The workers sit and share stories with me about a lifetime of mill work. Many tell me of their grueling commutes to the mill, as most can no longer afford to live in the center of the city. Sushila lives in the northeastern suburb of Vikhroli, and her body wears the marks of movement and exhaustion, as well as loneliness and isolation. She tells me: "It's tiring to travel up and down. I have to get up at 4:00 AM and leave the house at 5:00 AM. I reach [the mill] by 6:15 or 6:30. I take a shared rickshaw and catch the 5:30 train. Earlier, I had a few companions, but now that the mills are closing, friends are no longer working down there." On the one hand, the difficult commute has taken a toll on Sushila's body. On the other hand, she says the mill's central location affords her an opportunity to be in the city: "The city is gazbazlela—chaotic, noisy, with lots of commotion, but in a nice way." I ask her what will happen when she is retrenched and she shudders: "When you are at work you are always traveling and meeting people. Being at home, I don't know how time passes. I spoke about increasing my term to my union leader. He said let's see. He will speak to the owner and we'll see. But I hope my legs last that long." Even as this central location provides the exciting chaos that Sushila loves and allows her to participate in the life of the city, the mill itself is viewed as a dead zone that stands in contrast to other urban spaces being transformed into shopping malls, high-rise apartment buildings, hotels, and other desirable sites of middle-class consumption. Dhanraj workers experience a very different city than those who occupy the central city beyond the mill gates.

An Archive of Experience

If you want a person to believe that he is dreaming, when in fact he is locked to a chair on drugs, you have to remove his body from time. You have to feed him to keep his mind off his body. Or do you? I can't figure out which is the right indicator of being in time: feeling hungry or feeling satiated. But I do know there is a discrepancy. —RENEE GLADMAN, *The Activist*, 2003

At first it is very difficult to convince my informants to talk about how they experience their bodies, even as they share stories of pain and degeneration with me all the time. There is an ambivalence present within the trafficking of experience, as though the personal must be apologized for. As if "experience" cannot compete with "reality." In drawing on "experience," I am indebted to Joan Scott, who reminds us: "It is not individuals who have experience, but subjects who are constituted through experience" (1991, 779). I do not frame "experience" as a substitute for history, nor do I see my ethnographic traces as an alternative to accepted metanarratives of urban transformation, which are "true" in their own way. Instead, I see the experiences of my informants as a way of destabilizing the very construction of recognizable history: this is not a replacement. This is a disruption.

And an expansion.

In thinking through the ambivalence of experience, I find Walter Benjamin's use of *Erfahrung* (long experience) and *Erlebnis* (isolated experience) to be a helpful way of illuminating the conflict between seemingly traditional and modern engagements with experience.[11] For Benjamin, *Erlebnis* represents a modern framing of experience, understood through the emergence of industrial capitalism. *Erfahrung*, on the other hand, represents a more traditional form of communally understood experience, which draws on mimetic resources stored within the body. In distinguishing between these two forms of experience, I also draw on Paulla Ebron's framing of "public memory," which she defines as "the process by which a group of people who were once dismissed and never thought of as part of a 'public' might become visible to themselves and to others."[12] I place Ebron's "public memory" alongside Benjamin's framing of *Erfahrung* (long experience, stored in the archive of the body) as a frame through which to theorize Dhanraj storytelling. In this way, I challenge how mill land mythology *appears* to privilege "personal experience," framed as *Erlebnis* (isolated experience, accessed through perception and circulated as "knowledge" about the textile industry). However, this appearance is a deception, as such a formation of "personal experience" (commonly understood as the stories of the mythic out-of-work mill worker, unemployed after the 1982–1983 textile strike) forecloses access to Dhanraj public memory, which is often harnessed through accounts of ongoing material breakdown (bodies, buildings, neighborhoods).

This account of breakdown is a performance, but I understand that the workers do not practice this recollection for my benefit. Instead, they seem to be reinserting themselves into the "now" for the benefit of themselves and each other, as if these cyclical and meandering forms of remembering and forgetting, these forms of public memory, place them in spaces widely understood as past tense. This is a powerful practice: storytelling processes in Dhanraj refuse a chronological recounting of worker experience and instead unmoor memory from a logical timeline. Here at the mill we are in the realm of heterogeneous time.

Still, I am often frustrated by this lack of chronology, particularly when it comes to Sushila's stories of family, employment, and physical ailment. The stories are ephemeral and disembodied from anchoring dates and events: they often shift when repeated and refuse my need for order. If I ask Sushila when her back started to ache while standing, she shrugs and tells me, "For a while now." When I wonder when the walk from the station to the mill began to feel too long, she tells me, "For some time now." I claw desperately at some semblance of "fact": my inability to chart the changes in her life is maddening to me, my need for an organized trajectory mildly irritating to her. Perhaps I am asking the wrong questions. "Do you remember how old your children were?" I should have asked her. "Was Saraswati still working in the mill?" "How were your knees at that time?" Sushila's past is measured by narrative memory: she tells me the events she remembers, in the order she remembers them.[13] Dates shift and emotions transform and then return again, perhaps to somewhere familiar.

Even so, my presence as an outside audience is not without benefit, even if I fight against the cycle of remembering and forgetting. As mill workers at Dhanraj reveal to me their aches and pains, they do so to justify their current engagement with work and employment, constantly threatened by the city changes all around them. I am shown their contribution to the city through the toll it takes on their bodies, and they watch me write it all down. This allows memories of pain and insecurity to be transformed into experiences of presence and legitimacy. Sara Ahmed reminds us that "pain can shape worlds as bodies, through the ways in which stories of pain circulate in the public domain" (2004, 15). Aching limbs are framed as justification *for* the self, not exploitation *of* the self. Current employment is framed as continuing contribution to the urban economy, not as the stagnation of development through corruption.

Similarly, memories at Dhanraj often appear to leap *backward* over time, compressing the idle present with the grueling past. Sitting with Dhanraj workers almost always leads to discussions concerning that accumulated exhaustion, even as they are held at leisure beside our resting window. While "today" (and yesterday and last week and two years ago) is slow and monotonous—symbolic of the decline we are immersed in—the *memory* of productivity and exhaustion contains both suffering and pride, and these feelings are carried into the present moment.

This accumulated exhaustion, this archive of the body, draws on a form of affective experience in conflict with the narrative of mill work circulating throughout the city at large. In fact, I am often told that the experience and memories of Dhanraj workers cannot compete with the larger narrative of absence: Dhanraj is merely a holdout, as a more authoritative form of experience indicates the mills are all closed. And yet here we are, sitting in the back of the mill, discussing the raw material (poor quality) and the feeling of the morning's work (aching and paining). Anachronistic though they are, these industrial workers are working in the "now." This allows modernity to be both a space of promise, hope, and opportunity *and* a realm of disappointment, abandonment, and decay.[14]

The archive of the body is a sensuous space that relies on long experience (*Erfahrung*) as a key for access.[15] Because of this, such resources of experience and memory cannot relate to time in traditionally recognized ways. Instead, time becomes intertwined, layered, mimetic.[16] This form of mimetic play—mill workers' shared stories of pain or repetitive touching and rubbing of injured body parts—activates a set of resources unavailable to "rational" mining.[17] This experience echoes more traditional forms of call-and-response: voices "tangled within a complicated transhistorical dialogue" (Muñoz 1999, 61). Sushila will speak of a doctor's visit, and Manda will show me a scar from where a machine sliced her arm. Sudarshan will rub his tired feet, and Sitaram will tell me of his chronic shoulder injury.[18] Similarly, all the workers at Dhanraj share each other's ailments, forming a constellation of suffering and pain that roots them in the present while simultaneously connecting them to a very different past. This mimetic practice is a form of script, which is repeated collectively in my presence as evidence of a nonsensuous correspondence.

For cyborg industrial workers, this call-and-response appears to me as a way to account for elements/ailments that constitute this group of otherwise disparate individuals as a collective force. As so many feelings become normalized as bodily experience, shared stories of aches and pains remind workers at Dhanraj that their bodily sensations may be (and often are) a result of decades of industrial labor. These reminders result in workers cutting into the stories of others with their own remembered ailments, or reminders to coworkers of their experience of pain and injury. When Manda tells me her legs ache, Sushila rubs her own feet. When Sudarshan points to Manda's scar, Raj reminds Govinda of an accident years ago. When doctor's appointments are mentioned, related ailments from the past are remembered. The power of this storytelling cannot exist without the participation of the crowd. This form of long experience relies on sensations to trigger memories that otherwise remain buried (or sleeping) in the bodily archive.[19]

An Archive of Pain

But now and then his thoughts as they moved about would come upon the memory of it which they had not noticed, bump up against it, drive it further in, and Swann would feel a sudden, deep pain. As if it were a physical pain, Swann's mind could not lessen it; but at least with physical pain, because it is independent of thought, thought can dwell on it, note that it has diminished, that it has momentarily ceased. But with this pain the mind, merely by recalling it, recreated it. To wish not to think about it was still to think about it, still to suffer from it. —MARCEL PROUST, Swann's Way, (1913) 2002

As cyborg workers share a lifetime of industrial experience, this "long experience" (Erfahrung) reveals itself to me as a memory archive of pain. In engaging pain as archival material, I draw on anthropological literature invested in the body, even as I also look beyond its boundedness.[20] In doing so, I'm drawn to how these stories of pain, in addition to forging temporal and community ties, can also speak to the uncanny nature of the industrial cyborg body. In thinking through Dhanraj worker testimonies as forging identity through shared (embedded) industrial pain, storytelling practice at Dhanraj becomes both a form of resistance and a symptom of dislocation.[21] Both engagements emerge as I sit with Dhanraj workers in the slow monotony of unproductive afternoons: I hear an anxiety present in talk of hard work, a need to articulate the current contributions of this skeletal workforce and—more than anything else—repetition and sharing of ailments and physical breakdown.

When I first meet Sushila in November 2008, she tells me she fears that retrenchment will immediately turn her into an old woman. And she is right—when she leaves Dhanraj a year later (December 2009), the rapid transformation is uncanny. I begin to spend more and more time with her in Vikhroli and, like the lively ruins of Dhanraj, I find myself watching a body breaking down. It seems as though her body doesn't *work* anymore, because it isn't *working* anymore. I struggle with this: her doctor tells her to rest and enjoy her retirement, but resting is precisely what is accelerating the destruction of her body. Her aches and pains seem to be increasing at a rate that far surpasses what I expect is the "natural" aging process. Watching this is painful for me (and undoubtedly much more painful for her), and I begin to dread my long treks northward.

It's Sunday afternoon, and I have come over for lunch. After sitting with me for a few minutes, Sushila groans, braces herself on the edge of the bed, and prepares to lift herself from the plastic chair. As she untangles and straightens her body, I can see the strain and pain running through her arms and legs and down her back. She pauses with slightly bent knees, breathes deeply in through her nose, and shuffles into the kitchen. Squatting down next to her daughter-in-law, she prepares to serve our lunch.

I remain seated on the one single bed by the window, half of me pretending to gaze out the apartment, across the veranda, and into the park stretching out across the street. But the other part of me keeps an eye and ear on Sushila, not wanting to draw attention to her pained movements and make her self-conscious, but still very aware of the effort put into moving her aching body through everyday tasks—kitchen duties of cooking and cleaning, as well as care for her ailing husband and the responsibilities of directing and overseeing her daughter-in-law within the small space of their two-room apartment in Vikhroli.

Sushila was retrenched several months earlier, and her body has been visibly transformed by this short passage of time. She is softer and rounder and looks years older: no longer traveling daily into the city and walking along the rows of machines for hours, she instead sits at home, works in the kitchen, struggles to share seemingly endless time in a shrinking space with her daughter-in-law. She tells me the flat has never felt as cramped to her, now that she occupies it for the majority of her day. She had foretold this future, and together we watch its actualization.

Like the possibilities enclosed within the lively ruin of Dhanraj, my afternoons with Sushila in Vikhroli offer flashes of insight into the processes of bodily decay playing out across and within her body. The decay of the mill and the breakdown of the body become entwined: they are insights into the end of industry. Similarly, the stories Sushila's body tells me in her quiet Vikhroli flat echo the stories the workers tell me on the floor of Dhanraj. As I watch Dhanraj slowly wind down its semiproductive life, I simultaneously watch exhausted workers grapple with the future of their bodies, broken down to their present form after years of hard labor. As I sit with Manda, Sushila, Kishan, Sudarshan, Raj, and the others, I am told of hard work, of demanding quotas, of furiously moving machines. I am told about these things as though they are happening *now*, even if such productivity has not existed in the present moment for decades. But what I learn, as I sit with the workers for extended periods, punctuated by moments of productivity, is that the archive of the body continues to store this pain, exhaustion, fear, and insecurity alongside pride, excitement, and feelings of usefulness. Simply because we are sitting *now* does not mean that the past twenty, thirty, or forty years of seemingly endless labor are no longer present.

In this way, I am driven by Sara Ahmed's suggestion that "rather than considering how the feeling of pain is determined (by, for example, previous experiences), we can consider instead what the feeling of pain *does*" (2004, 24). Through worker testimonies of pain and degeneration, the affectivity of embodied work-related sensation reveals the experience of time in and upon the body. Stories of pain and degeneration come and go in Dhanraj: through both remembered pain and pain experienced in the present. These traces of feeling leave shadows, disappearing and reappearing at random. Through the telling, these stories are wrapped within these rhythms of remembering and forgetting, as the two are reliant on each other for their presence and absence, their emergence and disappearance: what Benjamin describes as the "Penelope work of recollection."[22]

These memories of pain recalled by workers on quiet afternoons are timeless flashes, disembodied from chronologies and legible histories. We are not talking about injury or the natural progression of aging but are discussing a feeling of wearing away and a feeling of being replaced:

as bodies become more productive, they become more efficient as industrial cyborgs. As flesh bodies become hybrid bodies, the feeling of industrial embodiment becomes more painful. By drawing on the language of "industrial embodiment," I am working toward an understanding of what it means to age in and through anachronistic technologies.

Of what it means to become a body through a relationship with industrial machinery.

Of what it then feels like for both body and machine to become obsolete.

Of what it means to live through bodily breakdown both through physical wearing away (aging) and through the disembodiment of one's cyborg apparatus (dismemberment).

Of becoming a beheaded chimera: only goat's body and serpent's tail and no lion's head to breathe forth fire. Cold chimneys and ashy breath: this, I think, is the *feel* of industrial embodiment.

This feeling of breakdown reflects the outdated machinery left in the mill: Who is caring for these old bodies and these old machines now that they are unvisible?

"They Worship the Machines Because They Give Them Bread"

Even the machine is nodding off
Sealed workshops store diseased iron
Wages concealed behind curtains
Like the love that young workers bury at the bottom of their hearts
With no time for expression, emotion crumbles into dust
They have stomachs forged of iron
—XU LIZHI, "The Last Graveyard," 2011[23]

The harvest festival of Navaratri is approaching, and I am being prepared for the last day, known as Dusshera, which I will celebrate in the mill with the workers. In Mumbai (and across Maharashtra), the festival falls on the tenth day of the month of Ashvin, which in 2009 falls in the last week in September. As a harvest festival, the goddess Durga is called upon to bring power back to the soil. On the first day of Navaratri, clay images of the goddess are displayed, and on Dusshera (the tenth day) they are immersed in the sea. The last day also marks the victory of Lord Rama over Ravana, but for the workers of Dhanraj this portion of the story is secondary. People visit each other and exchange sweets, as well as the leaves of the

Aapta tree, which symbolize future prosperity and wealth. On the day before Dusshera, tools (and nowadays, machinery) are not used but instead worshiped in a special *puja* (ritual).

Raj explains to me that the image of the deity is kept and worshiped for nine days, the period of time in which it has power and life. But on the tenth day the power leaves the image, and it has to be destroyed (submerged) before something happens to it. He continues:

> For the period of ten days when you do the puja, you offer rice and wheat and whatever you want [to the idols]. And during that period, for those nine days, the deity has power, has life. But this life cannot survive for more than ten days. So it is dead, you cannot keep it. So that is why you immerse it. You cannot continue to keep it, because if something happens, or if it is mutilated in some way . . . that cannot happen, so you immerse it. You immerse it just like you immerse Ganpati.

With all the future hopelessness I feel in and around the mill on a daily basis, on this festival day we will celebrate the availability of work, regardless of its insufficiency or fleetingness.

On the day of the puja, I show up with two boxes of sweets and a leafy branch from the Aapta tree. Manda and Sushila are wearing their best saris and have elaborate flower garlands woven into their hair. I'm asked to take picture after picture of my friends, standing in front of their beautifully decorated machines. While the preparation (cleaning, painting, flower arranging, etc.) seems to take hours, the puja is over in a matter of minutes. Manda tells me she is most excited for the food.

As we eat our *mithai* (sweets) and drink our chai, conversation turns to the subject of wages. The revelry of the day is punctuated by the larger reality present all around us. Dilip tells me:

> In the sixties and seventies we made only 300 or 400 rupees a month, but that was a lot: we were a rich industry. We earned much more than government workers. We made enough. Compared to other government jobs, we would get a lot. It was sufficient, more than other jobs. Now it is the opposite: we get much less, we are at the bottom. Now BMC [Brihanmumbai Municipal Corporation] workers and sweepers earn much more: maybe 50,000 per month. But we don't get more than 7,000 or 8,000 per month. Sweepers starting now will

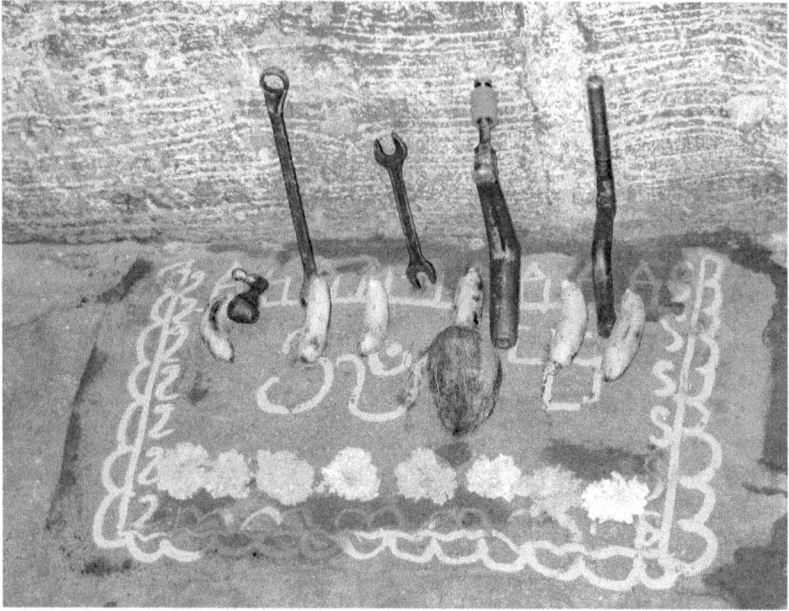

FIGURE 2.4. Blessing the tools for Dusshera.

FIGURE 2.5. Sushila decorating the winding machine for the Dusshera puja.

FIGURE 2.6. Sushila and Manda posing with their garlanded winding machine.

make 12,000 to 13,000 per month, and can earn up to 30,000. They make so much more.

Raj jumps in:

> Now, the interest of the owner is that he has a license to work here. And because of the mill he can operate these godowns and these tiny factories. His earnings are not from the mill but from these auxiliary operations here. The mill owner before I came to work . . . was really good. He used to say that the workers should never go unhappy from the mill. A worker should not curse you and go. That we should get the maximum money, that we should be happy. He would come sometimes, to the puja. The owner now is not like that. Even though I never met him [the former owner], I always heard he was a nice man.

The workers know that there is nothing invested in them: that their eventual retirement will lead to the redevelopment of the mill and the erasure of industrial remains. Sometimes this knowledge is met with sadness, and sometimes this knowledge is met with anger. On the puja day we have mithai to sweeten the bitterness, but even milk and sugar can't completely coat the hopelessness and frustration rumbling under the surface.

I run into Mr. Lal on my way out of the mill following the Dusshera puja. He laughs when he hears where I've been. "They worship the machines because they give them bread," he tells me with a cynical smile. I'm struck by his mocking tone and dismissal of his employees. Where does he think their bread will come from when the mill is gone? I find the same disregard in his tone when he speaks of his workforce. I ask him about who the workers are, and he tells me it should be no concern of mine. Perhaps because he doesn't know who they are? Or perhaps because he sees them as extensions of the machinery he is neglecting? Flesh and steel melt into each other and become simply another problem he must contend with. There are no individuals here: instead there is an aging workforce and a series of failing machines.

Cyborg workers disrupt previous identity borders, and I find that the boundedness of the body doesn't make sense anymore. Machines have value and bodies have value, both only as productive and unproductive entities. During my first year in Mumbai, before Sushila is retrenched, her health steadily declines, and her aches and pains infiltrate every conversation in the mill. The day after she has X-rays or blood tests or consultations with ayurvedic doctors, her health is all she can talk about. Usually these concerns are articulated through her concerns over money, as her husband is also unwell and the two of them together incur devastating medical bills. I begin to notice that Sushila talks about money trouble a *lot*, while none of the men ever talk about money trouble with me at all. They tell Sushila to take early retirement, but she replies that she is not yet sixty (she is only fifty-eight).[24] She joined the mill in 1978 and has completed more than thirty years of work: this is very likely her last year at Dhanraj. She explains to me: "I want to tell my bosses that I can work another year and a half, but now my legs are going so . . ." She looks either sad or scared when talking about retirement. But the men say she lives too far away: with her leg trouble, she can't sustain the travel. They tell her that when she retires she will be much more rested: she can wake up whenever she wants and take walks and not be exhausted. She smiles with her mouth but her eyes look sad. She asks, "What can I say?" Raj tells her: "Now that your children are all grown, you can start a new project." To me he asks: "Why don't you take her to America?" Everyone laughs while Sushila fidgets in her discomfort.

Later that day, Sudarshan and Sushila tell me about the worth of their bodies: if a worker dies, his or her family will get fifty days of paid compensation. Raj smiles his cocky smile and says with a laugh, "We should have negotiated for sixty or seventy." Kishan, ever the philosopher, looks out the window and asks: "So, should we all die?" Manda stares at him for several moments: "Just thinking about it, I get heart palpitations."

But safety concerns are very real at Dhanraj. Sudarshan tells me: "The machines have become very old: very old. They are damaged now, so work is dangerous. The management knows this, but slowly they are shutting down the mill. So they won't take care of it. We all know this is dangerous but what can we do? If someone is injured, they are sent to the hospital immediately but still . . . Actually, now it's luck by chance: not so many people are working, so . . ." The bodies of workers, like the bodies of the machines, are breaking down. And through the neglect of the mill machinery, as well as the negligence of mill management, the workers at Dhanraj see their own irrelevance reflected back: their bodies will break down along with the machinery.

Conclusions: Genealogies of Pain

Trace and aura. The trace is appearance of a nearness, however far removed the thing that left it behind may be. The aura is appearance of a distance, however close the thing that calls it forth. In the trace, we gain possession of the thing; in the aura, it takes possession of us. —WALTER BENJAMIN, The Arcades Project, 1999

Every day at Dhanraj I can see the impermanence of the industry I immerse myself in: aging bodies and aging machines surround me, and nothing youthful or modern enters as a replacement for decay. Workers complain about aches and pains, and the machinery echoes this protest with a deafening shrill.

When I first begin visiting Dhanraj in November 2008, winter is approaching and the mill holds the coolness of the air. The second floor is dark and loud, but the interiors are a pleasant respite from the sun. But the following June the rains have not yet come. It is not just the heat; it is the humidity as well. The cotton fibers fly around the machines and stick to our damp skin. I sit on a wooden desk and drink tea with Sushila and

FIGURE 2.7. The empty lot, destroyed by fire, awaiting its future.

Manda during their break. Our skin glistens with sweat and glows with the white fibers, leaving the impression of a partially plucked chicken.

The steadily increasing temperature outside makes the interior of the mill even harder to handle, and I marvel at the workers' ability to function in such intense heat. After lunch we sit in the back room near the window, looking out over the now empty lot, destroyed by fire so many years ago. The stretch of grass outside the window will someday be a high-rise apartment building, perhaps a hospital, or a tower of corporate offices developed by Mahindra in conjunction with the mill owners. But at this moment it is an empty space that carries fresh, cool air to our grateful faces, necks, and backs. A breeze moves through and we freeze, smile, let it cool our skin.

There is music coming from the shoe factory, but all is quiet with the women making bags across the hall. Manda raises her voice above the radio and shouts for the workers to lower the volume. She shakes her head and glares at the door. "Those two girls . . . ," she begins, indicating the two women walking in and out of the shoe factory. "They flap around too much." The younger one, Anuja, dressed in a cream and lavender *salwaar kameez*, walks back out and across the hall of the mill. "She has too much fat accumulated," says Manda, laughing spitefully through the gap in her teeth. Finally she stands up and marches over to the factory door, yelling to the manager to turn down the volume.

The men sitting around us tell Manda to calm down, that the music keeps the girls awake. But Manda is back on her feet, apron in hand, pulling her skirts up to her knees: *"Bhadwa!"* (Pimp!) she yells at him. *"Jhavdav tyala!"* (Your ass should be spanked!) He yells something back, and she storms back toward us, claiming under her breath that she will "beat up" the *madar chod* (motherfucker). Initially she is amused by her own brazen assault of the manager, but then she becomes angry and storms off.

The men tell me that Manda often berates the girls: her usual jolly manner transforms to rage in their presence. I wonder aloud if perhaps their youth and continual employment irritate her, and they look at me quizzically. I change the subject, but the effects of the material and built environment shifting all around us are impossible to deny: young workers in new economies creep into a decaying space where machines rust, industrial buildings crumble, and aging bodies break down and are discarded. All around us skyscrapers and cranes puncture the skyline, creeping closer every day. The only things these older cyborg workers have to hold on to are their ephemeral experiences and traces of pain.

A year later Manda will be retrenched, and she will no longer be able to stand on her aching legs at Dhanraj. But she will still be a storyteller. I will go to her home, and she will tell me about everything that continues to hurt. And all of the new pains, as well. At first I think she is giving me information, but then I realize she is telling me a story, and I continue to struggle with interpretation. What is she really telling me? What have I not found yet? Gladman's linguist-traveler explains to me: "Though my stay was nearly over, I had not reached that level of departure where any Ravickian artifact would do. What I brought back needed to represent exactly what it was like to be here" (2010, 101–102). Maybe I don't understand Manda's eight words at all. I simply cannot access, through the gap in our experience, what it feels like to be a worker: the sensation of breakdown in an anachronistic cyborg body. But I do know that the negatives always come before the photographs. Manda tells me: "My legs ache from twenty years of standing." I still do not know what it means to write what it feels to be there, in the haunted realm of memory, in the shadows of cranes and construction, in the unseen realm of bodies-out-of-time. What I do know is that everything I'm searching for, the aura that remains, exists somewhere within the archive of the body, within the negative of those eight words. And they have taken possession of me.

3

The Archive
of the Chawl

For the real houses of memory, the houses to which we return in dreams, the houses that are rich in unalterable oneirism, do not readily lend themselves to description. To describe them would be like showing them to visitors. We can perhaps tell everything about the present, but about the past! The first, the oneirically definitive house, must retain its shadows. For it belongs to the literature of depth, that is, to poetry, and not to the fluent type of literature that, in order to analyze intimacy, needs other people's stories.—GASTON BACHELARD, *The Poetics of Space*, (1958) 1994

To dwell means to leave traces. In the interior, these are accentuated. Coverlets and antimacassars, cases and containers are devised in abundance; in these, the traces of the most ordinary objects of use are imprinted. In just the same way, the traces of the inhabitant are imprinted in the interior. Enter the detective story, which pursues these traces.—WALTER BENJAMIN, "Paris, the Capital of the Nineteenth Century," in *The Arcades Project*, 1999

Arrivals: Living Insecurely

Prem Kumar reads the skyline and hears the city.

We sit together in his home near the old Jupiter Mills, a construction site once home to one of Central Mumbai's many textile mills and where Prem Kumar worked for many years. His employment ended in 1980, but he has paid close attention to the neighborhood's changes since then. From his kitchen we can see the new buildings rising out of the compound. "Just look at that building [he points to Jupiter Mills], there is no place for

FIGURE 3.1. The construction site formerly known as Jupiter Mills.

us there." He pauses for dramatic effect, locks eyes with me, raises an eyebrow. "Those buildings have glass windows. People like us do not live in buildings with glass windows . . ."

He sighs and moves away from his unit's own tiny window, covered with iron bars but otherwise open to the breeze. "There will be no place for the poor. It's like a cycle. When I look at all of this I say it is progress, but this progress is not good for the poor. Places where chawls have been broken down and replaced with big buildings . . . right next door to these big buildings are these huge towers . . ." His voice trails off as his eyes scan up, following the new steel towering over his own low-lying building.

I ask him if he plans to leave the neighborhood, and he shrugs, as if to defer my question in the same way he defers a decision. "We'll see," he tells me, with sad eyes. Prem Kumar could have been a poet, but instead he drives a rickshaw.

Prem Kumar occupies his home alongside an expectation of eviction, although the nature of that eviction is unclear to him. Perhaps it will be through redevelopment, maybe it will be through demolishment, possibly through another unknown coercive measure enacted by the city. He has already witnessed his original home being torn down—Prem Kumar lived for five years in a transit camp in Sion while his family's chawl was redeveloped, the central courtyard and breezy galleries (hallways) replaced by more units, more tenants. The open space that makes chawl living bearable was replaced with more concrete, maximizing the living space for individual units, not communal territory.

And yet Prem Kumar repeatedly tells me he will never live anywhere else. His story of home and shelter is seemingly one of nostalgia and precarity. Beginning from this place of past loss, current threat, and future instability, this chapter-archive explores how it feels to be precarious in a rapidly developing, formerly industrial region of the city by addressing how the crisis of housing plays out across the lives of former and current textile workers in Central Mumbai.[1] In mill land Mumbai, the space of the chawl is a site where life is lived "elliptically": this is a space of waiting, of treading water, of a refusal to engage accepted temporal movement. I approach these ways of being through a temporospatial optic I call "chawl time": by understanding these tenement buildings as lively, by framing mill workers as *vitally* anachronistic, and by arguing that life lived in such a way is "queer," I challenge the history of rapid urban transformation through the presence and experiences of my informants.[2]

The archive of the chawl uses time stories about housing both to reveal the inconsistencies of "modern time" and also to destabilize notions of what it means to be "at home" in this modern, contemporary moment.[3] By focusing on the archival material of temporality, this chapter-archive argues that in mill land Mumbai, forward-looking capitalist development produces an environment in which certain communities must refuse an engagement with such trends. This is not a question of resistance (James C. Scott 1987) but instead one of disavowal. Narratives of survival replace narratives of progress; stories of future hopes make way for stories of past potential. The challenge of surviving the current moment overwhelms possible investments in the future. Chawls become contentious sites of memory and materiality—a space where the nostalgia of perceived past stability meets the reality of development and displacement.[4]

In this way, "chawl time" reveals itself as a site through which time operates in contrary and disjunctive ways. Through traces of "pastness" left on housing structures and within memories, I draw attention to how former and current textile workers occupy and inhabit space in transforming industrial areas.[5] These transforming industrial areas are changing dramatically, and some former mill compounds (many of which once enclosed worker chawls) have made way for high-rise apartment buildings, shopping malls, upscale restaurants and nightclubs, and office buildings. However, the majority of Central Mumbai still retains its industrial feel through the low-lying mills and chawls yet to be redeveloped. For working-class communities still residing in these neighborhoods, the disjunction between the occupied material space of mills and chawls and the looming material space of cranes and construction results in a habitation of space and time that diverges from the temporal expectations of progress and development. By framing domestic life in these spaces as "chawl time," former and current textile workers, still residing in Mumbai's downtown chawls, exist both in this contemporary moment of rapid redevelopment and revitalization of former industrial spaces *and* in a perceived past moment of industrial activity and working-class stability.

This chapter-archive understands the chawl as a temporal archive of history and habitation: by acknowledging how time, through its interconnection with memory, operates differently in the chawl neighborhoods of Mumbai, working-class narratives challenge the dominant postindustrial narrative of urban restructuring and class-based development, even as such communities remain marginalized due to their seeming anachronistic subjectivities. In accessing this triangular relation between time, space, and memory, this archive relies on the "landscape biographies" (B. Voss 2008,) of three chawl dwellers: Prem Kumar, Sushila, and Manda, who work in the mills and live in the chawls.[6] Simultaneously, this lens disrupts the political implications of anachronisms as antimodern and instead resituates chawl dwellers within an allochronous space of modernity.[7] This temporal optic is critical in challenging urban narratives that erase individual experiences from larger, trend-based histories. Similarly, by focusing on life within the low-lying tenement buildings, I consider how "chawl time" reconfigures the expected trends of development, which would suggest immediate redevelopment in favor of high-rise apartments and upwardly mobile tenants. "Chawl time" illuminates the collision of alternative time spaces within progress-oriented development narratives.[8]

Museums of Domestic Decay

I have, right to this day, a photographically clear memory of standing on the concourse looking at my stained sleeve, at the grease — the messy, irksome matter that had no respect for millions, didn't know its place. My undoing: matter. — TOM MCCARTHY, *Remainder*, 2005

The chawl is a ubiquitous housing structure in Mumbai, often conflated with slums (known as *bastis*) and other forms of unregulated housing.[9] News articles routinely report deadly building collapses due to neglect.[10] Such news coverage furthers the notion that chawls are dangerous and in need of redevelopment.[11] Chawls are often referred to as "working-class tenements," not only referencing the multi-unit structure of the building but also suggesting its cramped and crumbling condition. However, avoiding both the images of impending catastrophe (presented daily by the local newspapers) and stories of successful stability (a nostalgic rendering often presented by residents and preservationists) allows for a focus on the chronic lived reality of most chawl dwellers.[12] This story speaks more to the insecurity of downwardly mobile working-class communities in a rapidly transforming, deindustrializing city and less to the literal fear of material collapse from structurally unsound buildings.

The most common type of chawls in Mumbai are wood and brick buildings, constructed for working-class migrants by mill owners and other private builders, beginning in the late nineteenth century. These buildings are found throughout what is now Central Mumbai and have been given both iconic and notorious status within the city's popular imagination. Structurally, the most common chawls consist of four adjoining rows of units, built around a central courtyard. They tend to be four to six stories high, with open hallways called *gallas* or "galleries" overlooking the open courtyards.[13] These structures have been compared to army barracks (Evenson 1995; Mehrotra and Dwiwedi 2001), and indeed the original design imagined each unit to house a large group of workingmen (often more than twenty individuals) who would sleep in rotation according to their mill shift. However, this imagining was dramatically transformed through the process of habitation.

In the late nineteenth century and early twentieth century, colonial authorities are sent messages that their lack of housing policy in Mumbai is leading to larger problems. In 1898, the city experiences a devastating plague outbreak, which is particularly severe in the cramped and unhy-

FIGURE 3.2. Chawl gallas.

gienic tenements occupied by workers. Similarly, the 1918 general textile strike and the 1919 food riots lead authorities to fear that worker tenements breed social unrest, as well as disease. As a result, the Bombay Development Department (BDD) is established in 1920 and charged with building upwards of one hundred chawls, although the number of completed units is dramatically lower. These chawls are made of reinforced concrete (instead of wood and brick, used in privately owned chawls) and lack the open-air galleries of private chawls. Instead, each building has wide interior hallways and shares an adjacent courtyard with a neighboring chawl (Caru 2011).

Throughout all structural incarnations of the chawl, *kholis* (units) are small, usually one hundred to two hundred square feet, and consist of a single room, used for sleeping and living. While many chawls now have indoor plumbing, gas connections, and in-unit toilets and washrooms, traditionally tenants shared latrines and taps that were located on the ground floor or alongside the gallery. Prior to in-unit gas connections, chawls had either communal kitchens or *khanawals*, eating houses often run by single women out of their own unit. Prior to the migration of families to the city, khanawals provide a place for single men to pay for a hot meal, and for women (many who were also, but not always, single) to create or supplement their incomes.

Living in such tight quarters is a skill mastered over time. Everything must have a place, and everyone who lives in a chawl must know where to find what is needed and how to get done what is required. Originally, chawls are not built to house families but to provide temporary sleeping spaces for migrant workers. As the majority of chawl units eventually became family homes, transforming such spaces into places habitable for families became the task of wives, daughters, and mothers newly arrived from the countryside (Koppikar 2010). The close proximity of chawl life presents new hurdles for women—the toilet blocks and public taps are challenging for women used to more privacy and subtlety, especially during their menstrual cycles. The limited number of latrines means that tenants are forced to wait in line for the toilet, as neighbors pass by and take note. Communal kitchens mean that the political struggles of family cooks expand to include negotiations between neighbors, as well.

Within popular imagination, chawls are described as unhygienic and cramped. Without a doubt, these overly intimate spaces are dangerous during epidemics, such as the bubonic plague and cholera outbreaks of the late nineteenth century. Today, the cycle of poverty remains a characteristic of chawl life in low-income communities. Most mill workers had and continue to have financial and social obligations to their village homes. This situation results in massive debt for migrants, who in turn take subtenants, with two or more families living in one unit as a result (Burnett-Hurst 1925). This overcrowding results in overwhelming pressure on the chawls' (barely existent) infrastructure.

While scholars such as Neera Adarkar and Kaiwan Mehta show how downtown neighborhoods such as Bhuleshwar and Kalbadevi, lined with the chawls in question, have some of the highest population densities in the world, they simultaneously call attention to the many contradictions present in studying the chawl *only* as a structure, devoid of the lives that animate its hallways, courtyards, and galleries, as well as the surrounding streets and markets. Despite the fact that "middle-class norms" are never applied to them, chawl social life transcends their bleak realities and gives birth to a vibrant character all its own. However, this "vibrant character" is disappearing through the redevelopment of Central Mumbai. This chapter-archive returns to the vibrancy of the chawl and, in doing so, rethinks the collision of time-out-of-space: the archival material of queer "chawl time."

The Queerness of Chawl Time

In their own inimitable ways urging us toward a disorderly and asynchronous collective, they might be heard to murmur: "Find the time, find your time." And that time is, after all, now. —CAROLYN DINSHAW, *How Soon Is Now?*, 2012

Every day, the downwardly mobile working communities of Central Mumbai see new developments all around them: raised flyovers and high-rises; mill compounds razed seemingly overnight. This message is sent and duly received: these industrial spaces might be alive, but they shouldn't be. New stories are being written now. When Prem Kumar reads the skyline and hears the city, he reads and hears of his absence, even as he feels and sees himself as present, as vital, as lively. When I ask him if he will leave, he shrugs—a queer gesture of embodied nonverbal language used to explain action as inaction. The language of inhabiting a space that shouldn't exist.

But what does it *feel* like to inhabit a space that shouldn't exist? In answering this question, I find that there is a form of consciousness that understands that "who we are is obsolete," even while simultaneously fighting hard to hold on to what remains. Throughout my time in Central Mumbai, I grapple with what it means to feel undead, leftover, a remnant, something out of time, something radically out of step with the present moment and the imminent future. The historian Reinhart Koselleck argues that our ideas about the future determine how we remember the past. Our lives, he writes, are littered with past futures because we are constantly experiencing a shifting of future possibilities: this is a past future, or a future past (Koselleck 2004, 255–276)—what James Ferguson (1999) has framed as the disenchantment of expectation.[14]

For Koselleck, experience is the realization of the past and is closely related to the category of expectation, which points specifically toward the future.[15] While the space of experience provides a link to a known but continuously shrinking present past, the horizon of expectation calls on an unknown, ever-expanding future. In thinking through Koselleck's framing of historical time, I am pushed to consider the seemingly nostalgic memories of my informants: this nostalgia is not romantic but instead the occupation of past possibilities in the present moment. What does it mean to hang on to hope, even when the time of such potential is long dead? Svetlana Boym (2001) draws on Koselleck's engagement with experience and expectation in order to complicate nostalgia, situate it as an emotion in time, and extricate it from the burden of sentimentality.

Boym writes of nostalgia not just as a longing for the past but also (and possibly more so) as the yearning for a present that threatens to disappear.[16] Invoking Koselleck, she explains, "Nostalgia, as a historical emotion, is a longing for that shrinking 'space of experience' that no longer fits the new 'horizon of expectation'" (Boym 2001, 10). In Mumbai, the textile mills were once an idea of the future, but they are no longer the *current* idea of the future. Living in a chawl is no longer a desirable life; working in the mill is no longer a ticket to future possibilities. And even as my informants know this, and even as some of them continue to live in this futureless discomfort, they tell stories of nostalgic yearning for what I *initially* thought was the time in which these worlds *were* desirable and full of possibility. But these are ambivalent places, as well as places of condition: when you are a worker, you work in a mill and live in a chawl. So what becomes of this life when one of these spaces is gone? Or both? Is it the ongoing disappearance of this material world that enables such nostalgia?[17]

Boym's work is helpful in conceptualizing the nostalgia I encounter, as well as reworking Koselleck's notion of experience and expectation. While I originally read mill worker nostalgia alongside an unrealistic romanticization of the past (in which work and housing were available), I later realize that the nostalgia I witness is instead a lamenting of dashed future possibilities, or futures past: a sense of disappointment and dislocation reminiscent of Ferguson's (1999) Zambian mine workers. While my fieldwork reveals the hardships of mill land life—in terms of both living and labor—my informants simultaneously mourn the loss of a more desirable future: the disappearance of their past material world does not invoke a nostalgia for the *experience* of the past, but instead a nostalgia for the *expectation* of the future. As their "space of experience" no longer fits the new "horizon of expectation" necessary for survival in Mumbai, Dhanraj workers struggle to capture a moment (or collection of moments) in the past that can continue to connect them to a space of future possibility and a larger horizon of expectation than that which they confront in the contemporary moment. This urban debris is one of both material sediment *and* historical moments.

I take seriously these temporal and spatial ruptures, and move through the stories of worker nostalgia in search of something deeper and more profound. As the shrinking "horizon of expectation" dashes worker hopes for legitimacy in Mumbai, the Dhanraj workforce emerges as devastatingly anachronistic subjects in a city they believe they themselves built through the sweat of their labor.

As I sit with my informants in their downtown chawls, I am shown how these spaces are more than simply housing structures: they are also temporal archives of layered histories and embedded memories. These archives hold a radical temporal resistance: even as the crowded, decaying nature of the buildings make them less and less habitable, the compression and expansion of chawl living becomes as much about time as it does about space. Given the looming threat of redevelopment and displacement, this archive catalogs the experience of spatial occupation when the current moment is haunted by future threats. Such future threats are, I suggest, resonant of S. Lochlann Jain's prognostic time: a time that demands "we adopt its viewpoint, one in which the conclusion haunts the story itself" (2013, 40). What does it feel like to live within this haunting? How is time understood when tenants may be required to leave their homes very quickly? How has the language of redevelopment highlighted potential revitalization projects while masking the inevitability of displacement and resettlement?

Through an engagement with nostalgia, I argue that "chawl time" is a form of "queer time." In doing so, I draw on chawl dweller stories to show how a singular temporality of "progress" pushes my informants into a seemingly past-oriented time, even as contemporary mill work is a critical element of informalizing capitalist modernity.[18] In opposition to such exclusion, chawl time operates through a tactic of remembering, which draws a past moment of aspirational modernity and urban participation (factors allowing for the possibility of mill workers becoming modern subjects through their labor) into a "postindustrial" present, where chawl-dwelling textile mill workers have become anachronistic.

Current work on temporality, in particular by Homi Bhabha (2012) and Gurminder K. Bhambra (2007), draws upon postcolonial studies and intersects with the field of queer theory, which considers the histories of communities previously excluded from progress-oriented and reproductively minded narratives.[19] The geographer Natalie Oswin, on the subject of queer time in Singapore, writes: "I argue that while it is of course necessary and politically important to examine the deployment of 'queer' as an identity category, queer theory's poststructuralist critique of the notion of sexual identity pushes us to examine how certain subjects come to be seen as abnormal or 'queer' while others are considered 'proper.' . . . We must therefore attend not just to the deployment of 'queer' as an identity category but to the process of 'queering' as a facet of governance" (2014, 427).

I take this call seriously in framing chawl time as "queer time." Elizabeth Freeman writes that "queering" time "may be to trail behind actually existing social possibilities: to be interested in the tail end of things, willing to be bathed in the fading light of whatever has been declared useless" (2010, xiii). Similarly, chawl dwellers are trailing behind Mumbai's conception of progress and have been declared useless as productive urban citizens.

In particular, this framing is helpful in thinking about how time is inhabited as "chawl time."[20] Freeman argues that the necessity of this trailing emerges from failures of recognition: that we can only know in *retrospect* what is actually queer. In many ways, industrial workers are always *chasing* modernity but cannot actually reach it in time to occupy its ephemerality. While industrial labor once promised the potential subject position of "modern citizen," for most of the industry's history mill workers were temporary migrant laborers unwelcomed by the infrastructure and ideology of the city.

In the postindustrial moment, industrial workers may lament a past time when their industrial labor once promised them modernity. However, such a positionality reveals the absence of ever having inhabited such a subject position in the first place. Mill workers are only celebrated in their present state of absence. Similarly, it is only through the loss or absence of industrial employment that industrial workers may recall a modern past— it is through memory and nostalgia, but not through occupation and experience. In similar ways, I argue that chawl temporality occupies a parallel space, trailing behind the temporal position of "progress"—"chawl time" is both a trailing behind and also a palimpsest (Huyssen 2003) or chronotope (Bakhtin 1981).

More abstractly, chawl dwellers remind us that waves of historical progression are socially and culturally constructed. Worker presence in Central Mumbai draws attention to this ceaseless fabrication. While outside of the mill lands I constantly consume a story that places textile mills and workers in the past tense, I continue to encounter mills and workers through my fieldwork—these workers continue to exist and produce, albeit on a very small scale. Small though it may be, this presence is important, as it alerts me to the cracks and fissures of an assumed seamless history—while Mumbai continues to develop, remnants of its past remain in the present. Chawl time, therefore, is like queer time because both coexist uncomfortably with (the myth of) "chrononormativity."[21] Chawl time resists the drive to conform to the contemporary urban trajectory of development and displacement, even as tenants struggle to remain connected to meaningful forms of habitation. If the queer subject fails to be productive because they (at least historically) cannot be bound onto normative notions of domesticity and familial structures, then chawl dwellers fail to be progress-oriented because they insist on binding themselves to notions of living and working that are *now* archaic (the synchronicity of factory work and chawl life) but were once *actually* the ultimate expression of a chrononormative life.

The marker of a modern subject is someone who has expectations for the future and a desire to control that future. With this in mind, chawl dwellers are the ultimate nonmodern subjects, as they remain bound to a past temporality and look not toward the future but instead backward, toward the moment when imagining a future was still possible. However, by "feeling backwards" (Love, 2007), they may, instead, be actively resisting a future that has no room for them. By drawing attention to the vitality of anachronistic chawl dwellers living in Mumbai's textile mill neighborhoods, I do not mean to suggest that forward-looking development is or should be the norm, nor do I intend to reinscribe poorer communities as nonaspirational in relation to the engines driving modern capital forward. Instead, I use these frames to destabilize temporal narratives that naturalize unidirectional renderings of progress and participation, both through material presence in the contemporary moment and through the collapse of time through memory and recollection. The queerness of chawl time emerges most clearly to me as Sushila draws me in to the collisions of time and home that structure the trajectory of her life.

An Archive of Spatial Ruptures

ACT ONE: PALIMPSESTS

There had to be a secret society of people working on the invisible architecture. How could there not be? There were phantom structures being built on top of and in between . . . what would you call them? Real structures, concrete structures? There had to be a cohort taking measure of these entities, tracking them across the city, reading them against ancient texts. . . . I had no choice but to relearn the book, to dismantle everything I believed about it and search out new choreographies. —RENEE GLADMAN, *Houses of Ravicka*, 2017

Sushila is my gateway between the museum and the archive: a threshold between opportunity and regret, a pause between the past and possibility.

She becomes a ghostly guide, leading me from her quiet apartment building built by the Maharashtra Housing and Area Development Authority (MHADA) in the northeastern suburban neighborhood of Vikhroli to the downtown chawls of her youth: first her childhood home (alongside her former neighbor, Prem Kumar) in Elphinstone Road and then her marital home in Lower Parel. Through these visits, I learn that the chawls are not just containers of lost memories; they are gateways to another city. As I find myself in chronotopic structures full of material life accumulated over generations, I learn how "vibrant matter and lively things" animate and activate what could otherwise be seen simply as object accumulation.[22] From these spaces of vivid "things," Shannon Lee Dawdy's "patina" provides a window through which the archive of the chawl can "summon a triangular relationship between time, materiality, and the social imaginary" (2016, 4). This accounts not just for a material and affective leakage but for a temporal one, as well.

The first time I visit Sushila's childhood home (and Prem Kumar's current home), I feel as though I am moving through time: the rows of low-lying buildings duck beneath the construction site of the sky, and if I keep my eyes level I can pretend the skyscrapers aren't hovering above me, blinding sight with their reflective glass windows. Sushila leads me down the lively lane running beside the hole-in-the-ground formerly known as Jupiter Mills, along a series of single-story *beti* chawls facing a line of redeveloped MHADA buildings. Outside the many units the walkway is full of women washing clothing in large plastic buckets. I occasionally glimpse men—wearing only shorts or *lungis*—squat and pour water over their heads. I see no women bathing here. A friend greets Sushila, a cousin she hasn't seen in quite some time. They disappear into a building on the left, and I awkwardly take in the street scene around me as I wait. Sushila emerges alone ten minutes later, smiling.

We pass by two more buildings and stop beside a bus stop. To our left, standing in place of the chawl of Sushila's birth, is a twenty-five-year-old structure called Shivaraj Bhavan. It is unremarkable—it looks like every other building on the street. There is a mural of a bearded man in white and gold royal regalia on the wall to our right. A garland of flowers has been tacked to the wall, as though resting around his shoulders. It is Shivaji, one of the founders of the Maratha Empire and the mythical warrior whose name has been given to so many places throughout the city.

We walk up the stairs of Shivaraj Bhavan, to the third floor, and enter

FIGURE 3.3. The lane outside Shivaraj Bhavan.

Prem Kumar's unit. To my right is a crowded single bed, occupied by two young girls and a middle-aged woman. Next to the bed, in the corner near the door, stands a cupboard crammed with papers and books and suitcases and piles and piles of saris and salwaars and trousers and children's clothes. There are school exercise books in the cabinets and family photographs and a small porcelain puppy with a red ball in its mouth. I am seated on the bed and look across to the opposite wall: a bookshelf sits there, slightly askew. Again, it is overflowing with all the worldly belongings of an extended family. The walls are brightly colored and covered with pictures of relatives and deities: above the cupboard hangs a portrait of a stern-looking elderly couple. An altar sits above the bed, and I see Mahalaxshmi and Ganesh and a painting of Sai Baba, a garland of marigolds hooked around the frame.

This accumulation is a regular sight within the chawls and redeveloped buildings I visit: material objects carry a history, and when I look around I can see the layering of time all around me.[23] The images of gods span multiple lifetimes: some are old painted pictures inherited from grandparents who lived in the unit before it was redeveloped. Some were carried from

FIGURE 3.4. Mural portrait of Shivaji.

the Konkan, while others were bought to Mumbai generations ago. The faded darkness of these pictures sits alongside brightly laminated plastic reproductions and velvet-painted imitations, bought recently from the market down the street. The patina'd photographs of deceased ancestors sit alongside these altars, linking the family lineage to the gods and goddesses repeatedly invoked and revered by that family for protection, guidance, and good fortune.

This layering of temporalities, through both accumulated objects and painted (and repainted) walls, shows signs of wear across lifetimes: bright colors chipping to reveal older, faded colors. The original building material peaks out from dented edges and chipped corners. These walls support newer pressboard cupboards and older steel cabinets, stuffed with old silk and new nylon saris; plastic toys and porcelain antiques. New schoolbooks sit alongside old document cases that hold employment records, records of housing disputes, newspaper clippings. When I look around Prem Kumar's unit, I see a palimpsest: the ghosts of the original chawl, the traces of family from an earlier time, layered efforts to bring brightness and beauty to an otherwise drab interior.

FIGURE 3.5. Inside Prem Kumar's chawl unit. This view from the door shows
the entirety of the interior space, save the single bed, to the right and pushed
up against the wall.

Prem Kumar tells me that Shivaraj Bhavan was redeveloped by MHADA in 1977: prior to this redevelopment, the building was a five-story chawl with two wings. With 17 units per wing, the building had a total of 170 units; of these, 44 units were 300 square feet, and the remaining units were 180 square feet. Prem Kumar and his family were living in one of the larger units, but they lost this space after redevelopment: contrary to their hopes and expectations, the MHADA intervention transformed their 300-square-foot home into one that was only 180 square feet.[24]

Twenty-five years into their life in Shivaraj Bhavan, however, Prem Kumar and his family have adjusted to their cramped surroundings. Balancing such struggles with limited space is written across the walls of Prem Kumar's unit. While at first I am confused by what lies before me, with careful attention I eventually see how the seeming disarray is really a system of organization, perfected over generations. As he sits cross-legged on the floor before me, his teenage son at his side, Prem Kumar tells me:

> I live here with my two brothers, two families, ten people. It is me and my wife and our son and daughter, my older brother, his wife and their two sons, our mother, and our younger brother who is unmarried. We are not happy with the unit area. We feel very congested. . . . But we don't want to shift because we've spent our whole childhood here. Our whole world is here. We love this area but not the building. We love the local people, everyone is so cooperative, there are hospitals and markets and schools; everything is nearby.[25] The western and central rail stations are near. We are living in the center of Mumbai, and this is to our satisfaction.

As Sushila sits quietly next to me, I think about the difference in these two friends: for Prem Kumar, space is a sacrifice worth making. His family resisted and continues to resist the movement taken on by Sushila and her family. They remain, exercising claims upon this space supported by a century of dedicated labor. Like most of the older tenants in Shivaji Bhavan, Prem Kumar and his family worked in various textile mills before the strikes of 1982–1983. He tells me that, before redevelopment, approximately 50 percent of the chawl tenants were connected to textile mills.

After our visit with Prem Kumar, Sushila leads me to the unit her father sold before shifting northward, first to Borivali and then to Kalyan. We ascend another flight of stairs, past the four common latrines and community tap, into a unit only slightly larger than the one inhabited by Prem

FIGURE 3.6. The Mandal men's chawl unit, which I initially mistook for a tailor's shop.

Kumar and his family. Looking inside, I am confused: Is this unit used as a tailor's shop? The longer walls to my left and right are lined with pegs, and from these pegs hang rows and rows of men's trousers. Straight ahead, almost acting as a curtain before what I guess is the kitchen, hang men's work shirts, faded shades of blue and yellow and cream. Four large, tall wooden tables line the left side of the room, and six men in their early twenties sit cross-legged on top of them. I express my confusion, which is met by Sushila's laughter. My naïveté hangs embarrassingly in the cramped space of the old flat.

Sushila explains to me that her father sold the flat to another Maharashtrian man, also from Ratnigiri district on the Konkan Coast, near to their family's ancestral home. In turn, the man—an investor—rents it out to young migrants from his own village. In this way, Shivaraj Bhavan is actually housing a new wave of Maharashtrian migrants to Mumbai: in this case, twenty young men occupy the tiny flat, sleeping on the wooden tables and hanging their clothes from the various pegs and hangers across the walls. The very same story was in operation more than one hundred years earlier: young single men seeking textile mill employment flocked to the city and holed up in tiny units (mainly chawls) with dozens of other young men in search of the same. It was not until much later that whole families joined in the urban migration and chawl units went to these traditionally structured families.

As we walk back onto the street, Sushila lets her storytelling meander through a collection of memories. In 1965, twelve years before Bhadak Chawl becomes Shivaraj Bhavan, Sushila is married and moves into her husband's family's unit in Shri Nagji Chawl in Lower Parel.[26] In 1968, she begins working in the mills: first at Phoenix Mill, where she is a *badli* (temporary) worker for ten years. When the mill burns down in 1978, she is laid off with no compensation. After her termination, she joins Khatau for two years and then Jam Mills in Lal Baug for six months, but both positions are terminated due to cost-cutting measures within the mills. It is only then that Sushila finds work at Dhanraj, again as a badli worker. She explains: "Back then the mill owners didn't do any contracts with their workers, everything was temporary. When they didn't need us, we'd just lose our jobs." Sushila doesn't find permanent employment with Dhanraj until 1999, after the mill is forced to reopen and provide contracts for all its workers, in accordance with the demands made by the RMMS.

ACT TWO: GHOST STORIES

My house exists and has walls but it is also invisible, I wanted to tell you how I came to live here, so I went out to the outskirts in order to see. I wanted to make clear what is meant by the word invisible, what is meant when someone says being unseen does not make you a ghost, particularly when you're a house.—RENEE GLADMAN, *Houses of Ravicka*, 2017

Sushila takes me to her marital home only once, and I feel most haunted here, in the empty lot that formerly cradled the Shri Nagji Chawl.[27] The outside gate looks unremarkable from the road, and if I were alone, I would not stop. But since Sushila is with me, I follow her through the gates and onto the flagstone path leading into the compound. It is cracked and worn; many of the stones are missing. The lot is strewn with rubble and rubbish and boys playing cricket in the hot April sun. At the far end of the compound is a blue tarpaulin tent where a group of women are making tea. They glance at us momentarily before returning to their work. The boys carry on with their game.

The entryway walls are covered with paintings of Ganesh and Sai Baba:

FIGURE 3.7. The crumbling ghost walls of Shri Nagji Chawl.

FIGURE 3.8. An abandoned pot/vessel on a sea of rubble inside Shri Nagji Chawl.

FIGURE 3.9. Cranes looming above the Shri Nagji Chawl compound.

lovely colored tiles garlanded with marigolds and strings of creamy pearls. I stand for a moment and allow the sunlight to dapple the packed dirt beneath me before I continue on, out of the shadows, and toward the spot where Sushila's marital home would have stood.

She points to the right, and I imagine the low dirt hill as a stranger's home, and then—after a time—her own home. At the age of fifteen she is married to a man twelve years her senior and moves into a ground-floor unit in the very spot where I am standing: only 120 square feet and already housing twelve other people.[28] There is a wall clumsily constructed at the edge of the property, consisting of corrugated metal, rust in color, held together by chicken wire. It does not manage to block the two-story chawl standing adjacent to the property. Sushila's unit would have looked right into the kitchen window of her neighbor, a window now blocked by this temporary barricade. There are water stains on the stone exterior walls, plants creep up the water pipes, rotten wooden shutters hang precariously off their hinges. I imagine this is what Sushila's building looked like before it was torn down. I ask her, and she shrugs.

Instead, she is looking straight ahead, out of the compound, above our heads. I follow her gaze past the cricketers, past the chai women, and out of the lot. I see a huge crane: it cuts across the skyline with an authority that none of these smaller buildings can possess, more than suggesting that *this* is the new face of Mumbai. Just to the left of the crane I can see a recently constructed building of high-rise apartments, a tower of flats in contrast to the low-lying units (and ghosts of units) around me.

I turn around, I tilt my head up, I see what remains of the building. I see the wooden railing hugging the veranda. I can see Sushila looking too, now: perhaps she is remembering the days when she would sit on the veranda in the evening. The paint is peeling: I can see the gray stone underneath the faint yellow flecks. This section of ruin seems like an afterthought of carnage, and I wonder why it remains when the rest of the building has been razed. There are doorways leading nowhere, windows without walls, plants pushing through the floorboards and up through a roof without a ceiling.

We walk out, back to the street, take a left, and immediately enter a tiny lane leading to another chawl. This one is long and linear and built on opposite sides of a bright narrow lane. There are five old women squatting on the smooth stone curb, all wearing saris of violet and lilac. Above them sits a garlanded bust of a bearded Shivaji, and around them hangs the laundry of ten or so units: pinks and greens and blues and more purples. Sushila leads me next door to the home of her friend Saraswati. The two women are pleased to see each other and reminisce over the times they worked together as winders when they were newly married. At that time they were badli workers, and many days saw them returning early from the mill, when no work was available for them. I think of the few times I've been to Phoenix Mills, now High Street Phoenix, a shopping mall with attached restaurants and nightclubs. I ask the women to tell me what the mill *looked* like, but they don't seem to remember any details. These memories are too old, my interest too banal.

Saraswati laughs when I ask her if she wishes for more space, like Sushila has in Vikhroli. She looks around at her tiny unit, littered with the bodies of family, friends, and random children from across the hall. "I would hate Vikhroli," she tells me. "This is my home; I never want to live anywhere else. In two years, if there still is a building here, it will be demolished and there will be a new building [built]. I'm excited for that to happen." She tells me she will wait out redevelopment and suffer the camps so that she can come back here. She hopes for more space for her family, better facilities. Such redevelopment has not yet happened, so she holds on to this *pos-*

FIGURE 3.10. The lane outside Saraswati's chawl.

sibility: the chance that the future holds potential for her life to be better, even as the *eventuality* of her landscape is hopelessly clear. In this way, Saraswati lives within a performative speech act of hopefulness that sits in quiet dissonance alongside Sushila's experience (among many others) of a conflicting empirical eventuality.[29] Somehow there is hope and comfort in the chaos of downtown. And promises of invisibility.

Sushila brings me to the threshold of queer "chawl time." However, her life in Vikhroli and the time she has spent living away from the chawls of Central Mumbai have reoriented her relationship with the temporality of mill lands. She can tell me only of "how we used to live." I turn now to Manda, whose daily rituals in her own chawl in Lower Parel instead reveal "how some of us continue to live today."

The Chronotope of the Chawl

I wanted to say language leaves a trace, makes a simultaneous trail, of us and of the crisis. My walking leaves a trace, also my saying I walked. And, this is important, because, though these marks do not render precisely the picture of our crisis, they do show where there are still people. —RENEE GLADMAN, *Ana Patova Crosses a Bridge*, 2013

Manda's home in her Lower Parel chawl is far from romantic—one room that serves as both bedroom and kitchen: a cupboard, a faucet, a woven mat on the floor. Piles and piles of pots and pans and dishes and utensils. The two of us sit on the floor of the flat, while her husband crouches in the doorway: there is little room for him in the small space he shares with his wife. At night he sleeps outside or with friends so that Manda can almost stretch her legs out at a right angle from her body within the room that is their home.

When I visit Manda, we rarely stay in her unit after drinking our tea. The building still has a courtyard, and we stroll through it on our way to visit neighbors. While I know that Manda, in part, enjoys parading her foreign friend through the hallways, in view of other tenants, I also know that her daily routine simply involves numerous visits to numerous friends— chai sipped out of stainless steel tumblers and gossip gambled and given away.

After she tires of her neighbors, Manda moves to the street. On hot days we visit the ice cream vendor and eat our dripping confections on one of the concrete benches built around Ambedkar Road's many trees. As we walk Manda greets some shopkeepers, ignores others, and argues with everyone we meet in her usual joking manner. The stretch of lane around the chawl contains just as much "home" for Manda as the unit she sleeps in. The routine of walking is one of interaction and familiarity: Manda *always* leads me first to her chawl neighbors and then to her street

FIGURE 3.11. Playing games in Manda's courtyard.

neighbors. Home is not just four walls, but instead a neighborhood community. Manda is known here: she is aunt, sister, mother, friend. She gives and takes recognition as she moves, and that is a freedom she cherishes.

When I walk the streets with Manda, we engage in an old form of sociality, which connects her to the community of Girangaon. While her chawl unit, in and of itself, is virtually uninhabitable, she shows me how chawl *life* is far more expansive than the tiny unit she cooks and sleeps in. We link the unit to the building through our visits, and then walk the busy streets in a social circumambulation that connects Manda to her history.[30] Roaming with Manda feels like a citation, marking her connection to a long lineage of social practice in Girangaon. This citational action is one of repeatedly reinserting herself in the contemporary moment of the city. Without that daily practice, her presence could be all too easily erased.

However, our walks also feel defiant and are performed as though an audience—perhaps the city—is watching. As we walk, Manda asserts her right to occupy the streets, to live in her chawl, to inhabit Lower Parel. She marks her territory through connection and conversation. This tactic requires constant repetition, and over time I grow to know her path and her allies. Once she has asserted her presence for the afternoon, we return to her cramped quarters for more storytelling and more chai.

Manda teaches me that "domestic space" leaks out of the units and courtyards of the chawls and bleeds into areas often misunderstood as "public space." In the chawls, "home" extends onto the street, challenging a neoliberal understanding of domesticity and respectability.[31] In this way, Manda shows me how her own movements throughout her neighborhood (and the city in general) result not in a difference between "public" space and "private" space but instead in a relationship that shifts daily and requires constant attention and cultivation.

Such movements also result in a nostalgia that valorizes the chawl as a space of openness and opportunity. The women I encounter in the various chawls I visit tell me stories about visibility and familiarity that hail the tenement buildings as bastions of safety in an otherwise dangerous city. Through my time with Manda, in particular, I am shown that women have more mobility in neighborhood chawls than in idealized domestic spaces, like the single-family apartment building. While redevelopment brings promises of more square footage for individual apartment units, I am shown how such promises expose the contrast between the idealized and the real. The potential gain of larger individual units isn't worth the loss of galleries and courtyards. The promise of newness and modernity isn't worth the threat of high-rise apartment buildings, understood as spaces where family units become isolated from their neighbors.

Visiting Sushila in Vikhroli feels very different from visiting Prem Kumar in Elphinstone Road or Manda in Lower Parel. I don't feel like I am in Mumbai when I am in Vikhroli, and I realize that is precisely what Prem Kumar and Manda are scared of: what Edward Said described as "a discontinuous state of being" (1984, 163). But the chawls are still a space of community, a place where one's perceived self-narrative matches the chaotic built environment and maps onto the bodies of family and neighbors living in close proximity. Through the lens of Mumbai modernity, chawl dwellers are crafted as anachronisms, indicative of a community no longer in step with the direction of the city. However, an alternative temporality—queer chawl time—challenges a homogeneous occupation of time and space. Instead of remaining anachronistic, chawl dwellers reveal fictions of the Mumbai modern, similar to how light filters through the crevices of a seemingly solid structure. I find that these cracks and fissures are chipped away at not just through occupation and traversals but also through the trafficking of memories. This trafficking is a form of nostalgia, but it is far more powerful and generative than the sentimental fictions often attributed to the term.

To Live in Water

Cyborg writing is about the power to survive . . . on the basis of seizing the tools to mark the world that marked them as other . . . to subvert command and control.
—DONNA HARAWAY, "A Cyborg Manifesto," 1991

The promises of forward-facing capitalist progression also bring with them the potential erasure of low-income communities, and many of my chawl-dwelling informants are well aware of the risks. While Saraswati tells me she is eager for her building to be developed, Manda is terrified of what such a scheme might entail. Waiting out redevelopment is a gamble, and not all chawl tenants are willing to chance the indeterminacy of transit camp life. While Prem Kumar spent only five years in Sion, many tenants find themselves stranded in camps indefinitely.[32] Additionally, returns may result in chawl dwellers encountering new buildings with unmanageable maintenance costs. While repairs are often welcomed, I am told that "necessary reconstruction" is what is feared, as years in transit camps and hikes in maintenance costs are factors that contribute to eventual displacement. Much of this "necessary reconstruction" involves transforming compounds of cramped chawl units and spacious courtyards into slightly *less* cramped, but more numerous, apartment units through the elimination of the courtyards and an increase in building height (through increased Floor Space Index allowances). One particularly insidious development trick is the installation of elevators as a result of increased building height: quite simply, the installation of elevators results in rising maintenance costs, which are often enough to make the monthly fees unaffordable for low-income tenants. Taken together, redevelopment looks more and more like displacement and less like revitalization for in situ communities.

Here I draw on Colson Whitehead's novel *The Intuitionist* (1999), in which Lila Mae Watson, "the first colored woman in the Department of Elevator Inspectors," exists in a world of verticality: a world where physical ascension is linked to evolution, both socially and spiritually. In Lila Mae's city, verticality might signal modernism, elevators might suggest accessibility. But in the mill lands of Mumbai, such subtle infrastructural changes can result in dramatic displacement: poorer tenants simply cannot afford the maintenance fees associated with such developments. What better way to displace such tenants than to create a situation in which they must choose to sell their units when redevelopment results in building with unaffordable maintenance costs, due to the addition of elevators? For chawl dwellers, tall buildings equal "seemingly" self-imposed displacement and relieve planners and developers of the burden and responsibility of eviction.

In the chawls of Mumbai, unlike the unnamed city where Lila Mae lives, verticality equals the death of urban citizenship for the poor, as an elevator has the power to transform the economic demographic of a building far more efficiently and subversively than eviction or displacement. Interestingly, there is no elevator in Lila Mae's building. While she services the elevators of the growing, modernizing city, she resides in a low-income, predominantly black neighborhood: the infrastructure (or lack thereof) tells stories to and about urban residents (C. Whitehead 1999, 29–31). Indeed, I find throughout my fieldwork that through in situ redevelopment projects (i.e., redevelopment projects in which tenants will be temporarily moved to transit camps while their building is razed and rebuilt), building owners and developers can appear accommodating to their low-income tenants while actually creating a building that is newly unaffordable to such communities.

Both displacement and redevelopment are looming threats to the chawl dwellers I come to know. The move to Vikhroli is isolating for Sushila and reminds Prem Kumar (as well as Manda and other current chawl dwellers at Dhanraj) of many of the reasons to hold on to the downtown chawls or redeveloped buildings they live in, regardless of the material state or looming insecurity of their home. In particular, Manda often expresses a desire to remain unseen by the state (in this case, MHADA), irrespective of the unlivable conditions she often experiences in her home. She lives in BDD chawl number 19, which was built in 1923 and initially used as a prison. Her neighbor Paro's unit has a rod running along the front wall, which is used to hang clothes and extra cooking equipment. I ask about it, and the women laugh. Paro tells me, "During the British time this building was a jail. Prisoners used to be tied to the rod and beaten. A lot of people were

FIGURE 3.12. The palimpsest of Paro's prison/chawl.

scared to live here: they had to be bribed. Some were almost given their units for free."

Manda and Paro often talk of their emotional attachment to this building, haunted by colonial ghosts. And it isn't just the past that torments the present—living on the ground floor (as Manda and Paro do) involves a chronic sense of impending disaster. During the monsoon season, water comes up to waist height on the ground floor, and many tenants live in the galleries (hallways) of the second floor until the waters subside. On July 26, 2005, Mumbai (as well as coastal Maharashtra and parts of Gujarat) experienced a devastating flood commonly referred to as "26 July." This event resulted in more than five thousand deaths. I am told that the water was up to the loft, and tenants were forced to live in the gallery for almost a week.

Paro tells me that every year—since her wedding in 1982 when she moved here—there is some problem with the monsoon. She is often cooking food in hip-deep water. She tells me:

> In this building there are thirty-two chawls. This building is built over a creek with sewage. We prepare and pack clothes just in case it starts raining and we have to take our stuff upstairs. The government doesn't really do anything, but after 26 July they gave five thousand rupees to each unit. The Shiv Sena came and gave them milk or bread or *vada pao* whenever there are very heavy rains. But only once during the year. Money was only distributed once. That time lots of things were ruined. They [the government] don't pay attention, even though you can read about it in the newspaper. For so many years we actually *live* in water.

I ask the women if they want the building to be redeveloped, but they both adamantly shake their heads no. Manda tells me: "Developers are putting pressure, but no one will agree. This building has a big gallery: a new building won't have such a nice gallery. It will have less space: the big courtyard will be destroyed. There will just be more buildings."

Neither woman wants the building to be redeveloped, even though the first floor is rendered uninhabitable every summer. However, it is worth emphasizing that their immediate fear is not displacement; it is instead returning to a building without galleries and courtyards, without the open communal space that makes the chawl a home. The eventual displacement of resettlement is real and present, but not necessarily imminent. In this way Manda and Paro live "elliptically," meaning, to draw on Lauren Berlant, that their attachment is not toward a future but instead is stuck— a nonaspirational state of existence.[33] In thinking of chawl life as elliptical, I am able to use stagnated time to challenge the teleological narratives emerging from displacement: this is the queerness of "chawl time."

When I ask Prem Kumar if he plans to leave his home and move north, his response is a shrug. In recounting Berlant's work on the ellipsis, Darren Byler (2012) explains that "a 'shrug' is a rhetorical response to a non-rhetorical question of the body—an embodied letting go of future promises in favor of life in the durative present." This bodily movement is not merely a way to avoid my question. Instead, it is a tactic to passively resist an engagement with time as an active, future-driven exercise. In an area of the city where industrial debris and deindustrializing development collide on a daily basis, the temporal space of the chawl plays out in the ellipsis: the ". . ." of a city experiencing both rapid transformation and frustrating stagnation. This elliptical occupation of time and space—this chawl time—is queer, particularly in a city widely understood to embody chronic and rapid progress-oriented development.

Conclusions: City out of Time

The city . . . does not tell its past, but contains it like the lines of a hand, written in the corners of the streets, the gratings of the windows, the banisters of the steps, the antennae of the lightning rods, the poles of the flags, every segment marked in turn with scratches, indentations, scrolls. —ITALO CALVINO, Invisible Cities, 1972

The archive of the chawl is a leaky archive: while the buildings themselves provide the most obvious archival containers, practices of habitation resist this boundedness and demand that we look beyond domestic interiors for a sense of "home." In this way, the communal courtyards, the gallas and the neighborhood streets provide archival spaces of resistance to hegemonic framings of "modern time." One day, as we walk home along Ambedkar Road, Manda motions to the cranes and towers overhead: "Jeev jaato majha." (My heart burns.) The fear of more buildings drives many conversations I have with her, as well as other chawl-dwelling workers at Dhanraj. Manda is a chawl dweller. Hardships or not, she doesn't want to be anything else. The chawl is not merely a building that exists in the present moment; it is also a site that invokes a particular time. Through the queer lens of "chawl time," this archive has destabilized a naturalized frame of forward-focused temporal progression. Drawing again on Reinhart Koselleck's critical point, our ideas of the future determine how we remember the past. For chawl dwellers who can't *see* a future for themselves within the island city, the draw of the past becomes increasingly powerful. Every low-income person I know living in Central Mumbai understands their home as some sort of ticking time bomb, destined to explode and exile them to suburban neighborhoods lacking the inscriptions of memory and the proximity of community. The archive of the chawl, then, is the repository of that remembered moment when home was solid and presence was unquestioned, regardless of whether such a time truly existed. These stories of time and expectation become the temporal artifacts housed within the archive.

In contrast to the imagination of the global city from a zoomed-out perspective of large-scale development and far-reaching connections, these stories of Central Mumbai's chawl dwellers approach globalization, urban restructuring, and shifting class dynamics from the ground up: these are affective stories of infrastructure, the sensorium of "chawl time."[34] Mumbai's chawl-dwelling communities—former and current industrial workers who do not see themselves as participating in the future of the city—are out of step with forward-thinking capitalist progression but are still vital and present and modern. They have created their own temporal patterns, which invoke nostalgia and memory as a "rebellion against the modern idea of time, the time of history and progress" (Boym 2001, xv). To live in the chawls is to embody the rebellion of the ellipsis (. . .).

The traces of past histories remain layered on the city streets of Central Mumbai chawl neighborhoods. When I walk the streets with Manda, I feel the ghosts of her history and memory alongside us, creating a buffer between our two bodies and the screams coming from construction sites, towering cranes, new flyovers, and multiplying skyscrapers. It is as though such overwhelming city messages can be ignored through movement— through the galleries, across the hallways, and along the busy city streets. So Manda keeps moving, and it is this movement that delays the inevitable resettlement so many of her neighbors have already experienced. It is this movement that speaks to "how some of us continue to live today." As though, if she keeps up the frenetic energy of chawl living, the inevitability of the future can be kept at bay. At least for a time.

4

The Archive
of the Strike

Identity and contradiction of thought are welded together. Total contradiction is nothing but the manifested untruth of total identification. Contradiction is nonidentity
under the rule of law that affects the nonidentical as well. —THEODOR ADORNO, *Negative Dialectics*, (1966) 2007

Disidentification is about recycling and rethinking coded meaning. The process of
disidentification scrambles and reconstructs the encoded message of a coded text in
a fashion that both exposes the encoded message's universalizing and exclusionary
machinations and recruits its workings to account for, include, and empower minority
identities and identifications. Thus, disidentification is a step further than cracking
open the code of the majority; it proceeds to use this code as raw material for representing a disempowered politics or positionality that has been rendered unthinkable
by the dominant culture. —JOSÉ ESTEBAN MUÑOZ, *Disidentifications*, 1999

Arrivals: Vulnerable Encounters

Kishan and I like to walk. We don't usually leave the mill together, but
we will meet up in Rani Baug gardens and zoological park, several blocks
down from the mill, at 3:00 PM when the morning shift is over. Kishan gets
chai, I buy the tickets, and we make our way into the shady expanse of the
park. Sometimes we end up on the stone benches lining the walkway, but
mostly we keep moving. During our walks Kishan tells me the stories he
can't articulate within the mill, among the other workers: stories of isolation and alienation, discrimination and threats of violence. The experience

FIGURE 4.1. Walking in Rani Baug gardens. Photograph by Kabi Sherman.

of being an outsider in a hostile city he *wants* to call his home. One day he explains to me: "Heart of hearts, I think I am a Bihari. I belong to Bihar, I was born in Bihar. Deep inside I feel like a Bihari. But I have been living in Bombay, I have worked here, this is where I have filled my stomach, and my family's stomach. That is my birthplace, but this is my workplace. This is where I belong. This place has given me work. I am here now, so this is where I belong."

Kishan is a sixty-year-old textile mill worker from the northern state of Bihar. As a labor migrant from one of the poorest and most stigmatized Indian states, he elicits a range of reactions from his Maharashtrian co-workers at Dhanraj. As I come to know Kishan over the course of my fieldwork, his stories of injustice and cruelty at the hands of his coworkers contribute to a larger narrative of Maharashtrian xenophobia against North Indian migrant workers that I hear circulating at Dhanraj.

He tells me that, as a North Indian labor migrant, he is now only allowed to be a winder at the mill, a menial job historically occupied by women. However, he also explains that this is a relatively new development, resulting from employment reservations enforced after the Great

Textile Strike of 1982–1983. Kishan's history of mill land labor is one of great demographic change: he explains that before the strike, North Indians made up the majority of mill workers. However, after the strike an 80 percent reservation for Maharashtrian workers is instituted throughout the mill lands. After the strike, he finds himself not only marginalized as a North Indian but also "feminized" through his employment position as a winder. This intersection of gender and xenophobia creates a work atmosphere of resentment and marginalization: a powerful identity-based hierarchy on which Kishan occupies the lowest rung. As we walk, Kishan presents memories, histories, statistics, and philosophical musings on the relationship between the current North Indian minority and the Maharashtrian majority within the declining industrial workforce of the city. Kishan reminds me, time and time again, that he is welcomed neither in the city nor in the mill and will therefore eventually return to his extended family in Bihar when the time comes to retire, even as he has spent his adult life chasing the identity and subject position of "Mumbaiker."

Kishan is convincing. He is articulate and politically engaged: seemingly vulnerable but lacking in sentimentality. He draws the city for me, and through his stories I become "caught" (as Jeanne Favret-Saada [1977] would argue) in the narrative of self he spins for me (after all, paranoia is contagious).

However, Kishan is also far from the innocent victim he presents to me through these carefully crafted stories. Over the course of my fieldwork, I watch as he slowly reveals himself as socially and politically problematic in both the mill setting, specifically, and his social realm, generally. And, throughout our time together, I begin to notice that there is something a bit . . . *off* with him. At first I can't quite articulate this instinct of mine, but I do feel uneasy around him. He is quick to anger, fascinated by violence, and dismissive of women and Maharashtrian men, whom he finds effeminate and weak. However, I try to ignore these feelings and instead focus on the stories he tells me—after all, that is what anthropologists *do*.

The Maharashtrian workers warn me about Kishan: they tell me he is a bad sort of man and that I shouldn't be alone with him. But when I ask them why I am told: "Bihari men are like that." This, therefore, strengthens my resolve, and I find myself spending more and more time with him. I listen to more and more of his stories: stories about how the 1982–1983 strike changes the demographics and atmosphere of the mill lands. Stories of his own marginalization.[1] At first I think I am hearing the "alternative truth" about the mill lands: a challenge to the larger narrative of identity politics and representation in Mumbai.

But then I realize I am getting something else: Kishan is *not* telling me the "truth."[2]

This realization creates an ethnographic crisis for me: How do I interpret his stories if they are designed to manipulate and control me? How do I think through the gaps between individual action and structures of feeling? How do I grapple with my own position as documenting anthropologist when a key informant both reveals a compelling narrative trajectory and simultaneously exposes the inconsistencies, contradictions, and inaccuracies of their own testimonies? If Kishan isn't telling me the "Truth" (in a singular, objective way), then what *is* he telling me?

This crisis is not new in the realm of anthropology and ethnographic fieldwork. In his ethnographic novel, *After Life*, Tobias Hecht grapples with the challenge of a dishonest informant he calls "Bruna Veríssimo." When she is first introduced, Bruna tells the author-anthropologist: "Go ahead, ask the questions. I know how to answer" (2007, 1). What is first interpreted as a willingness to participate is later remembered as something much messier. After a decade of interviews and collaboration, Hecht realizes: "Though everything Bruna was telling me was plausible, a substantial amount happened to be untrue" (5). This realization results in Hecht's own ethnographic crisis, which leads him to fictionalize his relationship with Bruna: the ethnographer becomes "Zoe," and the informant becomes "Aparecida." The ethnography becomes an "ethnographic novel," akin to historical fiction: Hecht reasons that this landscape of reality exists, these stories *could* be true. But they didn't happen to his informant; they are not her immediate experience. Hence the utilization of the novel form.

Such fictionalization gives Hecht liberty to push the limits of ethnography and ethnographic data: the interior life of the fictional ethnographer is exposed, the various stories collected over years of fieldwork become composite sketches, and the crisis of truth and transparency is explored. Toward the novel's conclusion, the ethnographer-as-Zoe wonders:

> How do we know what anyone else is thinking? . . . She does not have the answer. She was trained only to observe, to listen. She does both those things. . . . There are the things we see. But do we know what is behind them?
>
> I have no idea what Aparecida thinks, Zoe admits to herself.

But this is what I think she thinks, she continues: I am a client.
Is she not in the business of selling fantasies, of satisfying fantasies?
. . . So she has tried to guess my fantasy, Zoe thinks. (170–171)

Zoe thinks she is trained to observe, to listen. As though this is all she was trained to do. As if the field is a laboratory setting in which she has control. If this is her simplistic understanding of ethnographic fieldwork, then how unsettling to realize *she* has been observed, *she* has been listened to. The two women — ethnographer and informant — have been reading each other, reflecting back to each other what they think the other wants to see, wants to hear. And so it is, in part, the same for me with Kishan: how much more captivating for *me*, the ethnographer, to be fed a story of racism, regionalism, disenfranchisement, alienation.[3] Of a marginalized subaltern subject struggling to survive as a second-class urban citizen. Like Hecht, I know this narrative reflects the larger experiences of North Indians in Mumbai. This is why I am so eager to believe Kishan's stories. But also like Hecht, over the course of my fieldwork I start to realize these stories don't *exactly* map onto the direct experiences of Kishan's life.

However, this doesn't mean they are not his reality.

And this doesn't mean they are not my ethnography.

While such questions lead Hecht to fiction, similar questions lead me to the archive: I argue that my archive of the strike is full of the untruths provided to me by both North Indians and Maharashtrians in Dhanraj. By "untruths," I refer to a series of histories, identities, and memories that — while contradicted and challenged by more verifiable events — are critical in constructing a sense of self and meaning for my informants. Much archival material is left out of the museum because it is contradictory, unverifiable, or incomplete. Therefore, if I understand untruths as archival material, Kishan must be telling me something important. The story here cannot just be that he is a liar: instead, my time spent listening to North Indian testimonies of identity and belonging echoes the lively ruination I understand to be the material space of Dhanraj. Kishan's untruths represent a dying, yet still vital, narrative. Perhaps this material is insignificant in the museum space. But it is critical within the archive. There are lessons here if I pay attention.

While the question of truthfulness and trust may sit at the heart of all ethnographic inquiry, several scholars have specifically addressed truth in ethnographic fieldwork and the effect of trust on our relationship to our informants. In thinking through this scholarship, I am particularly taken by Lee Ann Fujii's exploration of "metadata," which she defines as: "the spoken and unspoken expressions about people's interior thoughts and feelings, which they do not always articulate in their stories or responses to interview questions. Metadata can take both spoken and unspoken forms. They include rumors, silences, and invented stories. Metadata are as valuable as the testimonies themselves because they indicate how the current social and political landscape is shaping what people might say to a researcher" (2010, 232).[4] By arguing that this archive is full of "untruths," I draw on Fujii's "metadata" to take seriously the unverifiable stories that, even so, make real meaning out of people's lives.

How can such untruths further reveal the experiences of nonrecognition, of being unseen? "Truth" is undoubtedly a messy notion in Dhanraj, across the mill lands, about the textile strike, and of mill worker identity (in addition to being a messy notion everywhere), but taking "untruth" seriously can help untangle these knots. Resorting to "ethnographic fiction" lets Hecht off the hook: he avoids grappling with the difficult questions posed through Bruna's imagination, embellishments, and fabrications. Why did she do what she did? How do untruths become critical ethnographic data? What do these stories tell us about the lives of our informants and the larger landscapes of their social and political worlds? To create the genre of "ethnographic fiction" is to assume that ethnographic nonfictions are peopled by informants who "tell the truth" and that to find a deviation in representation results in an ethnographic impasse.

This archive of the strike, filled with ethnographic untruths, challenges what is allowed in the museum and what is relegated to the archive. In exploring this so-called faulty data, I am pushed to confront the way I pay attention to the stories I am told. For years I listen to my North Indian informants tell me their alternative histories of the 1982–1983 strike and their sense of alienation within the mill (in general) and the city (at large). I try to understand how their sense of disenfranchisement and alienation creates an alternative archive that is both affectively impactful and—at times—factually incorrect.

But then I realize: I am *listening*, but I am unable to *hear* what they are saying.

This chapter-archive is composed of the traces of identity and belonging constructed within the workspace of Dhanraj.[5] This archive of untruths makes visible these identity-based anxieties, both through memories of a past event (the Great Textile Strike of 1982–1983) and insecurities of the present moment/looming future (the decline of the mill lands and impending closure of Dhanraj). In exploring this particular archive, my questions are driven by two different levels of disconnect. First, the disconnect between my informant's claims and verifiable "truths" on the one hand, and then more ephemerally, the hidden/personal experiences and official narratives that circulate, both as rumor *and* as "truth," on the other hand. How do my Maharashtrian and North Indian informants at Dhanraj speak of each other with such disdain and distrust while simultaneously working together, day in and day out, with what appears to be affection, respect, and cooperation? How do two parallel "histories" circulate within a space that is at once unified (Dhanraj as a singular workspace) and divided (oppositional experiences along regional lines)? What work is being done through the trafficking of untruths invested in highlighting regional difference, even as the identity of "mill worker" is used as a unifying category? How are larger urban narratives of political divisiveness and regional conflict distilled in the space of the mill? How do I interpret the identity-based untruths I am told, specifically in relation to the 1982–1983 strike?

And what do I do with Kishan?

Against Identity

Objectively, dialectics means to break the compulsion to achieve identity, and to break it by means of the energy stored up in that compulsion and congealed in its objectifications. —THEODOR ADORNO, *Negative Dialectics*, (1966) 2007

Kishan and I meet in spaces of incoherence and incommensurability. First, like all textile workers, he works in a space deemed impossible by the city—a textile mill still operational, even as the more official narrative of Mumbai's mill lands claims no such functional spaces exist. Second, Kishan is a North Indian—a demographic majorly underrepresented in mill land history (regardless of the stories circulated by North Indians in Dhanraj). Early in my fieldwork, I find myself growing more and more interested in telling an ethnographic story of competing statistics from Maharashtrians and North Indians regarding regional representation within the textile mills: I want to "disprove" the master narrative. I want to champion my marginalized North Indian informants. It takes me years to abandon this project. Additionally, as a Hindi speaker, Kishan is relatively incapable of communicating with his majority Maharashtrian, ma-

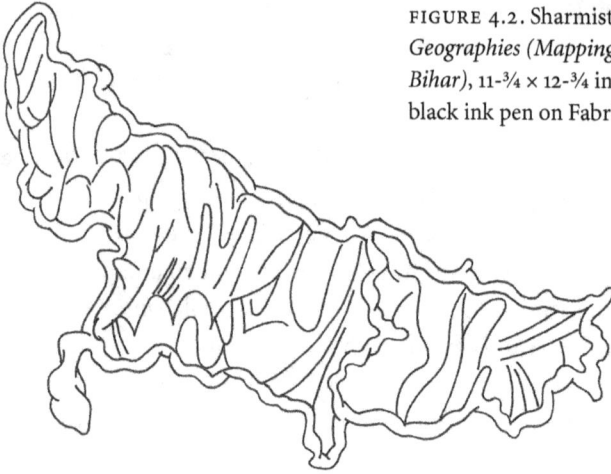

FIGURE 4.2. Sharmistha Ray, *Intimate Geographies (Mapping Uttar Pradesh and Bihar)*, 11-¾ × 12-¾ inches, porous point black ink pen on Fabriano paper, 2018.

jority Marathi-speaking coworkers. Third, and perhaps most important, no one likes Kishan. For months he explains to me that this is because he is Bihari—the most hated of the North Indians within a politics of xenophobia in Maharashtrian Mumbai.

With this in mind, it is important to reiterate that everyone who works at Dhanraj is a migrant of some sort: Most Maharashtrians at the mill are native Mumbaikers, but their families came to the city from rural Maharashtra two or three generations ago to reap the benefits of employment in the textile industry. Most North Indians are not born in Mumbai, but live most of their lives in the city. Kishan followed other family members from Bihar to the city of dreams and spent the majority of his adult years as a winder in Dhanraj. His children were born in Mumbai, and he considers the city his home. However, there is no migrant unity here: every Maharashtrian Dhanraj worker I come to know is a proud member of the Shiv Sena, a political party built on the platform of "Maharashtra for Maharashtrians." This association is not lost on North Indian Dhanraj workers, like Kishan.[6]

Indeed, my time at Dhanraj reveals resentment and distrust between Maharashtrians and North Indians: Raj, who is Maharashtrian, tells me, "When Biharis come to Mumbai . . . they are a problem. They are taking over jobs. . . . When you have people from your own country [*desh*], why don't you support them and give them jobs?[7] Everyone needs a job, but your residents should be given preference." Most of the Maharashtrian

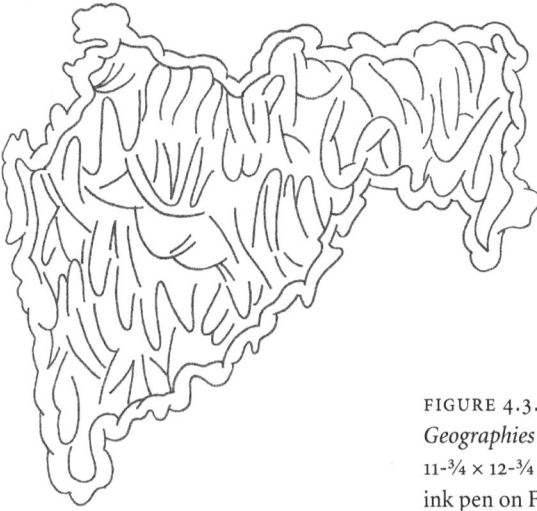

FIGURE 4.3. Sharmistha Ray, *Intimate Geographies (Mapping Maharashtra)*, 11-¾ × 12-¾ inches, porous point black ink pen on Fabriano paper, 2018.

workers at Dhanraj echo this sentiment. And while all North Indians are problematic, I am told that the Biharis are the worst.

To be clear: I am not disputing the xenophobia and alienation experienced by my North Indian informants. Indeed, I find that they are marginalized both in the mill and in the city at large. Mumbai has a dark history of xenophobia and communalism, and excellent scholarship is available on the subject.[8] However, even as this marginalization is all too apparent, there is no evidence to support the specific claims the North Indian Dhanraj workers make: that before the 1982–1983 strike North Indians outnumbered Maharashtrians in the mill. In fact, everything I read presents a simple Maharashtrian majority and North Indian minority, in terms of employment demographics.[9] When I abandon my need to "prove" an alternative "Truth," I find there is another space of interpretation: the space of "untruth." If Kishan (along with other North Indian mill workers) is rewriting the past in search of stronger justifications for the present moment, what do such untruths tell us, ethnographically?

North Indian testimonies of worker demographics take "the risk of being horribly wrong even as [they] risk being horribly right about unwanted truths" (Scappettone 2016, 102).[10] I assert that stories of a historic majority not only allow for my North Indian informants to speak about their vulnerability and isolation (within both Dhanraj and the city of Mumbai) but also facilitate the rejection of this vulnerable identity:

what José Esteban Muñoz calls a "disidentification." Muñoz defines "dis-identification" as "emergent identities-in-difference. These identities-in-difference emerge from a failed interpellation within the dominant public sphere. Their emergence is predicated on their ability to disidentify with the mass public and instead, through this disidentification, contribute to the function of a counterpublic sphere" (1999, 7).[11] In drawing on the frame of "disidentification," I do not want to suggest that North Indian narratives of belonging and identity in the mills provide an emancipatory or radical politics. Indeed, there is also a relationship between the "disidentifying" work in Kishan's narrative and the *North* Indian version of Hindu majoritarianism, in terms of non-Hindus peripherally employed in the mill lands (in particular Muslim men employed to stock and restock the godowns located on the third floor of the mill). While there is little space for Maharashtrian–North Indian solidarity in opposition to Muslim wage laborers, I did find that Kishan and Sudarshan are still also seen as "not-Muslim." However, I do believe that such a frame can realign an otherwise disempowering and alienating trope of "the other."

And so what interests me about the testimonies of my North Indian informants is not how they understand themselves *as* "North Indian" but instead how they understand themselves *to be understood as* "the other" by their Maharashtrian coworkers and how this "otherness" is rejected through performances of untruth. Questions about identity, particularly *cultural* identity, are historically central to anthropological inquiry, but I am unconvinced that explorations of caste, language, and religion (among other questions central in South Asia) will help me understand *why* North Indians tell me the stories they tell me (contrary to my Maharashtrian informants' claim that "North Indians are like that"): following Muñoz, I find this approach to be "especially exhausted."[12] While it would be unwise to reject identity as a critical form through which political, economic, and social realities come into being, here I instead want to draw attention to how identity can both be upheld as a critical form of social formation and also be revealed as untrue. The circulation of untruth—ephemeral stories of identity that cannot be mapped onto anything concrete—reveals the ambivalence of an identity that is both culturally rich ("North Indian") and socially flattened and dehumanizing ("the other").[13] Through North Indian stories invested in a rejection of identity, I argue that it is necessary to take seriously the juxtaposition and the dialectic of identification and disidentification.

In thinking through what it means to be framed as "the other," I draw on Theodor Adorno's work *Negative Dialectics*.[14] Adorno's meditation on identity reframes Hegel's dialectic of "identity of identity and nonidentity" to "nonidentity of identity and nonidentity."[15] In shifting the focus to "nonidentity," Adorno shows how negation "indicates the untruth of identity, the fact that the concept does not exhaust the thing conceived" (2007, 5).[16] In the realm of the archive of the strike, thinking through a negative dialectic involves grappling with the implication for North Indians, rendered "the other" within the landscape of a "Maharashtrian mill worker" majority.[17] What happens when *you* are, in fact, "the other"? How can North Indians fall under the category of "general mill worker" when they also become, through an inescapable identity category of "North Indian mill worker," "the other"?[18] Or, why is it that some general identities (at least for a time) work to contain and comprise the differences (the "others") out of which they are assembled, and others (or at other times) seem unable to stop the differences from creating friction (or perhaps even thrive on creating that friction)? The seeming success of the strike (for Maharashtrians) is as a unification of textile workers throughout the city.[19] However, this unification is incomplete and exclusionary, the point here being that there is a moment of industrial action that (for all its melancholy ends and failures) is generally seen as a last great hurrah for worker solidarity (the textile strike) but is actually premised on a constitutive exclusion.

Adorno claims that Hegel's positive dialectic is oppressive in its assumption that any collective action will be emancipatory or liberating in some manner. For Adorno, such collective emancipation is simply not possible. Instead, he goes back to the individual: back to an attempt to retrieve what has been lost of the subject in the struggle for recognition in which differences are subsumed to a greater good through a "higher" manifestation or representation of "the one" versus "the other." For Adorno, it is always critical to uphold the dissonance internal to any conceptual system and to refuse reconciliation.

My North Indian informants find themselves in a bind: while they *are* "mill workers" and suffer the communal nonrecognition experienced by *all* workers at Dhanraj, they are also "the other," in a way that cannot be adequately grasped through Hegel's dialectic of "identity of identity and non-identity" (because the identity of the latter does not resolve into any unity or institutional form of recognition, as Hegel would argue any "other" identity must do). And as such they also become the medium of the identitarian jouissance of their Maharashtrian colleagues. When Kishan tells me stories of a mythic past in which North Indians make up the majority of Dhanraj's workforce, we both know he is not telling "the truth."[20] But these "untruths," when read through a negative dialectic ("nonidentity of identity and nonidentity") are more about his refusal to hold a nonidentity in a manner that does not resolve with otherness in a Hegelian sense, and less about his claim that—demographically—the mill used to look differently. Or, put another way, his ambivalent self-presentation ("I belong in Mumbai, but in my heart I'm a Bihari") is more about acknowledging a nonidentity. For Adorno, such a nonidentity can never be adequately grasped linguistically; it can only be affectively experienced. Hence Kishan's self-account does not reconcile with the truth; but it also cannot merely be equated with "fiction." Reading through/with Adorno, the "untrue" is never fictional. It is rather *the most real*. By the same token, the "North Indian" or "Bihari" label that is put on Kishan by the Maharashtrian workers is an "identity" that he is refusing to hold.

In Dhanraj, these "untruths" are a result of this negative dialectic, emerging from a commitment to "nonidentity" over "identity" and "untruth" over "official story" (if by "untruth" we recognize something completely adequate in Kishan's self-narrative). In other words, the nonidentical is not a *lie* we tell ourselves, for that would fall back into the trappings of identitarian thinking, the very source of one's oppression. The challenge, then, is in negotiating the dialectical tensions between stories of fear, suspicion, and animosity and the daily grind of camaraderie, reciprocity, and openness. What do stories of dislike and distrust along regional lines mean within and for the daily lives of workers still employed at Dhanraj? How do stories of untruth destabilize our ideas about both the past and the present (if we think about "stories" here in the Adornian context of aesthetic representations that present a more apt description of our affective states than "true" statements, objectively and rationally)?[21]

It is particularly helpful to draw on Adorno's concept of the nonidentical because of his reliance on the work of Samuel Beckett (who underscored the absurdity of any reconciliatory identity in the "social situation") and Marcel Proust (who created literary representations of lost memory, retrieved only ephemerally and yet viscerally in the here and now).[22] In his essay on Beckett's *Endgame*, Adorno argues: "The less events themselves can be presumed to be inherently meaningful, the more the idea of aesthetic substance as the unity of what appears and what was intended becomes an illusion" (1991, 242). If reconciliation is not the point (because reconciliation is impossible), then the work of untrue stories can shift. Stories of identity, filtered through the event of the strike, become a metaphor (Amin 1995), linking workers to a previous moment when identity could be imagined differently at Dhanraj.[23] In considering how memory forges histories of identity formation in both time and space, I explore how the stories I hear, the histories I read, and the day-to-day interactions I observe in the mill present contradictory possibilities for regional and ethnic diversity in Dhanraj, but, in moving away from identity and truth and instead embracing nonidentity and untruth, North Indian workers reveal the double bind of economic and regional precarity in mill land Mumbai. And a rejection of the violence they experience as the constitutive "other."

These untruths push me to return to the dramatic/traumatic event of the 1982–1983 textile strike through remembered traces of experience: I am often told that this is a moment when "everything changed." I find that this event becomes a fulcrum for exploring economic and social insecurity in the mill lands. In doing so, I look to diverging accounts of union leader Datta Samant and the event of the Great Textile Strike. This history, both written and remembered, establishes a larger landscape through which alternative narratives emerge. These testimonies are forged through feelings of paranoia and uncertainty: What do these untruths tell me about identity-based vulnerability, economic instability, and the social erasure of industrial Mumbai? And how can I—as an anthropologist—remain in the realm of ethnography when encountering these untruths, akin to mythologies and magical origin stories?

An Archive of Regional Identity

Eddie and Ravan's lives ran parallel, that's all. And there is no greater distance on earth than that which separates parallel lines, even if they almost touch each other. One city, one chawl, two floors, two cultures, two languages, two religions and the enmity of two women separated them. How could their paths possibly meet?—KIRAN NAGARKAR, Ravan & Eddie, 1995

Before examining the power of the strike, I first turn to the question of identity categories at Dhanraj: What exactly is it that Kishan is rejecting? Both Sudarshan and Kishan (my two key North Indian informants) carry Shiv Sena membership cards with them for protection at all times. However, they both stress that their votes and loyalties go unquestionably to

Congress, the party in support of their Rashtriya Mill Mazdoor Sangh (RMMS) union. While both men talk at length about their insecurities as North Indians in the Maharashtrian majority of Dhanraj, they still managed to express a camaraderie and sense of ease within the mill compound itself. It is only later—in the safety of crowds and public spaces—that their identity-based anxieties emerge: conversations beyond the space of the mill always come back to issues of distrust and dislike of "the other." And when Dhanraj workers speak to me about their identities as "Maharashtrian" or "North Indian," I find that, irrespective of how such an identity is framed in the remembering and the telling, the 1982–1983 strike provides an anchor through which to understand "how things changed."

A prominent member of the GKSS tells me that, historically, North Indians working in the mills have made up around 15 percent of the workforce. "In today's environment, they feel insecure," he comments, but he also tells me that, when the strike was called, everyone participated. "There is no difference between North Indians or Maharashtrians." While this is a touching sentiment within a city rife with identity politics and xenophobic fears, the stories of workers at Dhanraj seem deeply invested in narratives of marginalization and majority, xenophobia and distrust, even as I fail to encounter anything more than accounts of majority versus minority identities.[24] Many conversations at the mill revolve around who once held and who continues to hold the ethnic majority in the mill lands, although such speculations are merely that: the numbers are unavailable, and rumor and memory become expertise in any demographic analysis.

Such speculation exists alongside the mythological archive of a greater and stable working-class past; although no evidence exists to suggest this past was either stable or great.[25] Instead, these memories are fueled by present insecurities and obscure the realities of the *badli* (temporary) system and the physical stress and exhaustion of actual mill work. As I sit with the workers in Dhanraj, they circulate stories of a past that contradicts the realities of industrial labor: with much less work to get done now that production is in decline, the long afternoons of rest, tea, and storytelling cook up a phantasmic industry that outshines anything conceivable or believable. Even, I imagine, to the workers themselves.

Upon this fantasy, both sides are able to project their own memories of majority: we are, after all, trafficking in potential fictions. Is Raj really convinced that no more than 15 percent of the city's mill workers were and continue to be North Indian? Is Kishan certain that North Indians made up 80 percent of that same population prior to the strike? Their convictions are concrete and their memories consistent. However, I grow to believe that the numbers *themselves* are less important than the message folded within. But what, I continue to ask myself, is that message?

The alienation and suspicion I feel and hear throughout my time at the mill appear as a collection of observations concerning how *we* are different from *them*, and who truly deserves to be recognized as urban citizens. And these conversations are not just about one's place of origin as location: instead, I am subtly taught the ways in which one's kinship organization, eating practices, home life, and work patterns indicate difference and signal belonging, adaptation, and rights. While my Maharashtrian informants are loath to discuss their caste affiliation, they generalize a connection to each other that suggests the Marathi-speaking workers of Dhanraj, who mostly hail from the Ratnagiri district of Maharashtra, understand themselves to be part of an extended "family." However, this extended family is only newly "Maharashtrian." Rajnarayan Chandavarkar's (1999, 2004) scholarship traces the historical endurance of rigid caste markers among rural Maharashtrian workers in Mumbai, as caste, kinship, and village associations first facilitate migration to the city and later provide social security for those who migrate. Housing, job placement, and social networks are all provided through "jobbers," who recruited workers from their own native villages and created larger networks from linked migration.

As urban citizens, they teach me how they transcend caste and clearly direct me to never ask about such crude things. However, caste becomes subsumed within other social factors. For example, Manda was born in the Ghati region of Maharashtra, in contrast to the majority of the mill workers, who are from the Konkan coast. "Ghati" (mountain) is a term used for migrants from the Western Ghats along the Deccan Plateau, whereas the "Konkani" are from coastal hinterlands, primarily the Ratnagiri district. "Ghati" is sometimes used as a generic term for Marathi labor, but is also used to refer to "uncivilized locals" by the merchant and business classes (primarily from Gujarat) for whom the Ghatis worked. Sushila, a Konkani, considers herself to be an educated and sophisticated woman in comparison to the roughness of Manda, who is illiterate and, according to Sushila, "wild and cunning."

While both Konkani and Ghati people are middle-caste agricultural workers, their cultural practices are subtly different and result in social divisions: in the chawls of the early twentieth century, *khanawals* (food houses or rooms) were separate for Ghatis and Konkanis in order to cater to their specific food cultures and habits. The coastal Konkanis are fish eaters, while the Ghatis are accustomed to meat. Similarly, both groups have different forms of theatrical, musical, and religious practices. In many ways, these cultural differences and ethnic stereotypes rationalize spatial separation of the two groups.[26]

It is the *North Indians* who refuse to let go of such things, I am told. Maharashtrians, it seems, adapt to the city through their disavowal of caste markers and their embrace of "Maharashtrian" (or, more specifically, "Maharashtrian worker") identity. Regardless of the stories circulating throughout Dhanraj, I realize that these caste lines continue to exist. However, my Maharashtrian informants, in "telling" me about caste, craft particular narratives and messages that transcend this category. In telling me *not* to think through caste, they present notions of "who we *should* be" and "who we *aspire* to be," which are used in contrast to North Indians, who are seen to be archaic, rural, and antimodern because of their reliance on caste distinction.

In addition to the social barriers between Maharashtrians and North Indians, the political landscape of the city is a strong force in (seemingly) erasing caste lines within mill-working Maharashtrian communities and further isolating North Indian communities: by the 1960s, the rhetoric of the Shiv Sena unified Maharashtrians across interregional lines through clear demarcations of the ethnic other(s). None of the Maharashtrian men at Dhanraj exhibit any sense of bias toward Manda, who, as a Ghati Maharashtrian, is a minority in a mill mostly employing workers whose families originate in the Konkan region. However, this claim is complicated by the fact that Manda and Sushila hate each other. In particular, Sushila is disgusted by the way Manda emasculates her unemployed husband by making him participate in "women's work" (cleaning the chawl unit, doing laundry). This, however, is not something that seems to bother the Maharashtrian men, who argue that if Manda's husband refuses to work outside of the house, he should help her inside the house. In contrast to this, Sushila's husband sits around at home all day, appearing to do next to nothing. While Sushila's son, a police officer, lives with them and helps out financially, Manda's children are struggling to make ends meet and can't afford to help their parents. Because my Maharashtrian informants refuse to talk to me about caste, class becomes a smokescreen that shields other biases.

Subtle geography aside, Manda's Maharashtrian identity makes her an insider in ways that Sudarshan's and Kishan's thirty-plus-year residencies never will. Manda and Sushila might not enjoy each other's company, but they visit each other's homes and eat meals together in social situations. Raj's wife frequently cooks for the other Maharashtrian workers, who all tell me she cooks "the best nonveg food in Mumbai." Sudarshan and Kishan—both pure vegetarians—are not part of these social gatherings.

When I spend time in the Maharashtrian chawls, I notice women coming and going: to work, to the market, to the units of friends and family. There is a comfortable banter between the Maharashtrian men and women: joking, laughing, bickering with ease. This is in no way an indication of full gender egalitarianism, but nevertheless such comfort between men and women in the space of the chawl translates to the mill. Manda and Sushila tell me they feel comfortable with the Maharashtrian men at Dhanraj, while respecting Sudarshan from afar and openly despising Kishan.

And this divide is abundantly clear through the paths that link the home space to the work space: none of the Maharashtrian workers at Dhanraj ever visit Sudarshan's or Kishan's home, and—while I am told offers have been extended—they have not played host to the North Indians, either. While Sudarshan, Kishan, and other North Indian workers are thought of quite differently within the mill, this lack of social interaction outside the mill seems to be the greatest dividing line between the workers. This extends to my own relationships: my most intimate encounters occur within the homes of Manda, Sushila, Raj, and their Maharashtrian friends and neighbors. Kishan and Sudarshan only invite me to their homes very late in my fieldwork, and I visit each of them only once.

And so Dhanraj North Indian workers give me few details about their domestic life outside the mill, although I know that the women in their families rarely leave the house. Kishan tells me, "In my caste women don't work, so my wife has never worked. Even if she is educated and capable of working, there is still no case of women working in my community." When I ask him if he thinks women *should* work outside the home, he shrugs, telling me, "In today's world it is hard for us to stay as we are. . . . Traditions change, neither for good nor bad. They just evolve and happen. Things change." He tells me that the city changes things and that the Maharashtrian women adapt to being poor in an urban area. "That is why they work," he tells me. "Life is too expensive." But Kishan feels that some sense of gender division is important and resents his own wife for the changes he has seen in her over the years. He tells me the city gives her a sense of freedom she didn't have before: she talks back to him, she favors her children over him.[27] He suggests that such things get in the way of his sense of what a family has been and *should* be.

When I begin fieldwork at Dhanraj, Kishan is a winder, a position considered to be unskilled. Additionally, it was historically (and continues to be) the only mill work seen as suitable and available for women. When I ask him how he feels about women working at Dhanraj, he tells me: "I have no issue." However, he immediately explains to me why he dislikes Manda so much, especially in comparison to Sushila: "There is a great difference between the two women; the only similarity is that both their husbands are drunkards. . . . The problem with Manda is that she is a poor slum-dweller kind of a person and she makes her husband wash clothes and clean utensils, things like that . . . things he should not do. That's the kind of person she is. She's the one in power all the time. Sushila is not like that." Manda's flexibility—while looked down on by Kishan (and Sushila)—references her own ability to adapt to the demands of the city. As the primary breadwinner in her family, Manda makes decisions based on survival and practicalities. While Sudarshan and (in rare moments) Kishan acknowledge the challenges faced by both women, Sushila provides an easier model to support. Even though her husband refuses to work (and later falls ill and dies due to alcohol-related complications), Sushila balances her role as dutiful and respectful wife with that of worker and provider. To the two North Indian men, Manda is less sympathetic because of her own gleeful disregard of gender norms and rules of respectability.

Interestingly, it is Raj who later defends Manda when Sushila complains about her emasculating behavior, telling Sushila that Manda has too much to do, what with her mill work and no daughter-in-law at home. He then tells me that working women should be given more respect than they receive and encouraged to "be their best selves":

Some people don't work: they sit at home and become lazy, and then they become weak. Working women are strong; it's better for her. A rich woman has maids and servants, they sit around, and they become lazy. But even housework is hard work. A woman doing housework is strong. If a woman has completed her education, it's an investment and she should use it. Now it's *kalyug*, everyone should work.[28] And now women are more efficient, they're going ahead of men. Where do you not see women now? They are in the military, they are drivers, conductors, teachers, they work in the airlines. Everywhere there are women.

Raj's wife is the primary breadwinner in their home, and his upward mobility is due, in large part, to her success (but that story is for another book). Perhaps this gendered flexibility also draws attention to the inability of North Indian mill workers to abandon their "essential" identity.

These subtle markers of difference create expansive divides between North Indian and Maharashtrian workers at Dhanraj. "Textile worker" identity reveals itself to be composed of "Maharashtrian worker" and "North Indian worker" identities, and the stakes are high: Who belongs in the city, who belongs in the industry? The scarcity of remaining jobs and the disappearance of affordable housing raise these stakes even further. This, I sense through whispered untruths and half-truths, can be distilled down to one question: After the strike, who gets to *be* a "textile worker"?

The Rise of Provincial Politics

If you are not to become a monster,
you must care what they think.
If you care what they think,
how will you not hate them,
and so become a monster
of the opposite kind?
—WENDELL BERRY, "Enemies," 1994

"If you want to understand the textile workers, you have to understand Datta Samant," Ashok, a former worker now active with the GKSS, tells me. I find this to be quite challenging, however, as very little has been written about Samant's life, save his immediate involvement in the textile strike.[29] In the 1960s and 1970s, Samant becomes one of the most prominent leaders of the Indian National Trade Union Congress (INTUC).[30] In late 1981, he is chosen by a large group of Mumbai mill workers to lead them in a conflict between the Bombay Millowners Association and the RMMS: this action is a rejection of the INTUC-affiliated RMMS, which had represented the mill workers for decades.[31]

Because the strike is never legally recognized, the fear of involvement for workers grows. But Samant plans a massive strike through his own union, the Maharashtra Girni Kamghar Union (MGKU), at the beginning of which an estimated 200,000 to 300,000 mill workers walk off the job.

This, according to mill land lore, causes the city's entire textile industry to be shut down for more than a year.[32] Samant demands that, along with wage hikes, the government should do away with the Bombay Industrial Act of 1947 (which regulated employee-employer relations) and derecognize the RMMS as the only official union for the textile workers.

Samant's seeming control of the mill workers makes Prime Minister Indira Gandhi and other Congress leaders fear that his influence will spread to the port and dock workers and make him the most powerful union leader in India's commercial capital. It is likely that these fears keep the government from giving in to Samant's demands, even as the city suffers severe economic losses. As the strike progresses through the months, Samant's militancy and the government's obstinacy block any potential for negotiation and resolution. As a result, many textile mill owners begin moving their plants to rural areas outside the city. While the strike is never officially called off, it falls apart after a year and a half.

In 1984, Samant is elected on an independent, anti-Congress ticket to the Lok Sabha, an election that was otherwise swept by the Congress Party under Prime Minister Rajiv Gandhi. He remains active in trade unions and communist politics throughout India in the 1990s and becomes a vocal opponent of the Shiv Sena and the Bharatiya Janata Party (BJP): while an activist for Marathi rights, he never supports the Shiv Sena.[33] In a 1996 interview, he explains: "These are my people, but they vote for the BJP–Shiv Sena. They empathise with me, but they never vote for me, they have become communal. Thousands of textile workers are begging on the streets of Bombay and Thane, but they do not want to vote for me. People vote for thugs, pro-management people" (Ashraf 1996).

With this in mind, it is important to understand the political climate in which these agitations of the 1980s emerge, especially the rise of the Shiv Sena.[34] The Sena was founded in June 1966, shortly after Maharashtra becomes a state, on a platform of regional citizenship (the state of Maharashtra for Maharashtrians), and stresses the importance of local concerns in the political landscape of urban India (R. Joshi 1970).[35] Dipankar Gupta argues that the Shiv Sena ideology is based on four points: first, that 80 percent of all jobs should go to Maharashtrians; second, that migration to Maharashtra from other Indian states should be discouraged; third, that to increase job opportunities for Maharashtrians and economic prosperity in the state, industrial production in Maharashtra should be expanded (a belief that put the Sena at odds with communists and trade union organizers, the historic political location of textile workers); and fourth, that India should be a Hindu nation (a Nationalist sentiment that also put Shiv Sena founder Bal Thackeray at odds with the communists, whom he framed as pro-Russia and pro-China, and therefore anti-India) (Gupta 1982, 41).[36]

While migrants from coastal (konkan) and mountainous (desh/ghati) Maharashtra had been moving into Mumbai since the nineteenth century (Chandavarkar 2009b, 60), the rural Marathi-speaking migrants of the 1950s and 1960s find themselves at a disadvantage in the labor market, in comparison to more skilled migrants from outside of Maharashtra (Hansen 2001, 45). While many of these migrants find jobs as unskilled temporary workers in the textile mills, the Marathi-speaking middle class in Mumbai is disenchanted to find that, even as they witness dramatic political changes on a large scale, their personal economic opportunities remain unchanged. Thackeray, a cartoonist by trade, represents these tensions in his cartoon weekly, *Marmik* (the essence), which he launches in 1963.[37]

Out of this economic disillusionment, South Indians become the primary target of Shiv Sena nativism in the 1960s, although waves of North Indian migrants continue to move into a city rife with housing and job shortages. In part, the Sena emerges from this anxiety of marginalization: as non-Maharashtrian migrants arrive in a city already stretched thin, "Maharashtrians as a community were, and felt themselves to be, subordinate on their own native soil" (Katzenstein 1973, 392). However, this Shiv Sena brand of nativism makes space in the city for *some* outsiders, as Thackeray himself writes that a Mumbaiker "not only includes Marathi-speaking Maharashtrians, but extends to all those of all castes, creeds and religion, who look upon Maharashtra as their homeland, who have been living here for generations together carrying on trade or business, contributing to the welfare and prosperity of Maharashtra and above all comingling their weals and woes with those of the sons of the soil" (Thackeray 1967). This sentiment makes room in the city for the industrialists but not non-Maharashtrian working-class migrants. In addition, it plants the seed for a contemporary Sena platform of development, in place of the older ideology of regionalism and xenophobia.[38]

Every Maharashtrian worker I encounter throughout my fieldwork belongs to the Shiv Sena. When I ask Raj why, he looks at me quizzically, as though I asked him what color the sky is: "I am Maharashtrian. This party is for Maharashtrians." The seamless link between identity and politics obscures a much hazier picture: the figures of Bal Thackeray and Datta

Samant are building two very different mythic Maharashtrian majorities, one capitalist and one socialist. However, these implications are obscured both by identitarian politics in the mill lands and Samant's untimely death. On the morning of January 16, 1997, four gunmen, believed to be contract killers, shoot Samant outside his home in the northeastern neighborhood of Ghatkopar. His death sparks rallies across the city, and a large procession of union activists gathers at his cremation. It's impossible to predict what might have emerged from his political life; however, his death does allow for Maharashtrian mill workers to politically support the Shiv Sena while circulating the myth of the saintly Samant.

However, this is not the case for the North Indians at Dhanraj. The first time I visit the mill, in early November 2008, Chandan, one of the compound's many watchmen, greets me at the gate. Chandan has been working at the mill for more than thirty years: he came from Bihar as a young man and, at the time of my fieldwork, is one of the oldest workers at Dhanraj. During the 1982–1983 strike he is kept on as a watchman and continues to work through the mill closings. He tells me: "I think the strike was a punishment for the workers. No gains for workers took place. Day by day, the industry came down. Now 90 percent of the industry is closed. No mill is working, aside from private sector. Had the strike not happened things would be different."

I ask him about Datta Samant, and he shakes his head. "Everyone was destroyed because of him and his strike, the textile industry died because of it," he says with residual anger. I am shocked to hear this, considering my extensive prefieldwork reading and interviews with GKSS members.[39] What I realize after talking with Chandan, however, is that *North Indian* workers do not share this unanimous support. Instead, they see their current marginalization as a direct result of Samant's political agitation.

Sailing in Two Boats

I like the generosity of numbers.
The way, for example,
they are willing to count
anything or anyone . . .
—MARY CORNISH, "Numbers," 2007

When I begin my preliminary fieldwork in Mumbai, years before I stumble across Dhanraj, I encounter only a story of heroism: the union leader Datta

Samant stood up for the workers and led them to strike in 1982. The evil capitalist mill owners, however, would never bend to the demands of the workers, and the strike led to the collapse of the industry. When I ask Maharashtrian workers at Dhanraj if they think Samant should have compromised, if they feel let down by his stubbornness, my question is often met with horror. "He did this for us," Sitaram tells me. "He was too stubborn, but he was stubborn for us."[40]

I love this story. The closeted Marxist inside me dances with joy.

However, the North Indians at Dhanraj have an alternate archive, which challenges this story and complicates the mill land narrative within a broader history of identity politics in Mumbai: Who, exactly, constitutes the "us" Maharashtrians speak of?

Most mill land histories assert that Mumbai's textile mills not only *are* employing majority Maharashtrian workers but also have—historically—*always* employed majority Maharashtrian workers. Even so, my North Indian informants confidently state that one of Maharashtrian Datta Samant's demands was an enforceable 80 percent reservation for Maharashtrians (similar to Shiv Sena ideology, citywide). The conservative estimates I encounter about the mill lands—that the workforce has, historically, been composed of 15 percent North Indian workers—are confusing, then, considering that Samant's reservation proposal allows for 20 percent non-Maharashtrian workers. This would seem to raise the percentage of North Indian workers in the mill lands. Diverging from the metanarrative of Maharashtrian presence in the mills, my North Indian informants counter this tale by claiming that prior to the arrival of Datta Samant, the textile mills were *not* staffed primarily by Maharashtrians but instead by migrants from various North Indian states: the cosmopolitan "Bombay" before the provincialized "Mumbai."[41] However, mass migrations into the city by North Indians, low employment rates among Maharashtrians, and the rise of Maharashtrian political movements (primarily as a result of the Shiv Sena and, later, the Maharashtra Navnirman Sena [MNS]) allow Samant to manipulate the city's regionalized anxiety and carve out a new space for Maharashtrians to claim as their own. According to my North Indian informants, it was not until *after* the massive strike of 1982–1983 that the mills of Mumbai transformed into a majority Maharashtrian space.

I love this story even more. Uncovering secret histories of marginalized migrant workers makes me turn cartwheels in my mind.

Sudarshan tells me:

The strike did not benefit the workers, it was the workers who had a loss. . . . But there were workers who supported the strike and supported Datta Samant. One, Datta Samant was a Maharashtrian and supported the Maharashtrian workers. And also he wooed the workers by saying, "I will get these benefits for you, I will make these demands." A lot of people were attracted by this. . . . As a leader of the union he made sure that the Maharashtrian workers were central. It was for them that he worked. Datta Samant was only good for Maharashtrians. It was his demand that the regional workers [Maharashtrians] should get 80 percent reservations in the mill.

When I ask Sudarshan to clarify this 80/20 percent distinction (in contrast to the widely circulating statistic that North Indians have always made up and still make up only 15 percent of the workforce), he tells me the number is a lie: "If now there is only 15 percent in the mill, it is because we are always the first to go. The union will make sure we [North Indians] are the first to go. But it wasn't like that before [the strike]."

I find that, whether within Dhanraj, at GKSS meetings, or around Mumbai in general, mythological stories about Datta Samant are ubiquitous. Most Maharashtrian mill workers see him as a tragic hero, while the North Indian workers unanimously see him as a thug. What I want to drive home here is *not* whether Datta Samant created a Maharashtrian majority or whether his strike had the best intentions of mill workers at heart. Instead, I see the stories of Samant as indicative of the stakes of marginal mill workers in the city. For my Maharashtrian informants, Samant is a figure who attempts to create a Mumbai with Maharashtrian mill workers at its heart.[42] The 1982–1983 strike allows for the struggle of previously disenfranchised workers to take center stage and to become both visible and legitimate. In many ways, Samant creates a space for the right of the Maharashtrian mill worker to exist, to be seen, and to have worth in the city. Today, as the mills close and the chawls are torn down or redeveloped, this memory of relevance is a powerful relic and is framed through the identity of *Maharashtrian* mill workers.

However, for the North Indian workers, Samant provides an alternative, though equally powerful, narrative of past belonging. If, as they argue, North Indians were a much more sizable minority (perhaps even a majority) prior to 1982, then Samant and his strike become the catalyst for the current North Indian marginalization within the last operational mills. Maharashtrian migrant mill workers are able to return to their villages during the strike while simultaneously remaining connected to the news of mill openings and job opportunities in Mumbai. Because of this network (through both Marathi newspapers and familial connections), many Maharashtrian mill workers return to the city as mill jobs become available in the aftermath of the strike. However, both Kishan and Sudarshan tell me that most North Indian mill workers simply chose to leave the city for good: the networks in Uttar Pradesh and Bihar were much weaker and the anti–North Indian sentiments of Samant too depressing to retain hope for future mill work. What this argument reveals is a North Indian nostalgia for an earlier, pre-strike time of North Indian legitimacy within the mills.[43] While the North Indian mill workers at Dhanraj acknowledge their minority status *now*, they simultaneously hold on to the image of a time in which their own belonging, their own right to the city, is stronger and less contested: a time when their own contribution to the textile industry is seen as central and not peripheral.

Regardless of whether such a time ever actually existed.

This negative dialectic ("nonidentity of identity and nonidentity") is a "refusal" (Simpson 2016) of mill worker identity as specifically/majority "Maharashtrian." Instead, North Indians remember a past time in which they were *also* "the mill workers" and not "the other." And not only that: they were also the majority. The strike, specifically remembered through the polarizing figure of Samant, becomes the solid moment that anchors their otherwise ephemeral and unrooted histories. Kishan remembers Samant's sudden rise to prominence with suspicion: he is initially optimistic about the potential and possibility of Samant's agitations but, like most workers, also aware of how precarious his situation is. He tells me:

> When Datta Samant first showed up, he seemed to really care about the workers. Even I initially supported him. But after the mills shut down (this one for seven years, I secretly worked at Phoenix Mills) then the majority of people supported Datta Samant, and so the strike went on. Even though I supported him initially, I didn't go for every meeting. Sometimes there were five hundred workers at the mill, but only twenty-five would show up. A meeting would be called and I would support it, but I would not attend it. I went to a few, just not all. What would I do, going there? I could lose my job.

And so Kishan also sees Samant as a polarizing and radical figure with no base of support. He tells me: "That's why he was not successful: he landed up from nowhere; he just stepped up and was there." Because the strike was never legally recognized, the fear of involvement grew. He adds: "I was afraid we would all lose our jobs."

Sudarshan echoes Kishan's concerns: "I never went to his [Datta Samant's] meetings or rallies." He chuckles, then continues: "All his work was unauthorized. The union that he formed—the GKSS—was not recognized by the court or by the law. So when there was a strike declared on 18 January 1982 and on 26 January, when the mill owners' association filed a case in court, the court held that the union was not recognized, and therefore the strike was illegal and it should not hold."[44] Kishan and Sudarshan, dedicated supporters of the Congress Party, also remember government support of their own labor: Samant's opposition to Prime Minister Gandhi is threatening to their own sense of self and deeply held political associations. Additionally, Samant and his allies may have been fighting for higher pay and better conditions for workers, but Kishan thinks they might not have even held the full support of Maharashtrian workers. He tells me that he sees the seemingly united body of Maharashtrian workers to actually be split: "I think the Maharashtrians were sailing in two different boats. They wanted to save their jobs, so they supported the Congress Union [RMMS]. But also, on another level, they were supporting Datta Samant's movement. They were sailing in two boats."

While most of the Maharashtrian workers at Dhanraj mourn Samant's death like that of a martyred saint, the North Indian workers like Kishan and Sudarshan see his murder as expected for a man they understand as a *goonda* (thug). Sudarshan tells me: "Datta Samant was very stubborn. He was successful with some companies, like Premier, who make cars. If the wealthy owner [of the company or mill] would not agree, he would get the guy murdered. He was the guy who was involved in the murder of the man who owned Premier automobiles. He was a thug. He killed the guy himself."

Lost in the Field

Early on, I learned to disguise myself in words, which really were clouds.—WALTER BENJAMIN, *Berlin Childhood around 1900*, 2006

One day, in the quiet of his office, Mr. Lal, tells me: "The textile industry was always with the Congress Party. Dr. Samant was a 'militant leader.' The textile industry had a labor force of 250,000 workers before 1982. The workers were a big vote bank." He chuckles to himself and says: "Prime Minister Gandhi couldn't even land in Bombay without Dr. Samant's permission! The government didn't want him to take over because of this power. The strike made conditions very bad for the workers and was embarrassing for the government."

He explains to me that after the strike the mills "were pushed to the edge. They were unviable. Power looms bloomed because this was so unorganized." According to him, "Dr. Samant created a strike and then he walked away. He never sat down to negotiate." There were 2,800 workers in Dhanraj before the strike. When I started fieldwork, there were only 108. Today there are fewer than 50. Like his North Indian employees, Mr. Lal believes he has Datta Samant to thank for all of his ill fortune.

Every textile mill in Mumbai contains records of workers: employment sheets with names and dates of service. For months I try to get access to Dhanraj's employment records but Mr. Lal never gives them to me.[45] In the meantime, I wonder what he remembers about the employee rosters: men versus women, Maharashtrians versus non-Maharashtrians, young versus old. He tells me he remembers nothing:

> I don't think we have the statistics. . . . Why do you want to segregate all of this? This is a problem of the Indian government. You should not be writing about this in a thesis. You will write it and you will create a problem. The Indian government would not like this. [*He begins to get visibly angry*] You are creating conflicts in the mind of the people. This conflict is already going on. Maharashtra doesn't want people coming here, the conflict of language and religion. I don't want to be a party to this. If I say how many Negroes in a factory and how many whites and lower classes . . . all of this creates confusion between different levels of people, and resentment. We have much more problems than black and white. If we say, why only 10 percent of workers are from outside of Maharashtrians? I don't think the government encourages this. What is the purpose, how does this serve your purpose? Is your purpose to cause conflict? That is all it does.

I tell him I don't want to cause conflict, I just want to understand what change looks like in the mill over the past few decades. But he never shows me the records. And so I am left with the generalities and averages that circulate throughout history books: historically, 15 percent of workers were North Indian, with 85 percent of workers being from various parts of Maharashtra. At the height of the industry, close to 40 percent of workers were women. While these statistics are open to subtle variations, it's likely fair to see them as some sort of reliable fact.

And yet.

When I speak with North Indian workers at Dhanraj, they still work tirelessly to convince me that there was a time—before the Great Textile Strike—when they were the majority in the industry. For years I believe there *is* a story to uncover here—a conspiracy of statistics that I must unearth and reveal. However, I am no longer convinced that even the North Indians believe this story; instead, I have grown to see how this form of storytelling is generative, even if it is also understood as factually inaccurate. North Indian workers present statistics and histories that cannot possibly be interpreted as factual: I am convinced that my North Indian informants know that the numbers they circulate are impossible to corroborate and impossible to believe. And yet they also reveal a foundational tension within Dhanraj, specifically, and Mumbai, generally: that so much of what it means to be a mill worker and a Mumbaiker is wrapped up in a traumatic history of communalism and regional identity.

As I become more and more lost and disoriented in the field, I return to the question of the archive and ask not whether these stories are *true* but instead what do these stories *do*?[46] I take these untruths—circulated by North Indian Dhanraj workers about the strike—as performative: while they may have no ontological status, they certainly constitute the reality of my North Indian informants.[47] The strike, then, as a "critical event," becomes a linchpin for identity and difference within Dhanraj.[48] This event provides a moment through which the everyday lives of textile workers are profoundly altered in every imaginable way: employment opportunities, housing options, kinship structures, political engagement, urban citizenship, and historical memory are transformed, and narratives of identity and belonging are "propelled into new and unpredicted terrains" (Das 1995, 5). This archive, then, is the event of the strike itself, and its documents and files are composed of memories and impressions forged across the lines of identity and selfhood.[49]

With this in mind, I have learned to take seriously the hidden messages lying beneath North Indian workers' histories (particularly Kishan's), regardless of their truth or falsity. North Indian mill workers are (and historically were) far more vulnerable than their Maharashtrian coworkers, and this vulnerability angers Kishan. I think back over our many conversations: What forms of silences and untruths and rumors did I miss as I focused instead on the potential metanarratives of regional demographics and alternative histories? One afternoon, as we sit in the shade on a bench in Rani Baug, Kishan tells me: "It is hard being Bihari in this city. Not just Bihar, but also *bhaiyyas* from Uttar Pradesh.[50] But it is also our fault because we are not united. If I try to kill a Maharashtrian tomorrow, ten people from his community will come to his aid and help him. But if one of them tries to get me, no one will come and support me. We are not united, this is our weak point." I decide not to ask him why all his examples of solidarity involve the potential murder of Maharashtrians. Instead I ask him if this division is possibly part of the problem: Why does he feel that allegiances must be drawn within ethnic bounds? "If everyone is united and everyone lives harmoniously, that is the best," he says and pauses. "But at least the brothers should live together. I should be united with those from my region. At least that should happen. Because I am living here now, I would die for this city. But after I retire I want to go back there. I would like to die there." Most of Kishan's immediate family has made their way to Mumbai: his wife and children live with him, although his extended family remains in Bihar. He has lived and worked in the city for more than thirty years. And yet he feels that, once his days of mill work are over, he should leave the city of his work and return to the village of his birth.

I roll his words around in my head. While Kishan nurtures his sense of victimhood, he also seems to harbor disdain for the Marathi-speaking Maharashtrian workers at Dhanraj. He tells me: "I understand very little Marathi, but I try to apply my mind and understand what they are saying. I know some words. But language is not the problem for me. I have never taken any interest in those people. Friendship means to love, you have to really love someone to be friends. . . . I don't have any friends at the mill. . . . Just talking to people does not make them your friends. There must be a connection so that friendship emerges." I ask him if he thinks there are tangible differences between Biharis (or North Indians) and Maharashtrians. He sits quietly for a while, and I wonder if he has heard me. I follow his eyes as he watches people walk past us, and I try not to watch him directly as he looks purposefully away from me. Just as the silence begins to feel too heavy, he begins:

I think that, working together, it should be [that] we are all equal, we are all brothers. It is like a fraternity, we are working together. I come from Bihar, I am a Bihari pundit [Brahmin]. And they are Maharashtrian. But they stick to their caste a lot, they hold onto their castes a lot.[51] And that shouldn't be done. I am here now, I'm going to be of help to them and they are going to be of help to me. My relatives are far away: it takes three days to reach [them], they will not be able to help me. But when I am in my workplace, I feel like these people want to hang on to their own community. They are casteist. They hang on to their community a lot. And they aren't doing this in your face, they aren't doing this rudely. But their stomachs are black: they look nice on the outside, but inside they are bad. They are not clean hearted.

Kishan's vulnerability is, at its core, a crisis of alienation. As "the other," he is an unprotected minority in a xenophobic city, an underrepresented outsider in an otherwise homogeneous work environment. His inclusion as a "textile worker" is complicated by his exclusion from the category of "*Maharashtrian* textile worker." And so he refuses this exclusion through the untruths he tells me: when he counters his current marginalization with a past majority status, perhaps he finds some more stable footing in the insecure environment he currently exists in. I hear in Kishan's (and Sudarshan's) "untruths" a rejection of identity/Being as absolute, a refusal to be reified as "other," and a demand to read history backward, through the future, in order to unsettle memories they feel have been formed as violence upon their now vulnerable bodies.

But I also know that a refusal does not erase the material reality of regional identity and the vulnerability emergent from such othering: these identity categories are very powerful, and I realize, after too much time has already past, that Kishan's untruths are his *only* line of defense against the everyday exhaustion of being an outsider, of being a Bihari, of being "the other." Unless/until he chooses to leave the city.

The stories I am fed by my North Indian informants reveal the failure of a positive synthesis (the identity of "mill worker" as a unified category) of identity and truth: instead of aligning a diverse group of migrants as "textile workers," the strike results in further alienation and a growing sense of "otherness" for North Indian workers, even as Maharashtrian migrants achieve the identity category in question. This destabilizes notions of historical time, as the strike also comes to serve as the decisive event that makes it seem as if a process that had, in fact, been a long time developing suddenly happened in the space of a year or two. With this in mind, the negative dialectic of strike narratives is an exercise aimed at grappling with the failure of the strike, itself: an unsuccessful attempt to unify workers, reinvigorate the industry, and erase "the other" by centering "identity" as the positive synthesis of a worker uprising. Instead, the event results in a fractured workforce, a zombified industry, and the privileging of *Maharashtrian* worker identity.[52] My North Indian informants, through the untruths they feed me, refuse this threefold othering not by altering the present, but by reframing the past, which then serves as a ground for a moral claim on the present. When Kishan and Sudarshan tell me that North Indian workers once constituted the majority demographic within the industry, I am now beginning to hear (at least) two things. First, they use this temporal shift to invent a time in which they are not vulnerable/ victims in Mumbai. And second, they suggest their precarity as "other" is relatively recent in the city's history (post-1983).

Even if this is clearly untrue.

Conclusions: In Search of Ethnographic Untruth

And the dust that
confuses countries
is in your eyes, and you
blink, and you blink,
and you blink.
—ROSA ALCALÁ, "Inflection," 2012

The Great Textile Strike is a *failed* strike: it is organized illegally (outside the purview of the RMMS), it is never technically resolved (it is officially still happening), and it doesn't revive the textile industry (although it does force many owners to reopen their mills and draw out the slow decline and painful death into the current moment). However, I don't immediately realize the reality of this failure or the implications of this result. *My* failure to understand *this* failure results, in large part, from the way I encounter the narrative: primarily from Maharashtrian workers who celebrated the event through their retelling. However, as this archive reveals, when I begin speaking to North Indian workers, I encounter a very different story.

In thinking through Kishan's testimonies of the strike, I am struck by how paranoid I find him: so many of our conversations happen in private, away from the mill, tucked in concealed corners of Rani Baug's gardens. He whispers to me, his eyes dart around, he worries that someone will see us, someone will overhear us. But then again, I am also paranoid when I am around him. At best, Kishan makes me feel uncomfortable. At times he makes me feel unsafe. In thinking about these moments of creeping paranoia, I am drawn to Eve Kosofsky Sedgwick's rendering of the concept, which she frames as a "theory of negative affects." By engaging it in this way, Sedgwick argues that "paranoia refuses to be only *either* a way of knowing *or* a thing known, but is characterized by an insistent tropism toward occupying both positions" (2002, 131). While I would undoubtedly characterize Kishan as paranoid (in a general sense of the word), my interest here is in applying to "untruth" the framework of Sedgwick's "paranoia" in an expansive, ethnographic sense: if, according to Sedgwick, "paranoia" is a theory of negative *affects*, then I argue that "untruth" is a theory of negative *effects*. These two are always entangled and create each other in and out of the other (the affects are efficacious, and the effects are affective). Kishan's stories of identity, in connection to the political climate of the 1980s, reveal how his "paranoia" (as affect) is materialized through "untruth" (as effect). And this, I find, sounds like a form of truth to me.

I still don't like Kishan: I don't trust him, I feel uncomfortable around him, and I think much of what he tells me is untrue. However, in this untruth I find far more than dishonesty: his untruths tell me important things. They tell me that he, along with the other North Indians I come to know at Dhanraj, refuses the identity of "other" in a xenophobic city. These stories tell me that, if "Maharashtrian textile worker" is now the "positive" result of the strike dialectic, then "North Indian textile worker" is the nonidentity of the negative dialectic both before and after the strike (when the heroic narrative begins to be unsettled). To throw out these layered stories is to refuse the messages left like traces in the telling: traces that give both depth and weight to the archive.

The Archive
of the Fire

If all that changes slowly may be explained by life, all that changes quickly is explained by fire. —GASTON BACHELARD, *The Psychoanalysis of Fire*, 1968

After that hot gospeller has leveled all but the churched sky,
I wrote the tale by tallow of a city's death by fire;
Under a candle's eye, that smoked in tears, I
Wanted to tell, in more than wax, of faiths that were snapped like wire.
—DEREK WALCOTT, "A City's Death by Fire," 1962

Arrivals: Celluloid Flames

In April 2010, the bilingual film *Lalbaug, Parel* (Marathi) / *City of Gold* (Hindi) opens in Mumbai. Ironically, it premieres at the plush PVR multiplex of High Street Phoenix, formerly Phoenix Mills, in Lower Parel. The film's melodramatic plot focuses on the Dhuri family, who live in "Laxmi Cottage" in Central Mumbai in the early 1980s. After the patriarch (along with many other male characters in the film) loses his job at the Khetaan textile mill because of the owner's greed, the film depicts a dystopian world in which workers commit suicide, sons become gangsters, and daughters resort to prostitution. For the working class, deindustrializing Mumbai is a place of chaos and disintegration, both morally and materially.

Toward the middle of the film, after negotiating the reopening of the mill with the owner and his scheming, conniving son-in-law, the workers congregate at the gate, eager to begin work again. Instead, they watch as the mill explodes into flames and burns to the ground: a daytime spectacle staged as a literal slap in the face of the worker-audience. Some men fall to their knees and sob while others riot, throwing rocks and bricks at the wall surrounding the compound.

In the film, the drama of postfire violence, anger, and despair culminates in a scene of mass suicide: an entire family hang themselves from the rafters of their chawl unit. The camera fades from the agony of immediate death and shows, in dramatic black and white, a montage of rusted, inert machinery covered in dust, along with the craggy and crestfallen faces of jobless men. These double deaths lead to the rise of an alternate union: one organized from within the community of jobless workers. The resulting strike creates and sustains angry hordes of men, intent on murdering the mill-owning family.

This fire scene in the film allows for a dramatic transition in which the families of Laxmi Cottage, once seen eating, bickering, and resting together in the safe and loving community of the chawl, become dispersed throughout the streets of the city. Children, no longer attending school, are shown foraging for food scraps dropped by careless passersby; men, no longer employed, sell off their household possessions out of financial desperation. There is no doubt within the narrative of the film that the fire is an act of overt arson and visual violence on the part of the mill owner and his son-in-law. Indeed, the film's tagline reads: "They clothed the city and the city in turn stripped them off." *Lalbaug, Parel / City of Gold* presents the desperation of loss and the violence of capitalist greed: the suffering mill workers and their families are thrown to the side by a mill owner who might as well have fangs and horns, so obvious is his inherent evil. The spectacle of industrial fire depicted in the film reveals a form of public mythic sentiment throughout the city, one in which the event of mill fires exposes the ugly head of capitalism triumphing over working-class aspirations. In the film a burning mill is a message, not an accident. And it is incredibly visible.

The sentiment of the film echoes a larger understanding of mill fires in Mumbai, as the past several decades reveal how owners profit from the nonindustrial development made possible through these flames. The first mill on record to burn down is Madhav Mills in 1965. Following this fire, a residential complex is built on the site, setting a precedent for nonindustrial development in the mill lands. In 1967, Moon Mills in Sewri goes up in flames, and the vacant land is used to build warehouses. In 1977, the city experiences its most famous mill fire with the burning of the ironically named Phoenix Mills at Lower Parel. This mill site becomes High Street Phoenix, one of Mumbai's first Western-style shopping, dining, and entertainment complexes and the site in which I watch *Lalbaug, Parel / City of Gold.* As with other fires in mill compounds in the city, the cause of the blaze at Phoenix Mills is never established, although as a result of the fire, the mill is closed for three years, and the seven thousand mill workers and most of the four hundred office staff members are rendered jobless. The 1977 Phoenix Mills fire generates government funds for modernization, allowing a new form to emerge from its flames. However, this is not *mill* modernization: instead, the money disappears into the pockets of the Ruia family, who own the mill compound. Over the next decade, the mill is slowly (and illegally) transformed into the space of shopping and elite residence it is today (Krishnan 2000).

In 1995, Dhanraj and Goldmohur Mills both experience partial fires. Although neither fire completely shuts down activity, Dhanraj does cut its weaving department, retaining only its winding department. In 2002, Matulya Mills burns down, and another large commercial complex is raised from these industrial ashes. Two years later, in 2004, Swadeshi Mills in Kurla burns, although no development has taken place there thus far. Khatau Mills in Byculla also goes up in flames in 2004 and is replaced by an exclusive residential complex. In 2005, another mill at Byculla, Sitaram Mills, is gutted in a fire. Moraraji Mills at Lalbaug is destroyed in 2006 by a fire and now houses another exclusive residential and commercial complex.

On Tuesday, November 24, 2009, a major fire breaks out at Dhanraj, completely destroying most of the buildings and machinery used in the production of cotton thread. That same year, Goldmohur (again) and Mukesh Mills burn to the ground. Both these mills were slated for modernization through the National Textile Corporation and, had they entered into this NTC agreement, would have reopened to larger-scale textile production. Instead, they are now in the process of nonindustrial development. With this in mind, it makes sense that workers see industrial fire as a message of destruction from mill owners and developers, even if the simplicity of this narrative obscures the reality of running an expensive and unviable business.

I find it easy to get swept up by worker feelings of frustration and betrayal, displayed so overtly in *Lalbaug, Parel / City of Gold.* However, mill

FIGURE 5.1. Dhanraj after the fire in 2009.

fires also reveal how mill owners struggle within the limitations of urban development in Mumbai's deindustrializing central neighborhoods. Once a mill becomes unprofitable, an owner cannot merely close shop, sell or develop the land, and move in the direction of Mumbai's shifting economy. While the talk of arson I encounter in the mill lands does not prove that mill owners circumvent the limitations of development laws and the financial burden of worker contracts by strategically burning their property, the prevalence of suspicious night fires and the avenues of development they open up demand pause. While minor mill fires occurred on a regular basis throughout the height of industrial production, they were generally small and easy to control due to the twenty-four-hour presence of shift workers. However, as the industry begins to decline, large-scale night fires emerge as mysterious and unexplainable threats. While development rules prohibit the redevelopment of mill land for nonmill activity for decades, the clearing of industrial land through mill fires often results in new *nonindustrial* forms of construction, since the buildings are already gone and the industry is in decline. While the specific fire at Dhanraj elicits minor interest outside the mill, the *idea* of mysterious night fires conjures images of evil capitalist mill owners, intent on destroying the livelihood of the city's dwindling working class.

For Dhanraj, this story is particularly complicated. Worker retrenchment and mill land development require money, and it seems this money does not yet exist at the time of the 2009 fire. Not only does the production of low-grade cotton thread *not* turn a profit, but production revenues also cannot sustain the cost of daily mill activity. In fact, up until the fire, Dhanraj is only able to pay workers wages and procure raw material by leasing two small, informal factories and several godowns on the mill property. Oftentimes, the necessary funds come from either development partnerships (for years Dhanraj is partnered with the development company Mahindra, but at the time of the fire, that partnership is wrapped up in litigation and essentially frozen) or misdirected government subsidies. However, Dhanraj already has a history of modernization schemes, which are documented in the public record. The mill uses government subsidies (allocated for projects to benefit the modernization *of the mill*) for non-industrial commercial projects (the "lifestyle" store selling expensive international antiques is the prime moneymaker on the mill property) and worker retrenchment (the exact *opposite* of its intended use) three times (the limit) before the 2009 fire. Because of this, Dhanraj no longer qualifies for additional subsidies, and the production of thread cannot cover the costs of workers' wages, let alone pensions, which are dictated by law and well protected.

So what is a sensible mill owner to do?

Whether arson or accident, fire can be a convenient bedfellow.

Burning Bright

You think, in the delirium: it was their dust that I breathed in. —CAROLYN STEEDMAN, *Dust*, 2001

Buildings in Central Mumbai appear soot-stained. It is not usually because of fire, but as I walk through the winding lanes, I still think of old flames pouring out of windows and doors, staining the walls black. Shadows of radiation, heat from fires, dirt from the traffic crawling through cramped alleys and pouring off the thoroughfares and falling from the flyovers. Chawls are blackened, stone walls seem charred. The city is not a burned

FIGURE 5.2. The soot-stained city in the smog.

city, but, then again, so many of the mill compounds have been eaten by industrial fires. Old industrial structures disappeared thanks to a convenient and mysterious spark. And so there is the mirage of fire on present surfaces and the destruction of fire beneath redeveloped or empty lots. Fire cannot still be seen where it once burned, but there still seems to be contagion in these spaces, as other empathetic buildings carry traces from neighborhood structures, as though bearing witness to the unvisible history of the neighborhood.

I return to Dhanraj a week after the November 2009 fire: even now the mill is still smoking and the smell is overwhelming, all-consuming. I meet Manda and Sushila outside the gate, and we wander over to a chai shop down the road. Manda tells me, "I cried when I first found out. What will happen to us now?" Both women tear up from the memory, and their fear and uncertainty are palpable. Later I view the extent of the damage from the rooftop of a nearby apartment building, which bears the misplaced empathy of darkened streaks and stains. The mill fire started on the top floor, which as it burned, caved in, taking each lower floor with it to the ground. The roof is now gone, and all that remain are four walls and a pile of rubble. One week later, it appears there is no sense in replacing machinery and rebuilding space slated for demolition in another couple of years. The workers tell me they will continue to clock in each morning for the next three months, but after that their futures are uncertain.

I assume Mumbai's mill land drama has come to a close and that the lot will be cleared for new development. Mills will become malls, and the old low-lying industrial city will be replaced by shining skyscrapers reaching up toward a "new" modernity. This assumption makes me sad. Dhanraj has been my field site for a year and a half prior to the fire. Talk of arson places a haze of paranoia over the mill. While no one tells me directly, I know that many workers are hesitant to talk to me, at least at first. Their jobs are now far more precarious than they were before the fire, and talking about an event cloaked in such suspicion might cast them as disloyal employees, perhaps the first expendable workers in what will surely be a chronic stream of layoffs and downsizing.

Throughout this chapter-archive, I attend to the modes of storytelling and the forms of information circulated throughout the mill after the fire. In doing so, I understand the fire as an event that cracks open an archival space through the circulation of rumors. In the wake of this event, rumor provides a social form: a way for Dhanraj workers to predict the future in an uncertain present. These rumors, therefore, are prophetic and reveal both tragedy and abundance.[1] In this way, the industrial fire at Dhanraj becomes an occasion to address the hidden complexities of industrial life in formerly industrial spaces while simultaneously taking seriously a deindustrializing landscape through which such mill fires are at once everyday (in terms of the history of the city) and extraordinary (in terms of the experiences of employed mill workers). Because Dhanraj is a space of lively ruination, the fire *seems* to accelerate the process of decay while instead simply obfuscating its ongoing slow death (Berlant 2007). Therefore, the fire, as dramatically evental catastrophe, obscures slower and less immediately visible structural transformations. Worker rumors bring us away from the spectacle and back to the everyday: through the circulation of rumor, Dhanraj workers alter the pace at which time moves in the mill compound.

While my core concern here is the ephemeral realm of affect and temporality, these rumors have structural implications, as well. The fire at Dhanraj disrupts larger narratives of rapid urban gentrification in global megacities. Through the story of the fire, the uncertainties of urban development clash with the demands on and desires of both the (seemingly) powerful mill owners and the insecure, downwardly mobile mill workers. Central Mumbai's future is revealed as insecure because of archaic industrial laws, decentralized urban development plans, widespread financial constraints, and an uncertain economy, both locally and globally. Against this context, the fire appears as decisive: something that cuts through slow and cumbersome processes that would otherwise be held up by laws and regulations. By understanding both the dependent and the discordant relationship between mill owners and their employees (in this case, such a relationship at Dhanraj), the dwindling yet lingering industrial workers in the city, and the extralegal strategies of mill owners still struggling to negotiate a future within a shifting economic landscape, this story disrupts a cleaner, easier narrative of development in Mumbai that is present throughout urban studies literature.[2]

This is not a gentrification narrative.

So what is it?

In this chapter-archive, I use the 2009 fire to shine light through the lens of the archive: here worker frustrations emerge and are articulated. Fears for and of the future coalesce in the rumors circulating within the mill: the spectacle of the fire melts into the affective landscape of Dhanraj and is transformed into a state of being. The fire itself takes on the atmospheric duration of a form of life. Therefore, this chapter-archive asks how a prefire world—one of rapid deindustrialization and impending doom— becomes instead an unrecognizable place of inertia. Time and space become frozen and mismatched, as expected trajectories of urban progression are transformed into indefinite moments of stasis. I am forced here to see not the future possibilities of transformation, but instead the ongoing ruination of a still-dying, yet simultaneously vital, space.

The narrative of a past working-class grandeur and contemporary industrial decline allows for both the stabilization of the city's recorded history and the distribution of an urban mythology. However the fire provides a disruption, as it joins things together that are otherwise separate. For Elias Canetti, the fire symbolizes the crowd. He writes: "Fire joins what was separate, and in the shortest possible time. Isolated and diverse objects all go up in the same flames. They become so much the same that they disappear completely" (1984, 76). Both the fire and the crowd (as rumor) want to grow: both feed off of contagious oxygen and energy. A flickering becomes a flame, and the event overwhelms the elements. These are spaces of power: both fire and rumor eat the landscape and transform process into narrative.

Similarly, in Mumbai fire stands in for a perverse negativity: the fire brings back the power of the mill in its negative form. Thomas Blom Hansen writes: "Fire may be ignited by someone but once it is going, it is a force in its own right, more in us than ourselves—something that is alien and yet overtakes us. . . . It is a force that exists in the community as a potentiality—but never identical to it. Fire is a paradoxical form of empty agency. Once fire gets going, it is a pure effect, lacking specificity or ontology and yet behaving as a type of autonomous agency—a pure transformation of something into nothingness" (2008, 34). When the mill dies, there is a great force in its death: as the fire consumes the physical building, it also consumes the *idea* of the industry, bringing back the ghost of the mill. And therefore Central Mumbai is a zombified city: industrial production haunts the halls of burned-out buildings, undead, unseen. This is a magic trick of smoke and mirrors, as production must continue even as the city says good-bye to its industrial past. Therefore, the mill on fire is a funeral pyre: a spectacle, a ritual, a moment of absolute transformation. Once the flames subside, the ashes reveal an uncanny form and an uncanny form of meaning. Rumor, then, is the perfect complement to fire: both rely on and leave indeterminate traces and, once they get going, are "pure effect, lacking specificity or ontology and yet behaving as a type of autonomous agency—a pure transformation of something into nothingness"—the element of impersonality and of contagious spread. With this in mind, this chapter-archive is concerned with the traces of fire and rumor: just as fire draws oxygen into itself to grow and move, the rumors circulating in its aftermath draw meaning into themselves as they spread and settle and move on, revealing "how uncertainty can be reproduced as knowledge" (Jain 2013, 221). This is a flickering alchemy.

Inside the Rumor Mill

Fire is an event, not a principle.—STEPHEN J. PYNE, "Fire: A Brief History," 2001

As rumor becomes an all-consuming form of communication after the fire, I once again resist my own urge to "discover" the "truth" at the root of worker stories. Instead, I push myself to pay attention to what I'm being told and how these stories are circulating. Rumor is, as Naveeda Khan (drawing from James Siegel's work on Indonesia) writes, "a story without a signature that is transmitted across bodies" (2006, 111). Rumor can be understood as "improvised news" (Shibutani 1966) that may "reveal the tensions and contradictions underlying uncertain social situations" (Bonhomme 2012, 215). Jonathan P. Parry writes of the "extraordinary velocity" with which rumors circulate, as well as the critical element of timing (2008, 243). In Dhanraj, this seems especially true. I find that once rumors of arson creep into common conversation as news stories to tell, they take off at an uncontrollable rate—perhaps similarly, I think, to the flames that consumed Dhanraj.

And even as rumor changes the ways in which information travels, rumor also alters the way time is understood. Through the deployment of rumor, workers engage an alternative temporality, as their control of narrative and information returns to a moment in which their participation in the future is expected, if not guaranteed: an alternative form of world-making, in the absence of the production for which they were hired. Plus, the expectation of fire is the immediate closure of the mill and retrenchment of the workforce, and that, strangely, is actually the opposite of what comes to be in the Dhanraj compound. After the initial downsizing, a decreased workforce is retained and employment continues: postfire employment is elliptical, as workers wait for the coming of the future that, contrary to expectation, is still slowed to the speed of industrial ruination. As mill activity belies the expectation of postfire futures, Dhanraj workers deploy rumor as a mode of storytelling that makes sense of a future out of time.

After the fire, I spend most of my afternoons sitting with Raj as he supplies me with endless amounts of information concerning the future of the mill, the motivations of the mill owner, and the expectations of his fellow workers. Raj cannot tell me who supplies his information and, really, it does not much matter. Dhanraj has always been a rumor mill because virtually no information is ever communicated directly to the workers. Because the industry is incredibly unstable, because workers are constantly facing retrenchment, because a sense of disempowerment pervades the atmosphere of daily activity . . . for all those reasons and more, the workers circulate their own narratives and find currency in the possession, transmission, and retention of information: these rumors appear as "true" as anything else in the mill compound.

While both gossip and rumor are present in Dhanraj, I want to disentangle the two from each other. In her lyrical "archaeology and pop-up opera," *The Republic of Exit 43*, the poet Jennifer Scappettone writes of rumor and gossip across the landscape of a corporate dump: "While the revamped Fresh Kills Landfill presents itself as dry, sterile, bureaucratic infrastructure, it's surrounded by juicy, clashing rumors and gossip. Gossip reintroduces the gory details of private life—disease, corruption, fallibility—into the disinfected infrastructure of public life; it sutures public and private back together after they have been cleaved away from one another by the decorum of official discourse. Gossip as talk reminds us . . . that infrastructure has lurid blind spots and leaks" (2016, 102). Two things draw me in here. First, Dhanraj is *also* a landfill: a landfill of industrial debris. After the fire, buildings and machinery become accumulated waste in the space that was once the mill. Second, by presenting the landfill "as dry, sterile, bureaucratic infrastructure," Scappettone allows for particular narrative forms to reinfuse this infrastructure with liveliness. While she uses "gossip" and "rumor" interchangeably, I find the definition (this speech practice reintroducing "the gory details of private life . . . into the disinfected infrastructure of public life") to be applicable to the rumor mill of Dhanraj after the fire. The stories I hear after the fire are deeply invested in this reintroduction and allow for the event of the fire to hold more meaning than citywide narratives of infrastructural transformation might make room for: outside the compound I am told that the industry is no longer. Inside the compound I witness new forms of being emerge into existence. Both of these narratives exist alongside each other: fire brings about finality, and fire brings about new ways of life. The difference, then, is positionality: Where am I located when these new forms come into being? And how do they circulate?

Unlike in the Fresh Kills Landfill, gossip and rumor operate very differently in Dhanraj. While my years at the mill involve hearing gossip traded between workers over tea by the breezy back window of the mill's second floor, Luise White notes that what sets rumor apart is that "people believe it" (2000, 57). While day-to-day Dhanraj gossip is usually "time pass"—something to do while waiting for the day to end or the machines to turn back on—industrial fire rumor is an exchange of "truths," even if the overall story cannot be traced to a reliable source or backed up with factual evidence. While gossip becomes a way of introducing a certain juicy vitality into the scene, rumor functions to make sense, to explain something perhaps unexplainable.

FIGURE 5.3. Dhanraj as a landfill. Clearing the debris after the fire.

Even as rumor and speculation circulate, no one is accused and no investigation is opened. No one outside the mill is interested in the event the following day. The fire elicits very little media attention, and I scour the internet and local newspapers for some trace of interest. Instead my curiosity is continuously met with indifference: nonrecognition—a "lack of desire, intimacy, and respect" (Hansen 2012, 97)—as the silence of the media mirrors forms of active forgetting I encounter throughout the entirety of my time in Mumbai. Even my friends and interlocutors in the mill land activist world are both unaware of and uninterested in the fire: only the Dhanraj workers seem concerned with excavating the fire's history. It seems the rumors that circulate among mill workers provide a means to understand the relationship between industrial fire, processes of deindustrialization, and the production of precarious workers. Exploring the political significance of rumor demonstrates how precarious workers understand the stagnation of time in the postfire moment, even as the expectation is that industrial fire will result in rapid redevelopment.

The archive, then, reveals how industrial fire contributes to this narrative of mill land finality while—in the case of Dhanraj—enabling mills to continue to function and workers to continue to work (albeit on a dramatically reduced scale). The museum narrative of decline and redevelopment might be circulated outside the mill gates, but this story does not work here inside Dhanraj. Particularly after the fire, the mill becomes archival because, even as stories of Dhanraj's finality map onto the expectations attached to mill land fires in popular imagination, nothing inside the mill compound is conforming to expected trajectories. The lively ruin of Dhanraj, in messianic form, is hidden through the expectations of acceleration and disappearance. By understanding the drive of postindustrial urban development through the case study of Dhanraj, industrial fire emerges *as* deindustrialization, and Central Mumbai can be seen as simultaneously industrial, deindustrializing, and postindustrial: stratification of economic, social, and political eras embedded in the landscape of Central Mumbai. Dhanraj's fire and continued operation, then, counter the fictions of deindustrialization that frame such a process as forward moving (Chakrabarty 1989; Chatterjee 2004) and instead draw attention to pockets of chronic stagnation/lively ruination within spatial and economic transformation. These spaces of lively ruination, such as Dhanraj, do not exist in contradiction to "modernity." They are *also* modernity.

Mill fires in Mumbai, while common and often suspicious, are generally cloaked in ambiguity and uncertainty in terms of intent and orchestration. While the fire at Dhanraj is officially ruled accidental, it is only the latest in a string of suspicious industrial fires that have occurred over several decades.[3] Outside Dhanraj's walls, the fire appears to "speed up the passage of time, to bring all life to its conclusion, to its hereafter" (Bachelard 1968, 16). An otherwise chronic and indefinite decline allows for something seemingly immediate to occur: if I consume news media, I read that Dhanraj production is no longer. This death is immediate. However, I see something quite different within the compound, as the rumors circulated by Dhanraj workers suggest both a continuation and an emergence.

Flames eat and fire produces.

This is a new form of industrial production.

But motivation aside, once started, a fire becomes its own force, regardless of the expectations that ignite it. And some traces have no origin.

As I wander through the postfire space of Dhanraj, I learn that the things I know pale in comparison to the things I do not know. I know that on Tuesday, November 24, 2009, a major fire breaks out at Dhanraj Spinning and Weaving, Ltd. It is a devastating fire that completely destroys the buildings and machinery used in the production of cotton thread. I know this is the second major fire Dhanraj has experienced in recent memory, the first being in 1995. I know that both fires happen at night, when no one is working and the chance of casualties or injuries is low. I know that no one is hurt or killed in either fire. While the police investigating the fire determine it is accidental, it is also the most recent in a series of industrial fires generally suspected to be the result of arson. I know that such large-scale fires, burning through a landscape of deindustrialization and rapid redevelopment, leave empty lots that the city's general public believes will never be rebuilt as industrial spaces. I *think* I know that one of Mumbai's last privately owned textile mills has shut its industrial gates for good. That, after all, is the story circulated by the media in the wake of mill fires. Knowledge becomes slippery after the fire: some events here I can know for sure, like what happens to the mill. Others, like who started the fire and how, I probably will never know. Instead, I am forced to focus on how newly displaced mill workers talk about the event and what they *think* happened.

As the smoke begins to clear, a collection of conflicting stories rises above the rubble and winds its way around and through the conversations I have with the workers. When I initially return to the mill a week after the fire, they are all quick to dismiss the assumptions of arson: "Why would someone burn their own property?" I am rhetorically asked, as though the simplicity of the inquiry corresponds to an obvious answer. "It was just an accident," I am told by other more suspicious workers. "Don't ask questions, it's already been determined." But a week later, this acceptance is replaced by concern. "What will happen to us now?" they ask. One morning, all the workers gather at the mill gate. Their union representative is meeting with the owner and manager to determine the futures of the current workforce. The workforce will likely be retrenched, and the workers are concerned about their pensions.

Before the fire, I spend my time at the mill with the morning shift (7:00 AM–2:00 PM), and everyone knows me. But hardly anyone from the afternoon shift (3:00–11:00 PM) knows who I am. One red-faced man in a faded yellow shirt points his finger at me and demands to know if I am a spy, sent by the mill owner. Many assure him that I am a friend, that I am on their side, that my sympathies are with them, with the workers. I observe quietly, struggling to comprehend this conversation among so many people screaming simultaneously in Marathi. I smile at him and assure him that I am not a spy. He asks me whose side I am on, and I tell him I

FIGURE 5.4. Mill workers surveying the rubble.

am on his side. He glares at me for the rest of the day, but after that I never
see him again.

After the fire, there are so many other people I never see again. At the
time of the fire, I had already watched as the tiny workforce was downsized to fewer than a hundred workers. This downsizing at Dhanraj is seen
as simply the last step in an ongoing process of converting industrial land
into spaces of middle-class consumption popularly known as the "mills

to malls" phenomenon. Dhanraj is one of the last holdouts of textile employment for the lingering yet massively diminished industrial workforce still clinging to the underbelly of Central Mumbai. Such mill fires and closures contribute further to the ongoing casualization of a community of workers teetering precariously between formal and informal employment. Retrenched workers disappear into the ether of Mumbai or into the expansive suburbs or impenetrable downtown chawls. Half the workforce is retained, while the remainder is let go. Those who survive this whittling down take on the role of the god's eye: perched on the second floor of the remaining mill structure, they look down on the day laborers sorting through trash in the main compound. The absence of exterior walls allows them to sit on benches or folding chairs, like theater patrons in the balcony, spectators to their own afterlife.

The Theater of Broken Machinery

[How] does one tell impossible stories? . . . By advancing a series of speculative arguments and exploiting the capacities of the subjunctive (a grammatical mood that expresses doubts, wishes, and possibilities) . . . —SAIDIYA HARTMAN, "Venus in Two Acts," 2008

In February 2010, I sit with Raj in the theater of broken machinery. Nearly three months have passed since the fire, and I have managed to find a new routine of monotony at the mill. From our perch on the mill's former second floor, we watch the day laborers clear wood and metal debris from the lot below us. Somehow our presence is believed to keep the workingmen honest. I know there is value in another man's trash, but it really does look like useless rubble to me. It is hot out, and I can see the men sweating and huffing below me. Fortunately, Raj and I are cooled and shaded by the stone around us. We settle onto our wooden bench to watch.

Very little has been communicated to the workers, and it is this uncertainty that breeds rumors. Men sit around in groups, speculating on their future. I ask Raj how he knows what is going on, and he tells me: "People talk." I ask him who these people are, and he just shrugs. "Everyone."

When Raj and I talk of the fire, he usually brushes me off, unwilling to take a stand in opposition to the party line: "Obviously an accident." That is, until this day in February. Suddenly, that mantra momentarily disappears and is replaced by something new.

FIGURE 5.5. The theater of broken machinery.

While twenty-two people have been retrenched, so far only twelve have received their money. Manda and Sushila, the two remaining women workers at Dhanraj at the time of my fieldwork, are the first to be retrenched. They tell me they are devastated by their loss of employment: their pensions are directed almost entirely toward the education of their grandchildren, and Manda struggles to find work cleaning office buildings and cooking in other women's homes to get by. Sushila's health is deteriorating, and she is unable to find work, so she relies on her oldest son to support her. Both women are married to men who have not worked in years due to alcohol abuse and poor health. However, Raj believes that most workers are quite happy to take their money and go. Everyone has been so fed up because there is no "actual" work being done, just a lot of sitting around. He tells me, "Most people are happy to move on, happy that the mill has closed. I won't be retrenched yet, but when I am, I'll take what they give me."

FIGURE 5.6. View of the burned mill from our perch on the second floor.

But that will not happen anytime soon: the owner is still planning to purchase four or five new machines. I ask Raj about this, and he smiles. "But this is really about his unauthorized godowns. The municipality objects to what he is doing, but they are all bribed after they make their demands. They come to the mill to check out production, and they see what this is really about. But they're happy after they receive money. They write what the owner wants." I am shocked to hear Raj speak so candidly with me, especially since we are sitting in the mill, not the safe and distant locales of his home or the corner tea shop. "Is it OK to speak about such things here?" I ask him.

He shrugs and answers:

> The workers don't have any problems with this. As long as we get our salaries, we'll have no objections. There is very little production in the mill, so our salaries come out of the money received from the godowns. We know this is a scam. The so-called new machines will be secondhand. The owner will paint them, shine them up. But for the authorities, the owner will give the bribe and the authorities will write reports saying that they are new machines. The bribes are done by the owner. The managers are doing the exchange of money, but the owner is driving it.

He tells me he is not sure who "these authorities" are, but he knows that management sends them gifts for all the holidays.

He leans back in his chair and surveys the mess below us: "The fire was quite good for the owner, but the owner still desperately wants to run the mill. He doesn't want his license canceled, so he'll get a few machines and the insurance payoff will come, but I don't know how much. I know that he'll get a lot of money. If he had five machines, he'll say he had twenty. He will multiply his losses, and he'll get more money. If he gives the authorities a nice envelope, they'll say whatever he wants." I feign surprise and Raj laughs. This is not the first time we have discussed the city's corrupt bureaucratic practices.

I tell him I am interested in how quickly the fire was deemed accidental by the police: the mill was still smoking when the police statement was released, and I am curious if this seems suspicious to him. "Of course the police were paid off. What do the police have to lose if the owner burns his mill? And as for the workers, we would never say it was arson. Even if we saw someone burning it, we won't say it was arson. We won't say anything against the owner." I hold my breath: this is the closest I have come to a confirmation from the workers. In the past, my mentioning of arson created a sense of chaos and anxiety, quickly rebuffed with "Of course not!" and "Don't say such things!"

We sit for a while longer in silence. I am bored. Raj is bored. The men are all bored. They tell me they feel useless and worthless. They have invested a lifetime of hard work, and now they sit around, monitoring the movements of young day laborers. Raj sighs and says: "Honestly, our heart is not here anymore. The owner is not going to have much production when the machines come. We will not be doing the kind of work that we want to do, we'll be doing the work that the owner tells us to do. We probably are not trained for this work. But if we don't do what the owner says, he will file a complaint. You can see we are stuck." His tone is irritated but undramatic. For a man who has been told so little, he seems to know a lot.

Raj assumes the mill was burned intentionally, guesses that money changed hands, and figures a big insurance settlement is pending. I attempt to draw him out, suggesting that maybe the fire was merely the result of a series of coincidences. Raj, however, is unconvinced. He tells me: "There is corruption everywhere; show me one place without corruption. If you want admission to college, if you want a job, if you want anything, you have to pay. Even if you want a job with the police, you have to pay one lakh to secure your station. If you're poor, you take a loan. And then you have to take *hafta* [a bribe] to pay off the loan." Corruption (like fire and rumors) is all-consuming: contagious. I read through his words: mill workers are constantly screwed by the city. Why should this be a coincidence when it could instead be yet *another* example of how poorer people suffer from the workings of the city institutions, practices, policies? Which interpretation falls into a logical historical trend?

Suddenly the manager walks up the steps and into the space where we are sitting. Raj sees him, and everything changes. His tone changes, and he sits up straighter. He turns to me with a dramatic wave of his hand, proclaiming: "Even though it may have really been an accident, the government will always say it was arson. People outside the mill might say it was arson, but we know that it was an accident. Maybe in 1995, maybe that was arson. But now we know that this was not, there's no benefit to the owner here. He was getting so much rent from the godowns: twenty-two lakh rupees per month." The manager looks around, catches my eye, descends the staircase, and returns to his air-conditioned office. Raj's eyes twinkle, and he flashes a devilish smile. He is enjoying this performance.

Raj asks if I would like some tea and snacks at the corner store. "Now this is our job, we are here nine to five, just like a government job. But unlike before, there are no restrictions on us. We can come and go as we want, we can go out and get tea, get *nashta* [snacks]. We walk up and down; all we have to do is watch these guys." I accept his offer, and we head out for a bit, eager to stretch our legs.

In this unstable environment, particularly around the time of union meetings, group retrenchment, and extraordinary events (in particular, the fires of 1995 and 2009), rumor becomes the primary mode of social interaction for Dhanraj workers. As workers speculate on the future, the rumors they circulate, while ephemeral, become crucial in locating stable ground in an otherwise insecure environment. When cotton production becomes impossible, the production of fire rumors takes its place: workers find that this circulation, as a way of making sense of things, is also a practice of making something. Of receiving recognition for expertise. Perhaps I am the consumer purchasing their goods.

While the rumor mill of Dhanraj begins to suggest that the fire was, indeed, the result of arson and that the owner is, after all, the one to blame, such conclusions are less important than the sense that this fire reveals everything: loss, betrayal, disavowal, irrelevance. In this way, the mill owner may have lit the fuse that burned the mill, but the fire itself contains far more than individual action. Therefore, the fire encompasses individual capitalist greed as well as the abandonment of a city that Dhanraj workers believed they built through generations of industrial labor. These rumors hold weight because the act of spreading such information keeps the conspiracy alive and allows Dhanraj workers to remain at the center of a story they were ousted from years before. It is here, within these circulating stories, that a renewed community is forged.

Smoke and Mirrors

Societies in fact reconstruct their pasts rather than faithfully record them, and . . . do so with the needs of contemporary culture clearly in mind—manipulating the past in order to mold the present. —MICHAEL KAMMEN, *Mystic Chords of Memory*, 1991

One hot and heavy March afternoon, several months after the mill reopens, I sit in the shade wasting time while the workers pretend to work. The air is saturated with moisture, but the rains are months away. Raj has taken the afternoon off but tells me to come by his home when I am done. Until then, I watch the men wander aimlessly up and down the rows of machines, occasionally catching my eye and throwing their hands up in the air for dramatic effect. Vishnu cleans his glasses every ten minutes; Dilip,

Sitaram, and Namdeo retreat to the corner to read the Marathi-language newspaper. Kishan and Sudarshan finally give up and take naps by the window, stretched out across used gunnysacks pulled from an overstuffed cupboard. At 2:00 PM, Namdeo offers to walk me to Raj's house, since the two live near each other. After another day of overwhelming boredom, the men are all eager to return home for the afternoon.

There is a curious tension present in the period of postfire uncertainty: the drama of the fire recedes into the total boredom of the aftermath. Perhaps it is this strange transition that feeds the vitality of rumor: remaining tied to an event of transformation sustains the otherwise static and numbing present. And so the rumor mill churns.

When I arrive at Raj's house, he emerges looking as dapper and well-groomed as ever, wearing a crisp white embroidered shirt and well-ironed powder-blue trousers. His gold chains catch the light, and he looks like a mirage, standing in the dirt courtyard framed by his light brown apartment building. He leads me inside, and his wife, Ketaki, welcomes me with an overwhelming lunch spread. It does not take long before I am again asking about the fire and pushing him on the issue of arson and rumor. He considers my question and then responds:

> He [the owner] might have burned it because of Mahindra [the development company]. His lawyers might have advised him [to do so]. Maybe he hoped that after the fire, all would be resolved with Mahindra. We would have believed that it was an accident, but everyone says it is arson. If he [the owner] has to do anything, he has to take permission from Mahindra. There is a court order that he can't do anything without Mahindra. He received a 44-crores [US$8.5 million] advance from Mahindra. He has taken the money and refuses to give up the property. Now Mahindra is not getting possession of the property because the owner was saying the mill is working.

He suggests that perhaps Mahindra and the owner burned it together. "Fires don't happen, they are caused." He tells me there has been some progress on the legal end—initially, Mr. Lal gave away the property for one-quarter of the price, and now it has gone up four times in value. Because the court said the owner could not back out, Mr. Lal then offered Mahindra all the money, plus interest and all expenses. But Raj tells me the court ruled that they have to work together: everything has to be shared fifty-fifty.

This, he explains to me, is why the workers decided the fire was a joint effort between the developers and the owners. After all, the mill security guards are hired through Mahindra, and a Mahindra Lifespaces sign hangs just behind the gate. Raj believes that the fire is motivated entirely by insurance money. However, Mahindra does not want to develop the compound, and the owner does not want to relinquish control. His son's lifestyle store, the workers all insist, is an illegal project. No permits were ever secured for its opening, so the owners argue that it is, in fact, the mill's showroom. Since I began fieldwork in 2008, the store has expanded to five times its original size, and business is booming. Workers tell me that without the front of the mill, the store could not continue to exist: the workers may be surveying an empty theater, but this is also the stage on which an actual business becomes possible.

In the context of such a space, the fire at Dhanraj takes on more meaning. The mill cannot cease to function, as the union will not overlook the extralegality of the lifestyle store if the production keeping the union relevant disappears. And so the mill space is downsized to make way for the growth of new economic opportunities. Over ten years of fieldwork (2008–2018), I watch the store expand from one to five buildings, spread throughout the mill compound. As of 2018, just enough mill activity is ongoing to provide legitimacy for the mill to continue, allowing for the retail store (as well as the sweatshops and storage godowns) to pull in the real money. The lively ruins of the mill even provide the requisite postindustrial *staging* for the lifestyle store. It seems, in the compound, a postindustrial aesthetic is becoming chic. And this transformation is only possible through the spectacle of industrial fire.

In some ways very little has changed, as both before and after the fire daily life at Dhanraj involves witnessing the intense intermingling of formal and informal economies. Before the fire, young women employed by the two informal factories—one producing shoes and one stitching bags—come in and out of the main mill compound while young men carry goods up and down the stairs leading to the third floor godowns. After the fire, young day laborers clear out both the carcasses of mill machinery and the shards of pottery once stored in these godowns. The remaining mill workers are savvy in discussing how such unauthorized economies trap them in the precarious employment situation they currently find themselves in. The low wages paid to mill workers and the high returns acquired through nontextile activity within the mill compound contribute to a bleak economic reality for workers and a productive period of limbo for owners. Raj argues that the mill owner benefits from the city's growing casualization because much of the mill's income is generated by informalized opportunities: "Now, the interest of the owner is that he has a license to work here [in the mill]. And because of the mill, he can operate these godowns and these tiny factories. His earnings are not from the mill, but from these auxiliary operations here."

At the same time, the fire triggers a circulation of rumors that help reframe and reexamine a world otherwise seemingly set: the receding of an old economy into a new economy, the destruction of an old landscape for the emergence of a new landscape. Prior to the fire, workers produce thread while assuming their days of industrial labor are coming to a close. After the fire, workers produce rumors engaged in untangling affect (fear) from impact (the transformation of the compound, the interplay of union and owner). Raj's understanding of Dhanraj's extralegal production makes him suspicious of any event (like industrial fire) that reduces textile production but preserves opportunities like small informal factories and godowns. The workers show me that what seems like a simple story of postindustrial urban transformation through industrial fire is in fact complicated by their low wages and the income generated through informalized, nontextile activity. Industrial mill fires become a convenient mode of expanding this productivity: while textile workers cannot work in an empty lot and an archaic industry cannot be expected to revive itself if machines go up in flames, the facade of production enables cheap labor to linger as a formal front while income-generating informal production flourishes.

By this logic, these workers are at once the spectators in the theater and the actors who allow the illusion to be enacted. Indeed, while the crude thread spun before the fire in 2009 was sold to local markets, following the fire, these bundles of spun, packaged cotton accumulate in the corners of the remaining buildings. I learn that it is actually economically savvy to pay the remaining textile workers to produce needless thread while simultaneously profiting from the unauthorized auxiliary industries providing a steady stream of income to the mill, such as shoe and bag factories. But both before and after the fire, the real money is coming from the lifestyle store.

FIGURE 5.7. Abandoned thread in need of a market.

The Archive of Shifting Developments

At once person-specific and interpersonal, expectation also takes place in the today; it is the future made present; it directs itself to the not-yet, to the nonexperienced, to that which is to be revealed. Hope and fear, wishes and desires, cares and rational analysis, receptive display and curiosity: all enter into expectation and constitute it.—REINHART KOSELLECK, *Futures Past: On the Semantics of Historical Time*, (1979) 2004

The fire and subsequent reopening of Dhanraj complicates a more straightforward narrative of deindustrialization, worker displacement, and racial homogenization so often articulated through revanchist processes described in urban studies.[4] Through the case of Dhanraj, it becomes apparent that teleological trajectories of urban development are unsettled, and a messier, nonlinear pathway is revealed. This pathway is lined with the conflicting interests of citizen stakeholders, whether they be mill workers, owners, or developers, and the current interpretation, enforcement, and (oftentimes) disregard of development law.

Additionally, to speak of the mill lands in the past tense is to overlook the critical economic contribution of unauthorized activity in these industrial areas, activity enabled precisely because several mills remain open and several hundred mill workers remain employed. In the case of Dhanraj, before the fire these unauthorized activities include two factories (one making shoes and one making bags) and several warehouses for storage of various goods. Additionally, assuming that mills are closed and workers dispersed relies on the notion that "gentrification" is a universal result of economic transformation in low-income enclaves, when such patterns are not actually evident in Indian cities such as Mumbai.[5] What emerges instead is a section of urban space that resists a revanchist ethos even as it buys into many of the tenets of urban renewal, redevelopment, and gentrification.

In a literal sense, therefore, the workers of Dhanraj are trailing behind the engine of progress in Mumbai. But within the complex structure of licensing and land use regulations, they are also enabling this progress, by providing the "front" behind which other kinds of moneymaking can take place. In that sense, the continuation of Dhanraj is a form of surplus value extraction—except that workers are not actually producing the valuable goods anymore. They are instead producing legitimacy through both their ongoing presence and their public disappearance: while the mill owner may profit from the fire or even (in the realm of rumor) may have lit the fuse, he is also held hostage by the current moment: he must pour money into the mill in order to reap returns in the future. This is a game of accumulation, and the owner is not winning quite yet.

This gamble results in the production and circulation of multiple worlds: the lively ruin of the mill may still be undergoing its process of decay, but outside the compound walls this process has been deemed complete and the era of industrial production has been rendered obsolete. Because Mumbai is understood as "postindustrial," because the official histories of textile production are entirely past tense, because the industrial workforce is understood to have dispersed and disappeared, Dhanraj workers are anachronistically problematic and therefore unseen.[6] Yet, there they are.

The recorded fire history of Mumbai's mill lands is one of razed mills and raised towers. Fire allows the low-lying industrial landscape to be replaced with shining skyscrapers, and fire within mill compounds implies motivations of greed and illegality. The land in question—centrally located and covering six hundred acres of prime urban real estate—is valued at Rs 30,000 (US$500) per square foot (Jha 2013). However, prior to 2003, development laws in Mumbai asserted that mill lands could only be developed for industrial purposes (D'Monte 2002). Because of such legislation, mysterious mill fires provide the perfect avenue for nonindustrial development, since a declining industry can arguably be retained but justification for rebuilding such an anachronistic industry is seemingly senseless. Therefore, mill fires result in the construction of highrise apartment buildings and shopping malls, a process that subsequently has helped transform the imagined demographic from industrial workers to middle class. Now that the development rules have shifted in favor of owners and developers, the only thing standing in the way of development is union contracts and the need for substantial financial overhead (to pay off worker pensions). Dhanraj must still keep the RMMS union happy for a few more years, but after that the development game has a whole new set of rules.

The new question is what kind of structures will rise out of mill compounds when workers and unions are finally out of the picture: Shopping malls? High-rise apartment buildings? Hospitals? Mr. Lal tells me: "We are business people. . . . It [our development] would be to maximize the profits. Because I am not going to come and live here. So whatever are the maximum profits, we will go in only for that. Anybody would. Therefore we have been deferring decisions whether to put offices, whether to put residential. Whether a hospital. We will see." Before the 2009 fire, I try to get access to Dhanraj's employment records, ones that Mr. Lal helpfully promises to provide "next time," each time I ask him, for months. Finally, after the fire, he tells me that they have burned with the mill.[7] When he sees I am clearly disappointed, and when I realize he has finally found a way to ensure I can no longer argue with him, I ask Mr. Lal what he remembers about the employee rosters: men versus women, Maharashtrians versus non-Maharashtrians, young versus old. As always, he tells me the identities of his workers should mean nothing to me, and the only change that matters is the change of new machines: "Instead of the workers sitting here idle, we will keep people working on the machines. But it is not for production. These people want to be kept occupied. We don't *have* to put [in] these machines. We are just bringing in machines so that the workers feel like we are doing something. So that they don't sit idle and take money for nothing. They feel that they are coming here and earning, not getting dole."

We sit in awkward silence for a moment, and finally Mr. Lal tells me: "It's a complete waste; even if I had to modernize, I would have had to pull everything down. I wouldn't have modernized it, it was dying. Even when we had the sixty-odd workers, the workers were still lying idle. There are no workers." He stares out the window. Our interview is over. I walk out of his office and into the ruins of the mill compound: I think I am beginning to see the process of decay I find myself standing in. While unacknowledged by the city outside the mill gates, the fire breathes life back into the dying remainders of Dhanraj, and the workers' rumors keep the spark going.

As the story of Dhanraj illustrates—and contrary to the official story of industrial decline and fire transformation—textile mills have been operating and employing workers within the city of Mumbai for years after their public death, even if the productive output has virtually disappeared.[8] Here I want to stress that my definition of productivity is one of employment and production: while Dhanraj cotton may continue to accumulate dust on the factory floor (because no market currently exists for its sale), the mill continues to employ workers, and these workers will continue to produce a product once the compound is cleared and new machines are brought back in. It is through this continuation of employment and production that I define Dhanraj as productive, not through a larger sense of capital supply and demand.

However, outside of Dhanraj's walls, I rarely hear this reality acknowledged.

In part this is because the sale and development of mill land are enmeshed in social and political controversy, exacerbating these conflicting urban ideologies. Issues of lost labor, workers' rights, environmental conservation, and the desire for open space complicate (and continue to complicate) how development can (and will) take place.[9] Over the course of fifteen years (1991–2006), the development rights of mill owners and the future of the mill lands are locked in legal battles that limit the use of half-empty lots and lingering industrial production. In 2006, the Supreme Court determines that owners are free to develop their land as they see fit, but this legacy of ambiguous legal interpretation has led to uncertainty (as rules are constantly being overturned and revised), and the risk involved in selling, renovating, razing, and rebuilding mill lands continues to paralyze landowners hoping to turn major profits from mill land development.

Conclusions: How to Make a Problem Vanish?

We're told we don't exist because they need us not to exist. They need to take control. ... Step one: establish that it's barren. Step two: destroy it.—CLAIRE VAYE WATKINS, *Gold Fame Citrus*, 2015

During my remaining seven months in Mumbai, I watch as the fire accelerates an already engaged process of downsizing and development. When I leave the city in June 2010, the burned lot is almost entirely cleared, but the restless mill workers are still aimlessly patrolling the property beneath a heavy cloak of inertia. They talk of new machines and the possibility of renewed production, but I wonder if this talk is really just a scam: a way for the mill owner to bide time and draw out decisions before the lot is sold to the highest bidder intent on creating a hospital or hotel in the congested neighborhood of Central Mumbai. I return to the city in March 2011 expecting to see the ground cleared for new development, since this is understood to be *the* reason industrial fires happen in the first place: to rid the lot of the past and make way (and claims) for new, sky-reaching towers. The fire turns out not to have been the decisive event that it was supposed to be: instead, I find nine secondhand machines, purchased from nearby defunct mills, run by a remaining skeletal workforce of seventy workers. The mill burns, but the veneer of production continues. Why burn a mill if mill closure is not the goal?

The next day, I visit Manda for tea and gossip. While she hasn't been back to the mill in months, she is occasionally in touch with several of the workers. She didn't know the machines had arrived that week, but she tells me she is not surprised by my news: "The owner wants to show the government that the mill is working. Now he can show [them] the new machines have come." She has been talking to Raj, and she knows the workers want to retire. "Everyone is fed up," she tells me. Under different circumstances, they would leave the mill and find new work. She insists there is insurance money to be collected, if it hasn't come in already. "He [the owner] hasn't suffered any losses. . . . Rich people insure everything." Manda flashes me her gorgeous toothless smile and winks: "They [the owners] don't suffer any losses, and that's why they cause the fire." She pauses, her eyes brighten: "All the owners get together and decide whose mill to burn this month." She laughs and claps her hands, exclaiming: "'Look: my mill burned down, I've suffered!' But really, this is a racket. They [all the mill owners of the city] are a group—they have their meetings every year, and

FIGURE 5.8. New/old machines, part I.

FIGURE 5.9. New/old machines, part II.

they plot together." She sits back, pleased with herself, and we chuckle as the joke settles upon us like a stifling blanket.

It is nice to laugh with Manda, and she seems to enjoy the distraction. She has been out of work for months and cannot find a new job. She doesn't want to clean other people's homes, and she lost her job washing floors at an office building after the manager suspected multiple employees of theft. She tells me she placed the entirety of her pension in trusts for her grandchildren's education and is living off the meager rent collected from the tenants inhabiting the majority of her flat. Still, she is not someone who invites pity, and she never plays on my sympathy. She is tough and scrappy and proud of her resilience. We sit quietly for a moment, and I sip the water she offers me. I find that the rumors have made their way here, as well.

In the film *Lalbaug, Parel / City of Gold*, the mill fire represents death, transition, dystopia, redevelopment, and economic transition. The film begins with the oldest of Mr. Dhuri's sons sitting on the roof of a new building in the central neighborhood of Parel. From his lofty perch, he tells his wife the story of his family and the tragedies they endured in the neighborhood of his youth. This is why he wishes to move into this new tower instead of finding a nicer neighborhood away from the chaos of Central Mumbai: even as the tragedy and poverty of his youth made room for the emergence of a wealthy and successful man, he wants to remember, he wants to remain close to his past. However, the workers of Dhanraj find themselves stuck in an elliptical time: the fire does not transform the compound in the way we all expected. And this is precisely the point: this stasis demands that the fire remains an arrested event, even years after the flames have been extinguished. The fire transforms the mill into a purgatory of expectation, and the event continues into the present moment.

The fire, as an *event*, arrests, even while trying to unfold, to do what it's supposed to do. But like the workers themselves, it finds itself suspended. Rumor wraps around the stories spread by workers to make sense of the stagnation and frustration they live within. Industrial fires in Mumbai often allow for the clearing of land, development of new buildings, and transformation of mill land into spaces of elite consumption. In the case of Dhanraj, the fire also allows for a final public death to overwhelm the realities brimming beneath the surface: that mills continue to operate, textile workers continue to work, and cotton continues to spin forth from archaic machines. These secrets enable textile mills to continue as profitable business ventures, even if the income is not generated from the production of cotton thread or textiles. Simultaneously, the seeming finality of the industry allows such mill activity to be rendered unvisible, through both the destruction of the fire and the city's circulation of mill land nostalgia. Such clarity is productive, even as the messiness of false loss lingers on the struggling industrial landscape.

The workers of Dhanraj find neither rebirth nor freedom through the 2009 fire; instead, they remain locked in an archaic industry that has died, been burned, but cannot immediately transform: a suspended phoenix. Through the circulation of rumors, the workers at Dhanraj remain actively involved in their own story, even as they are written out of it beyond the mill walls. Through the archive of the fire, these rumors remain in circulation for years after the event itself has been seemingly forgotten. In spreading these rumors, workers show how they are aware of their own growing futility in both literal and figurative ways: they are precarious workers in an unstable working environment, as well as irrelevant workers in a city convinced of its "post"-industrial status. However, the fire reveals a resistance to this dominant city discourse: even as the master mill land history asserts the absence of industrial workers in a new economy, the rumors circulated in its aftermath reveal how the workers in Dhanraj are still struggling to craft something entirely their own. And so perhaps the fire, after all, *is* doing something decisive, even if this runs contrary to expectation. That by fueling rumor, the fire is actually helping to animate a world that would otherwise be running dry.

Epilogue

The Archive
of Futures Lost

The archive: if we want to know what that will have meant, we will only know in times to come. —JACQUES DERRIDA, *Archive Fever*, 1995

The ruin of a building . . . means that where the work of art is dying, other forces and forms, those of nature, have grown; and that out of what of art still lives in the ruin and what of nature already lives in it, there has emerged a whole, a characteristic unity. —GEORG SIMMEL, "The Ruin," (1911) 1965

Departures I: Watching the Ruins Grow

There are green plants growing from the cold mill chimney of Dhanraj, and you can see them peeking out the top while sailing over the Lalbaug flyover. However, from the sidewalk the chimney is barely visible from below the flyover, and the shadow thrown by this skyward street confuses me in a space once familiar and recognizable. The flyover wasn't complete the last time I was in town, and now it takes me a moment to orient myself and locate the entrance to Dhanraj. I am back in Mumbai after four years away; it is December 2015. And then January 2016. I straddle the two years even as they fade into each other, this artificial organization of temporal progress. The mill is barely operational with fifty workers, and yet the workers still work, the union still advocates, and the thread is still produced. The market is now in Gujarat, but somehow this tiny center of production remains.

FIGURE E.1. On the street outside the mill, under the Lalbaug flyover.

In a year or two the Mumbai-based mill will shut down and production will be moved to Silvassa, a once tiny village, now industrial hub, three hours north of Mumbai. There are tax breaks there; water and electrical costs are much lower than in Mumbai. Perhaps this production will once again be lucrative without the exorbitant overhead of an urban operation. The Mumbai workforce will retire, receive their pensions, move on. Silvassa will grow its diverse industrial arsenal.

I turn off Ambedkar Road and tread a path I've walked so many times before. It is both familiar and very alien. Many of the temporary barricades that lined the interior lane during the majority of my fieldwork, made from corrugated sheet metal, have been removed, and I can clearly see fields once visible only through cracks and breaks in metal and concrete. Yet, these fields are being cleared of debris and are now almost entirely empty. Barren. The new owners of this land, Peninsula Development, will water the land, and it will become a hospital or a housing complex or a shopping mall, skyscrapers reaching up and over the hidden horizontal city. Further company for the expanding vertical city.

When the lane snakes around, bringing buildings into sight, I stop,

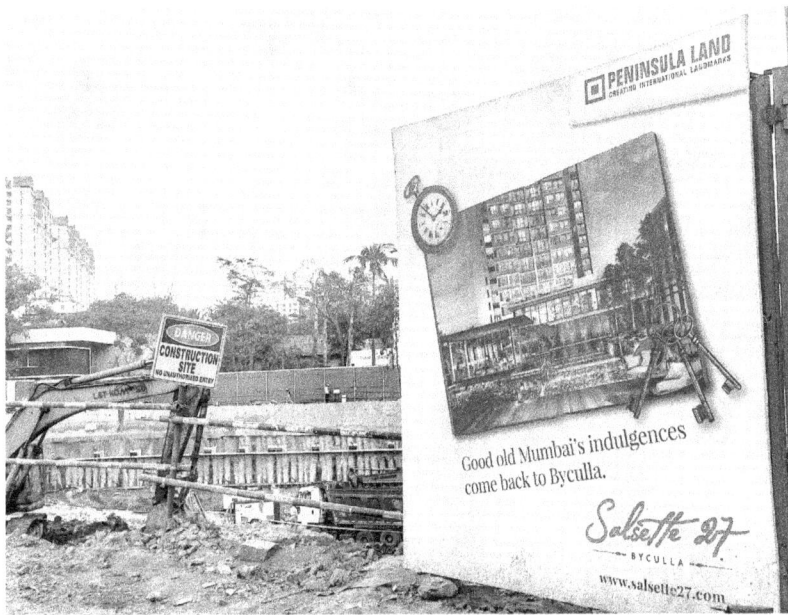

FIGURE E.2. Dhanraj-past/Peninsula-future: the mill as construction site.

gawk. It is as if someone scraped everything loose away from the structures, leaving only their roots and stubborn trunks. I am seeing skeletons:
a boarded-up canteen, steps leading nowhere, walls with no inside. The
mill is completely gone, at least in the place I expected to find it. Only later
will I find it has been relocated across the lane to a smaller building and
now functions in a former single-story warehouse.

When I backtrack and enter the new space of the mill, I am overcome
with an uncanny recognition. This is the mill of dreams: an altered version of something familiar. The same, and yet completely different. Recognizable, and yet entirely new. But familiar faces greet me: Sudarshan,
Govinda, Chandrakant. I discover that Raj retired, happily, six months
before. The shifts rotate now between morning and afternoon, so several
faces are familiar, while several others are brand-new. The only guarantee
the workers have is that it will all soon be gone.

After establishing that I'd been gone four years, that I am happily back
in town but only for a short visit, and that I had thought of everyone in
my absence, a new but entirely familiar table is cleared in the back so that
I can sit and watch. And wait. Chai is eventually served. Men work. I sit,

FIGURE E.3. Skeletons: the empty passageway (with the "new" mill peeking out behind the tarps to the left).

FIGURE E.4. Skeletons: the boarded-up canteen.

FIGURE E.5. Skeletons: inside the new mill, the mill of dreams.

and my body begins to remember how to coexist with the noise and the heat and the flying cotton and the sight of workers completely unprotected from dangerous material; barefoot or in chappals, standing on steel sheets lining the floor. Poor ventilation and no fans. Ears unprotected from the deafening whir of machines. Everyone smiles at me. Their audience is back.

Across the second threshold, behind the mill and away from the main road, sits Arvind's growing empire of art and design. The space of the store has grown in four years, adding an art gallery and furniture designer to its enclave. The near future will involve two more gallery spaces, a café, and perhaps a boutique hotel. These two and a half acres will provide beauty, quiet, creativity, and engagement to an affluent urban demographic interested in thinking about an entirely different form of production.

Later, as I wander out of the mill and into the lifestyle compound, I remember a similar moment, perhaps seven years ago. Four years before old Mr. Lal died. Long before I had ever heard of Silvassa. In 2009, the spring, maybe. April. On that day I sit with Mr. Lal in his office above Arvind's store. Moments before I had been browsing through the display of Rajasthani antiques, silver tableware, and contemporary paintings in bright, aggressive colors. These mornings are always uncomfortable for me: the waiting in the cool, expansive warehouse space, the cups of coffee in delicate china mugs, the disconnect between the activity of the mill and the quiet of the store. Mr. Lal always makes me wait, and so I find myself aimlessly wandering through the displayed stock of decadent home furnishings, presented for and sold to Bollywood elite, industrialists, and foreign collectors. There is nothing in these expansive rooms that I will ever be able to afford, much less the workers who pass by the store's massive doors on their way to work every day.

Arvind encourages me to browse, and I do, often first taking refuge in the bathroom at the back, where I clean train dust off my skin and arduously transform myself into someone suited to sitting in an air-conditioned office with power and money. I usually fail.

Or at least I feel like I fail.

The anxiety for me is how to move between the mill and the office, often in the same day, without alienating those occupying either space. Who do I make comfortable with my sartorial choices? Who do I suggest allegiance to through my comportment? This form of ethnographic code-switching is always at the back of my mind as I watch myself shape-shift into my idea of who my informants will feel most comfortable talking to. And this shape-shifting is not just a process of moving between spaces. It is also a process of moving between time.

What do we wear when moving between time periods established as "the past" and "the future"? What clothing is appropriate for time travel?

After some time, usually twenty to thirty minutes, I am led upstairs to the office of Mr. Lal. It is deep and dark and relatively empty, considering the accumulation of decor down below. Mr. Lal sits at a large antique wooden desk, a colonial map framed on the wall. Around this display the walls are cracked and worn and desperately in need of a coat of paint. The window is filled with ancient looking glass, which gives the room a hazy historical feel. Here we engage in veiled combat over our shining cups: I ask questions, he deflects them gracefully. We smile at each other and sip, preparing our next move. Below us the artifacts of excess wait to be placed in new homes. Across the pathway the artifacts of industry crank cotton thread from tired metal fingers.

This space is also a threshold between worlds: not in terms of the city's temporality but in terms of the temporality of production and consumption. Dhanraj has not been a recognizably productive industrial space for years, yet here in this office the perceived production of industrial labor facilitates the formation of a new form of consumption, one that establishes and enables particular forms of taste and distinction. In this way, the days in which I wait for Mr. Lal downstairs will often overlap with visits by wealthy clients in search of art and furnishings. In what other space does the anachronistic past of industrial production collide with the new order of elite identity through the consumption of items out of place? Amid the contemporary art and gilded goblets and crystal chandeliers sit rough renderings of gods and goddesses, intricately carved wooden doors (brutally dismembered and removed from their previous homes that were . . . Razed? Renovated? Who knows? . . .), and weathered, hand-painted tiles. These objects — certainly beautiful — are worth their exorbitant prices not simply through this beauty but also through their histories, whether mythological, remembered, or archived through historical documents.

This collision of time and space brings value to the buildings housing such splendors, as well. But unlike the objects displayed like hothouse flowers, these buildings are still alive, if also slowly fading from one life to another. While rarely do worker and patron meet, the buildings used to house these items, seemingly a *formerly* industrial space, are actually still *functionally* industrial. As the mill's downsizing, through mysterious fires and obscured negotiation, makes way for empty buildings through which this inventory can expand, such an expansion exists uncomfortably alongside the reality that such downsizing cannot be infinite — an island of winding has to remain in order for the legitimacy of such a retail space to continue, albeit through a gray area of extralegality.

Two forms of anachronism exist here — that of the industrial worker and that of the antiqued land. One cannot exist without the other, yet they simultaneously demand the other out of existence through their own presence. How can a gate on Ambedkar Road, several minutes' walk down the street from the zoological park inside Rani Baug gardens, cage such temporal disparity? How do mill workers understand the grandeur of anachronistic objects lining their former work space, even as their own anachronistic subjectivity fades like weathered cotton with every passing day? These questions have fueled this ethnographic project, and new questions emerge from the asking. Where can the proliferation of such questions take us?

These specific questions converge in an archive of lively ruination: How do some ruins grow while other ruins disappear? This ethnography has answered this question through the life, labor, and memories of the lingering Dhanraj workforce, rooted in the ethnographic archive. Through this ethnographic archive, the temporality of lively ruins reveals how the industrial remains in the postindustrial through stories of embodied time and place. The ruins of industry are buried beneath narratives of infrastructural shift: when we encounter global cities only through structural trends, we miss the liveliness of living *in* the global city. The ruins that grow emerge from recognizable trends within global cities discourse. The ruins that disappear are the unseen remainders of Dhanraj: lively and vital, a critical but unvisible foundation supporting the emergent vertical future. The story of a city cannot be told without including this unvisible foundation: lively ruins like Dhanraj.

Departures II: Watching the Ruins Disappear

Turns out, according to neuroscience, the more you actively "remember" something, the more the headstory you carry around changes. Every time you recall something, you modify it a little bit. . . . Eventually you are not remembering what happened at all, but your story or head movie about it. The safest memories are probably those embedded in the brains of people who have lost the ability to retrieve them. —LIDIA YUKNAVITCH, *The Chronology of Water*, 2011

Throughout this book I have used the plasticity of the present moment to reimagine time beyond a linear and forward-moving frame.[1] Seen through the prism of Dhanraj, the process of industrial decay occurring throughout the Mumbai mill lands reveals the messianic, uncanny progression of time: this form of temporal progression cannot be reconciled with the artificial eras of "industrial" and "postindustrial" capitalism (or any era limited by a human view of history). Simply put: time is not necessarily rooted in progress and linearity; that is merely the frame through which it is currently imagined, ordered, and drawn. Dhanraj is a location where the messianic potential of ongoing deindustrialization can be actualized.[2] By attending to the afterlives of an "industrial" past still remaining in the "postindustrial" present, new stories of what it means to be urban, what it means to labor, what it means to dwell, and what it means to survive emerge. Dhanraj workers tell this story simply by remaining.

The museum space of mill land Mumbai tells this story of linear progress: a narrative of transformation that moves the city in a direction already established as "the future." But beneath this armored layer of transforma-

FIGURE E.6.
Watching the
ruins grow.

tion lives the vampiric archive of the market—a hidden economy where the past still struggles to exist in the present and the present continues to drain vitality from the gradually perishing past. This hidden realm exists in the shadows of a developing future, one that looks beyond Mumbai for a space to thrive, even as it remains partially mired in urban quicksand.

On a quiet afternoon in January 2016, I sit in Arvind's office above the lifestyle store. Mr. Lal died the year before, the lifestyle compound is expanding, and the mill is slowly shrinking in its allocated space. The office where I now sit has been dramatically transformed: no longer the dark and cluttered space of the past, the office is now bright, with freshly painted walls, impressive art, and a polished mahogany desk, which sits in the center of the room. Arvind and I drink our coffee while he tells me of his plans. A boutique hotel in Thimphu, Bhutan. Art and design talks with makers from all over the world. Musical performances. The possibilities for the compound are limited, it seems, only by what he can imagine.

He walks me through the compound, and we stop outside the art gallery: a gorgeous space housing some of the hottest contemporary art from up-and-coming local artists, including the artist gracing the cover of this book, Digbijayee Khatua. I walk inside and seat myself on a sleek, smooth wooden bench. I stare at Khatua's images in front of me: an intricate diorama showing a city of chawls. The windows are cut out, and small paper people lean out. They hang paper clothes, they water painted plants. Some windows are boarded up, some walls are cracked. Beside the crafty structure I see immediately before me, to my left, is a razed site, perhaps another chawl? Now it is only a pile of paper rubble housing a two-dimensional stenciled bulldozer. What will that paper construction site grow in the imagination of the artist? The gallery is full of these transformational sites — there is life here in one building beside another building that has disappeared. Across the gallery even more lively buildings and ruined structures create a skyline of past lives across the wall.

What does this museum say to the Dr. Bhau Daji Lad Mumbai City Museum down the street? What does this nostalgic imagery of struggling vitality say to the photographs of PUKAR's "Barefoot Researchers," now stored in their own archive in some museum basement? I leave the museum and step out into the afternoon sun. Across the lane is a small construction site: a new gallery is emerging from a former industrial workshop. Like so many structures in this city, it will emerge far quicker than I expect. The next time I visit, it is already completed. Old news now, what's next? (But what if we lingered with the "old news" before following the seductive trail of "what's next?") I wonder what visual renderings of a dead city will hang on the walls of the new city.

The Dr. Bhau Daji Lad Mumbai City Museum and the art galleries of Dhanraj are material museums with actual archival spaces. Every element of the chosen story cannot make it onto the available walls: otherwise we would never make it out of the exhibit alive. The archives of the city museum are likely lined with artifacts and art that will never fit the prepared narrative and yet are stored and preserved "just in case." The Dr. Bhau Daji Lad Mumbai City Museum displays a particular past. The galleries of Dhanraj will only ever present a small selection of artistic futurity. The pieces are curated to display a particular form of new production. And so both conceal histories even as they teach us lessons about the past and the future.

The archives of the city are more ephemeral than the archives of these museums: they are disappearing, emerging, and transforming every day. The archive of futures lost is one of the most secure of the archives: the seal is strongest, the gatekeepers most vigilant. This archive has never been remembered, and therefore it is most intact. But that also makes it very hard to find.

So how do these archives laid out across these pages—the mill, the chawl, the body, the strike, the fire—tell us about the urban future? After Mr. Lal dies, Arvind and his older brother, Rohit, split the compound in two. While Arvind keeps control of the five acres containing his lifestyle enclave, Rohit takes control of the mill, selling off most of the land and retaining a small section where the diminished cohort of remaining workers continue to produce cotton thread. In January 2016, both Arvind and representatives from the RMMS tell me of the mill's eventual shift to Silvassa and the inevitable end of Dhanraj production in Mumbai. However, in December 2017, even as the Silvassa operation has begun, fifty-five Dhanraj workers remain employed by the ghostly Mumbai mill. The archive, for now, is still intact.

But what happens to archives when the buildings housing such history are demolished? Where will the archive of loss exist when Dhanraj, as a textile mill, is gone? While elements of these various archives are mobile and travel with their makers and keepers, the compound that linked them all together will soon erase most traces of what was collected within the mill gates. The lifestyle store draws on an industrial aesthetic for a romantic, antiqued patina (Dawdy 2016), but this really is nothing more than nostalgia and new capital. I may think I see flashes of the city in the gallery, but really I am only encountering memories made into monsters: the undead enslaved by the stories we choose to tell.

These archives, then, are an attempt to reframe both the past and the future through an engagement with destruction, decay, and transience: what Walter Benjamin termed "natural history." In claiming "natural history," I am drawing on Beatrice Hanssen's (1998) engagement with Benjamin's use of the term. Hanssen explains: "Benjamin's appropriation of the category [natural history] proved to be highly unorthodox. With this term, he first of all referred to a process of transience and to a logic of decay that radically undermined Enlightenment and post-Enlightenment conceptions of human history, anchored in categories of human freedom and historical teleology. . . . I argue that Benjamin's positive validation of natural history was meant to overcome the limitations of historical hermeneutics, whose category of 'meaning' (*Sinn*) remained grounded in the understanding of a human subject" (1998, 3).[3] This radical (re)interpretation of "natural history" is useful in (re)framing the lively ruins of Dhanraj:

Are we subjects to/of time or architects of historical change? And how can living through/within ruination challenge the limits of how current socio-political/economic epoch are narrated? Dhanraj is an allegory for both this question, as a concept, and this affective site, as a material world: through Dhanraj's archives, emergent meanings can take hold.[4]

And so this book is about the archives of Dhanraj, but it is not just a story of the mill I stumbled upon and chose to explore. Most residents of Mumbai live and work in obsolete economies. While India's new economies (and the powerful narratives of globalization and technological infrastructures) frame the country through future possibilities, any time spent in the city reveals how these new economies do not actually affect most city residents. And so the particular story of Dhanraj reveals how the narratives of development cannot eclipse the material reality of Mumbai: this is an old city vitally rooted in its own ruination. What seems anachronistic and decaying from the outside may indeed conceal a liveliness that enables the development of a new and modern veneer. But these two cities are simultaneous. They coexist critically, if also vampirically, as spaces of lively ruination.

When I stand on the quiet mill compound lane between the completed gallery and the emerging gallery, I watch as an informal workforce raises a new museum where an older archive has been razed. These young workers might once have worked in the textile mills. Now the material they produce is of a different sort: their labor does not create their own cultural capital. It instead invests, in unvisible ways, in a new form of cultural capital: the new city, the new economy. Young culture producers pushing up against and beyond the low-lying industrial city lying like a stain across the landscape. But this stain is what lets the city grow. What holds it up. These shadowy spaces between the city and the city. Between the past and the present. Between skin and bone.

Dhanraj is leaving soon.

Dhanraj is not going anywhere.

At the time of completing this book—in the winter of 2018—Dhanraj is still operating, workers are still working, and the city is still pretending they aren't there: the mill is both a shadow on the future and in the shadows of the future. So I sit between ruin and reincarnation: waiting for this industrial debris to be cleared and the next life cycle to begin.

Notes

Introduction

1. On its website, PUKAR describes the exhibition as follows:

In its heyday when all the fifty four cotton mills, located in Girangaon, were
churning out beautiful textiles, generations of mill workers contributed to the
economic, social, and cultural prosperity of the city and country alike and the
culture built around the textile industry became an integral part of Bombay's inimitable identity. Their life style inspired and nurtured many creative instincts
in Girangaon, fostering its rich cultural ethos. Mill workers' entertainment included public festival like the Ganesh-Utsav, Dahi Handi, Jakhadi, which became
very popular across the state and are famous even today! The mill workers also
staged brilliant theatre and sustained folk arts like Lawani, Tamasha, Bhajan,
Namaan, and Shahiri Powadas. All these art forms narrated the stories of their
lifestyle, their social and political upheavals, the freedom struggle of the country
and Samyukt Maharashtra Andolan. Today, with the onslaught of globalization,
Girangaon stands at a historical moment of unprecedented transformation, and
of lives and of the distinctive social fabric it once possessed. "Chawl culture" is
being replaced by "mall culture" and many indigenous residents are being dis-
posed. This exhibition is an attempt to preserve that rich cultural heritage of Girangaon and the moments of transformation by archiving and documenting it
for posterity. This Exhibition is a part of PUKAR Project titled "Mythologies of
Mumbai" that is supported by The Ford Foundation.

2. In *The Museum of Innocence*, Orhan Pamuk writes: "This is the greatest consola-
tion in life. In poetically well built museums, formed from the heart's compulsions,
we are consoled not by finding in them old objects that we love, but by losing all
sense of Time" (2009, 520).

3. My understanding of "the archive" emerges from a longer genealogy of scholarship invested in both a material and a conceptual framing of this concept. In particular, my analytic lineage can be traced through Michel Foucault (1972); Jacques
Derrida (1995); Carolyn Steedman (2001); Antoinette Burton (2003); Diana Taylor

(2003); Ann Laura Stoler (2008 and 2009); Anjali Arondekar (2009); Jennifer Gabrys (2013); Abigail De Kosnik (2016); and Jennifer Scappettone (2016).

4. See Papalias 2005; Stoler 2009; Povinelli 2011; Dave 2012; Garcia 2016.

5. In their introduction to *The Poetics in the Archive*, Paul J. Voss and Marta L. Werner argue: "The history of the archive, on the one hand a history of conservation, is, on the other hand, a history of loss. . . . Founded in order to preserve the official records of successive cultures but comprised of material 'citations' often wrenched out of context, the archive is necessarily established in proximity to loss—of *other* citations, citations of *otherness*. . . . The *poetics* of the archive . . . is a poetics of recollection, of re-membering, in which all proofs are provisional and subject to revision" (1999, i–ii).

6. This dynamism keeps the archive lively while also barring it from stratification—this archive of loss is not becoming a museum. While the museum and the archive are constituted vis-à-vis each other as a binary, I still understand them to be potentially nonbinary and capable of existing independently from each other. This is a matter of transparently uneven distribution.

7. In using the term "curated," I draw on the work of archaeologist Barbara Voss, who, reinterpreting the work of E. B. W. Zubrow, argues: "Curation affords an encounter with material remains that is qualitatively different than what occurs, for example, on the excavation site itself. The laboratory and curation facility is where archaeologists can come into direct physical contact with material evidence, not temporally constrained by the fleeting encounter of excavation but in a sustained and systematic manner that has the capacity to 'kick back' against applied ideas, models and theories. As any curator can testify, what develops in the course of that engagement can often confound or surprise, forcing modification of schemes of interpretation. This is where theories can be tested against a touchstone of reality, and remoulded in a collaborative and creative act of interpretation that takes into account the resistance of emerging evidence" (2012, 149). What Voss proposes archaeologists do with material remains I attempt to do with ephemeral (ethnographic) remains.

8. Here I draw on Diana Taylor's work in *The Archive and the Repertoire*. By "repertoire" Taylor refers to "ephemeral" remains, such as performance acts embodied by both actors and audience, while the "archive" is a collection of "enduring materials," which include "documents, maps, literary texts, letters, archaeological remains, bones, videos, film, CDs, all those items supposedly resistant to change" (2003, 3, 19). I am seduced by this distinction, and yet I am also interested in challenging it through Taylor's own critical postcolonial intervention. She notes that while "the archive and the repertoire exist in a constant state of interaction, the tendency has been to banish the repertoire to the past." This, she argues, is in part because these two nonbinary sources and spaces of knowledge have been constructed *as* binary, given how "the written and the archival" constitute "hegemonic power" and the repertoire constitutes "the anti-hegemonic challenge" (21–22). It is this frame that allows me to argue that the archive of loss does not become the museum of loss simply through documentation and display.

Additionally, my investment here is in transforming the balance of power within and across the archive, not constituting an alternative, embodied space of "the repertoire." By this I mean my definition of "archive" absorbs Taylor's "repertoire" while also challenging the seemingly hegemonic nature of "those items supposedly resistant to change." The archive of loss, then, encompasses performance, events, and memory while also arguing against Taylor in two specific ways. First, aging bodies, crumbling buildings, and ancient industrial machinery are as ephemeral as performance and enter into the "archival" space (or Taylor's "repertoire") in similar ways. Second, the archival space does not engage "enduring materials" democratically. Even within the "traditional" archival space (constituting "traditional" archival materials), what can be found, what has been lost, and what has already been forgotten constitute a stratified landscape of uneven distribution. My archive, as an archive of *loss*, is deeply invested in this uneven distribution.

9. While cotton was originally imported from the United States, the instability caused by the US Civil War enabled the Indian textile industry to flourish.

10. For more on this history, see Morris 1965; Tindall 1982; van Wersch 1992; Chandavarkar 1994; D'Monte 2002; Menon and Adarkar 2004; Riello 2013; Beckert 2014.

11. For a history of this strike, see chapter 4, "The Archive of the Strike."

12. India's balance-of-payments crisis of 1991, followed by a period of structural adjustment, led to a new industrial policy built around trade liberalization and deregulation. This program of economic liberalization included reduction and relaxation of policies regarding trade and foreign investing, as well as greater exchange rate flexibility. In addition, industrial activities such as mining, infrastructure, telecommunications, and banking, once controlled exclusively by the public sector, became open to private investment. The textile mills of Mumbai were directly affected by these new schemes.

13. In the next two years, ten different mills cycle through various stages of commercial redevelopment, but this process is again stalled in October 2005. Following floods of petitions from environmental NGOs, the Bombay High Court sets aside the 2001 amendment to DCR-58 and freezes the scheduled development activity on mill land in the Mumbai property markets. In early 2005, the National Textile Corporation (NTC) appeals the High Court's judgment and succeeds in overturning the ruling and freeing the land for development. Nevertheless, this development remains mired in uncertainty. In 2006, the NTC finds that mill owners are able to sell their remaining mills without contributing a sizable percentage to the public realm.

14. Dhanraj has a reputation for undertaking extralegal modernization schemes, which exist on public record. Three times now, the mill has used government subsidies (allocated for projects to benefit the modernization of the mill) for nonindustrial commercial projects (a "lifestyle" store selling expensive international antiques is the prime moneymaker on the mill property) and worker retrenchment (the exact opposite of its intended use). Because of this, Dhanraj no longer qualifies for additional subsidies, and the production of thread cannot cover the costs of worker wages, let alone pensions (which are dictated by law and well protected). This messy financial situation limits the options that are open to mill owners contemplating the

future of their land as sites of industrial production. What remains undisputed, however, is textile production cannot continue in Central Mumbai, and new development is imminent.

15. The Lal family, while ethnically Mewari and originally from Rajasthan, ended up in Bengal during the late nineteenth century. Before 1947, the family had eight jute mills in Bangladesh, but these properties were lost during the partition of Bengal in 1947. In 1958, the family acquired three Mumbai-based textile mills, including Dhanraj. Just as the partition dramatically altered their fortunes, so did the Great Textile Strike of 1982–1983. While the Lals managed to retain Dhanraj throughout, the other two mills were taken over by the NTC in the mid-1980s. This loss was dramatic: before 1983, they exported cotton all over the world: in the winter of 2009, early in my fieldwork, Mr. Lal tells me with pride that they even provided cotton to Bloomingdale's in the 1970s.

16. Unfortunately for Dhanraj owners, the mill's workers cannot be paid their entitled pensions until more money is freed up from the court case. In the meantime, the production of low-grade cotton thread is not even yielding revenues that can sustain the cost of daily mill activity. In fact, Dhanraj is only able to pay workers' wages and procure raw material by leasing the two unregulated factories (sweatshops) and several storage units ("godowns") on the mill property.

17. Kerstin Barndt writes: "Formerly industrial landscapes now seem suspended in time or even thrown into reverse: framed by nature and drawing on the aesthetics of ruin, the remnants of recent economic progress and decline fall back in time and are rendered instantly ancient in their resemblance to past ruins" (2010, 138).

18. Walter Benjamin writes: "In the ruin history has physically merged into the setting. And in this guise history does not assume the form of the process of an eternal life so much as that of irresistible decay. . . . Allegories are, in the realm of thoughts, what ruins are in the realm of things" (2009, 177–178). In thinking about allegories in relation to ruin, Beatrice Hanssen clarifies: "Allegory at once could figure the transience of natural history yet retain the fleeting promise of imminent reconciliation" (1998, 102).

19. By suggesting Dhanraj is an "uncanny" ruin, I flirt with Freudian and Lacanian psychoanalysis. I am taken by Mladen Dolar's sense of the uncanny and modernity. He writes: "What I am interested in is . . . the uncanny that is closely linked with the advent of modernity and which constantly haunts it from the inside. . . . With the triumph of the Enlightenment . . . the uncanny became unplaceable; it became uncanny in the strict sense. . . . It [object a, the unattainable object of desire] too [in addition to the subject], is most intimately linked with and produced by the rise of modernity. What seems to be a leftover is actually a product of modernity, its counterpart" (1991, 7). Similarly, I use the notion of Dhanraj as an uncanny ruin to write against Andreas Huyssen's anxiety about authenticity. Huyssen claims that nostalgia for ruins ties into their "promise of an alternative future" (2006, 8). However, I would argue that this is not the promise for an "alternative" future but instead a point of entry through which to access the *potentiality* of both the present and the future. After suggesting a link between authenticity and a Benjaminian reading of

"aura," Huyssen argues: "I posit the idea of the authentic ruin as a product of modernity itself rather than as royal road toward some uncontaminated origin" (12). By pushing Huyssen away from authenticity and nostalgia and toward a sense of the uncanny (read through Dolar), a sense of future potentiality through ruinous spaces may be re-formed. Throughout this book I reframe this uncanny ruin as a soothsaying space.

20. In particular, the last few decades has resulted in scholarship invested in defining neoliberal capital. A definition of this term will always elude us because the *theory* of what such language is capable of containing will never map onto the *materiality* of what it means to live in the world. Language has power in forming worlds, and this practice of naming constructs reality. These structuralist approaches ignore the absolute reliability of people and places to defy structures of order, surveillance, and control, even as they are also subject to them. There is a tension here that I am working through within Dhanraj. In particular, I am thinking about the work of David Harvey, especially *A Brief History of Neoliberalism* (2005), as well as Michel Foucault's work on governmentality (1991) and the birth of biopolitics (2008) and J. K. Gibson-Graham's work "Diverse Economies" (2008). In addressing the liveliness of ruins, I am also arguing that this scholarship reveals a need to define and redefine these eras, which stands in the way of addressing the stakes obscured through language: How do people occupy the categories being created? And how are they not occupying them? I avoid the language such as "the postindustrial" and "the neoliberal" because this is not the language my informants live within.

21. In "Ruinophilia: Appreciation of Ruins," Svetlana Boym (2008a) writes: "'Ruin' literally means 'collapse'—but actually, ruins are more about remainders and reminders. A tour of 'ruin' leads you into a labyrinth of ambivalent temporal adverbs—'no longer' and 'not yet,' 'nevertheless' and 'albeit'—that play tricks with causality. Ruins make us think of the past that could have been and the future that never took place, tantalizing us with utopian dreams of escaping the irreversibility of time."

22. This global crisis sits at the heart of current economic discussions under the Trump administration in the United States, but I am unconvinced by the questions being asked (such as, "Will this administration bring back coal and steel jobs, and at what rate?" and "What future is available for those once enmeshed in industrial production?" or "What would such a reemergence do for the American economy?"). What does it mean to shift such questions, so deeply enmeshed in current crisis, away from a taken-for-granted world and instead toward future potentialities? How might India (and specifically Central Mumbai) provide a frame through which to understand the United States? Much excellent work on deindustrialization in the United States has grappled with loss and memory: Kathryn Marie Dudley's *The End of the Line: Lost Jobs, New Lives in Postindustrial America* (1994); Sherry Lee Linkon and John Russo's *Steeltown USA: Work and Memory in Youngstown* (2002); Cathy Stanton's *The Lowell Experiment: Public History in the Post-industrial City* (2006); Caitrin Lynch's *Retirement on the Line: Age, Work, and Value in an American Factory* (2012); Christine Walley's *Exit Zero: Family and Class in Postindustrial Chicago*

(2013); Chloe Taft Kang's *From Steel to Slots: Casino Capitalism in the Postindustrial City* (2016). This body of work is critical in understanding elements of decline in industrial North America and raises important questions about the relation between loss and imaginable futures. I use this foundation to then also rethink how conceptions of time can be reworked within ongoing decline and ruination.

23. This is both about the *practice* of seeing and the possibility that some things cannot be rendered visible in the way I expect.

24. Avery Gordon tells us: "To study social life one must confront the ghostly aspects of it" (1997, 7).

25. Or, as Gordon explains: "A disappearance is real only when it is apparitional because the ghost or the apparition is the principle form by which something lost or invisible or seemingly not there makes itself known or apparent to us. The ghost makes itself known to us through the haunting and pulls us affectively into the structure of feeling of a reality we come to experience as recognition. Haunting recognition is a special way of knowing what has happened or is happening" (1997, 63).

26. I'm taken by Jason Pine's exploration of the allegorical implications of meth usage. He explains: "This ethnographic allegory is not only textual, but a textualization of an already allegorically inscribed material-affective geography. Through industry and ruination, a human body and a landscape compose a life tenuously holding together" (2016, 310–311). I see this engagement with bodies and landscapes as suggestive of ethnographic ephemera, in contrast to phenomenological readings of embodiment/bodies in space.

27. In thinking through affect, my engagements are formed through scholarship both within and beyond anthropology, including Favret-Saada 1977, 2012; Lacan 1991; Stewart 1996, 2007, 2017; Massumi 2002; Merleau-Ponty 2002; Sedgwick 2002; Mazzarella 2009, 2017; Berlant 2011, 2012, 2016; Dave 2012; Lepselter 2016; Ameeriar 2017.

28. In explaining what she frames as "affectsphere," Lauren Berlant draws on Colson Whitehead's novel *The Intuitionist* (1999). In the novel, Lila Mae Watson is an elevator inspector in an alternate New York City of the 1960s, a futuristic landscape of verticality that imagines discourses of racial "uplift" through the materiality of urban infrastructure. She is also the first African American woman working in a field otherwise entirely white and male, as well as a young Intuitionist in a field otherwise controlled by older Empiricists. As an Intuitionist, she "feels" the elevator's psychic vibrations through meditation. In this way, Lila Mae is part of a new but increasingly successful cohort of elevator inspectors challenging the traditional Empiricists, who practice their craft by inspecting the actual machinery of the elevator. Berlant writes: "Lila Mae negotiates the city landscape by feeling its atmosphere . . . she knows the street maps but what counts is the affectsphere, organized by the sensory pressures of the biopolitical. There is, she senses, a 'zero-point' of collective kinetic life. . . . That zero-point, a collective affective habit and norm of the city, is where history in the novel first reveals itself shaping the affective ordinary" (2011, 72). For more on this novel, see chapter 3, "The Archive of the Chawl."

29. In their editorial introduction to a 2012 curated collection of *Cultural Anthro-*

pology, Jessica Lockrem and Adonia Lugo argue: "Taking infrastructure as the object of analysis allows a different approach than that of neoliberalism, which has been criticized as a perspective that is too broad and can fail to consider everyday practices in local contexts" (2012). Also see Elyachar 2005, 2012, 2014; Anand 2011, 2012, 2015, 2016, 2017; Harms 2011; Appel 2012; Ghertner 2014; Bjorkman 2014, 2015; Zeiderman 2016.

30. This is not merely a call of "where are the people!" Instead, I seek to destabilize what counts as knowledge and expertise in anthropology. While they are not experts on engineering or urban planning, my Dhanraj informants *are* experts in living among ruination.

31. Here I am indebted to the scholarship of Anjaria 2009; Anand 2011, 2012, 2015, 2016, 2017; Doshi 2013, 2014, 2017; Doshi and Ranganathan 2017.

32. In *The Ravickians* (her sequel to *Event Factory*), Renee Gladman's narrator, "The Great Ravickian Novelist," begins: "To say that you have been born in Ravicka in any other language than Ravick is to say you have been hungry. That is why this story must not be translated" (2011, 7). And yet still I read *The Ravickians* in English (only partially because neither Ravicka nor the Ravickian language actually exists outside of Gladman's imagination).

33. In particular, see Herzfeld 1991; Confino 1997; Moore and Wheelan 2007.

34. In *The Archive and the Repertoire*, Diana Taylor explains: "Museums enact the knower-known relationship by separating the transient visitor from the fixed object of display. Like discoverers, the visitors come and go; they see, they know, they believe—only the deracinated, adorned, and "empty" object stays in place. Museums preserve (a particular) history, (certain) traditions, and (dominant) values. They stage the encounter with otherness. The monumentality of most museums emphasizes the discrepancy in power between the society that can contain all others and those represented only by remains, the shards and fragments salvaged in miniature displays" (2003, 66).

35. Recent work on memory has fought against the "memory archive," which models "memory as a static and stable place of storage, where past perceptions and experiences are retained and from where they can be retrieved" (Brockmeir 2010, 10). Such skepticism of the "memory archive" emerges from a sense of memory as alive; over time, memories adjust and grow, and the notion of a stable archive limits this dynamism. While I am sympathetic to this skepticism, I am also concerned by the subsequent abandonment of the memory archive: when speaking of the accumulation of memories, archives need not be interpreted as "stable spaces of storage." In fact, archival spaces remain dynamic through time and interpretation.

36. See Tuan 1979; Entrikin 1991; Lefebvre 1991; Merrifield 1993; Massey 1994; Soja 1996; Thrift 2000; Jessop, Benner, Jones, and MacLeod 2003.

37. In *The Mana of Mass Society*, Mazzarella writes: "By likening these collective forces to an *archive*, I want to invoke the sense of resources deposited and variably available for excavation and citation—for activation. By calling it a *mimetic* archive, I am picking up on the suggestion, crucial to both Adorno and Benjamin, that the mana-potential that resides in our collective experience-environment is some-

thing that we activate and apprehend as much by sensuous, mimetic tactics as by discursively citational means. It is at least as much unconscious as it is conscious. And insofar as we activate it sensuously and mimetically, we operate by way of what Benjamin, in a famously enigmatic passage, identified as the medium of the mimetic faculty: 'nonsensuous similarity'" (2017, 145).

Mazzarella's mimetic archive provides a methodology through which Benjamin's "nonsensuous similarity" can be collectively activated. Like astrology (Benjamin's example) and mass publicity (Mazzarella's example), my ethnographic archive of loss reveals how language and presence (the two foundations of ethnographic fieldwork) may activate linkages previously assumed to have been lost (but yet remain as mana-potential in the archive).

38. In using "resonance," I borrow from Susan Lepselter, who defines the term as "the intensification produced by the overlapping, back and forth call of signs from various discourses. The uncanny narratives here acquire affect, intensity, and meaning through their resonance and dissonance with other more familiar cultural narratives, those that can seem like the inevitable shape of the real and are less overtly marked as constructed narratives. Resonance describes the social, affective, and aesthetic dimension of a perspective based in apophenia, finding connections between signs, and often understanding that process as political. Here these connections are based on resemblance and repetition. This effect entails mimesis, but the resemblance is partial and fluid. It is *felt*. And the intertextual connections feel vertically layered, rather than horizontally bridged" (2016, 4). For Lepselter, these resonant threads, echoing Benjamin and Mazzarella, are "mimetic."

39. Returning to Mazzarella's "mimetic archive," the "residue" is "embedded not only in the explicitly articulated forms commonly recognized as cultural discourses, but also in built environments and material forms, in the concrete history of the senses, and in the habits of our shared embodiment" (2017, 8). Mazzarella then makes a claim for the mimetic archive to be "a reminder of what that concept [the culture concept] would have to be capable of in order to do what it must" (9). My archive of loss, then, takes Mazzarella's framing of the mimetic archive as an ethnographic challenge: What happens to this mana, this residue, these resonances, these ephemera, when we bring the promises of theory into the ethnographic everyday?

1. The Archive of the Mill

1. A warehouse, likely derived from the Malay word *godong*. At Dhanraj they are rented out as storage units.

2. Such claims are quite common and help owners navigate the archaic and restrictive development laws that limit their ability to legally keep up with a shifting economic market.

3. When I visit in January 2016, a huge sign hangs outside the compound on the main road, beckoning shoppers inside. There is no mistaking what now exists beyond the gate.

4. In 2011, one lakh equals 100,000 rupees. Thirty-five lakh rupees equals approximately US$77,500.

5. In her essay "Imperial Debris," Ann Laura Stoler frames "misrecognition" as colonial aphasia, "an inability to recognize things in the world and assign proper names to them" (2008, 210). Drawing on the language of a linguistic disorder, Stoler's sense of colonial aphasia suggests a violence lacking agency: the inability to speak, remember, and articulate the cause of such ruins is passive, even if the foundation of such ruins is rooted in intention and purpose. I disagree with Stoler's diagnosis: throughout this book, I show how, in the "postindustrial city," the ruins still materially visible are not a form of aphasia, or an inability to recognize, but instead an active *non*recognition of what remains.

6. I learn this relationship from my informants. It is for this reason that I am less invested in explaining, structurally, the changes occurring in Mumbai and more invested in exploring, affectively, the interpretations and subjectivities of my informants. My *own* "data" control the engine of this project.

7. In thinking of the agency of infrastructure, I am particularly taken by Julie Chu's work in China. Chu has shown how the destruction of infrastructure (in particular, housing) can mask the layers of state power and intervention present throughout displacement and redevelopment: as a building is transformed from a home into "an unlivable pile of rubble" (2014, 359), what originally appeared metaphorical (material as agentic) becomes an infrastructural attack. This movement from metaphor to assault is not an unawareness of infrastructural process but instead an understanding of the relationship between human and nonhuman actors in urban space: infrastructural shifts are seen and understood not only through policy but also through materiality.

8. Feeling backward from Hansen's framing of "nonrecognition," I read this struggle for recognition through Hegelian terms, as Mumbai becomes the master of the worker-slaves. In particular, I find Alexandre Kojève's (1980) interpretation of Hegel's story of the Lord and Bondsman (which he renames the Master-Slave dialectic) to be particularly helpful. For Kojève (translating Hegel), the desire for recognition becomes the absolute and most basic characteristic of humanity: he argues that human beings seek to be seen as free and equal agents, and only through mutual recognition can they lead truly satisfying lives. However, Kojève uses Hegel's dialectic to show how human beings simultaneously refuse to offer that recognition in return: as the two figures of Hegel's parable face off in battle, one of them will feel a stronger desire for self-preservation than for recognition. This decision renders that person a slave, as the victor becomes the master. Therefore this desire is always ambivalent and often pain inducing. In losing out on desired recognition, the slave-workers do not become *misrecognized*, they become *nonrecognized*.

9. Kojève's reworking of the dialectic is helpful because it moves us past Hegel's preoccupation with the Slave's desire to kill the Master (or the Bondsman's desire to kill the Lord). Instead, Kojève reveals how the Slave desires *recognition* and searches for this recognition through labor. However, while Kojève seems to suggest that the

Slave manages to find such satisfaction *through* labor, I argue—through my field-work with Dhanraj workers—that such self-recognition is not nearly enough. In-stead, the workers at Dhanraj constantly voice their need to *be recognized*: not just by themselves, each other, or even their employers but also by the city at large. While a literal translation of Hegel would identify the figure or figures in control of the means of production (the mill owner, the mill owner's family, the mill itself) as the Master, I argue that the metaphorical Master is actually the city, itself. In fact, my conversations with workers suggest this over and over again, as "the city" is believed to send messages to workers through the shifting skyline and transforming infra-structure. The dependency of Dhanraj workers on the possibility of recognition *from* the city sustains the dialectic and reveals the anachronistic nature of their subjec-tivity: they will never again be recognized as productive workers, and their own sense of satisfaction can only emerge through this unobtainable recognition.

10. Judith Butler explores the subject as "the *effect* of a prior power and as the *con-dition of possibility* for a radically conditioned form of agency" (1997, 14–15).

11. One of Butler's central inquiries (through Althusser and Foucault) is how "power that at first appears external, pressed upon the subject, pressing the sub-ject into subordination, assume a psychic form that constitutes the subject's self-identity" (1997, 3). She argues that identity is actually shaped through power, and to resist would result in a dismantling of the self: because power both forms and sub-ordinates a subject, subordination can be seen as more desirable than failing to exist at all (6–7). Butler's argument leaves her open to critiques connected to questions concerning agency and resistance, but what is particularly useful in terms of Dhan-raj workers is how "the peculiar turning of a subject against itself that takes place in acts of self-reproach, conscience, and melancholia . . . work[s] in tandem with pro-cesses of social regulation" (18–19). Working off Foucault, she shows how subordi-nated individuals may become passionately attached to, and in turn desire, their own subordination.

12. What is helpful to think through here is that the very definition of Hegel's slave is someone who prefers life to death and therefore chooses to stay alive as a slave rather than risk death in an attempt to become the master. However, in drawing on Kojève's and Butler's work, I argue that the workers' desire for recognition is a desire for that which will bring them most harm (at least psychically): a desire for and an attachment to an impossible recognition. Butler argues: "If wretchedness, agony, and pain are sites or modes of stubbornness, ways of attaching to oneself, negatively articulated modes of reflexivity, then that is because they are given by regulatory regimes as the sites available for attachment, and a subject will attach to pain rather than not attach at all" (1997, 61).

13. This is a blind refusal, however: Dhanraj workers were not seeking recognition from visible out-of-work workers because they told me they were unaware of these activists in the first place.

14. This is in contrast to Kojève's claim that "for only in and by work does man finally become aware of the significance, the value, and the necessity of his experi-ence of fearing absolute power, incarnated for him by the Master" (1980, 23).

15. Miéville (2009) calls these cities "topolgangers," as they are two cities, existing simultaneously in the same time and place, and their topographies mirror each other. And yet still they cannot (or, more accurately, they are forbidden to) see the other.

16. Walter Benjamin explains: "In Freud's view, consciousness as such receives no memory traces whatever, but has another important function: protection against stimuli. 'For a living organism, protection against stimuli is an almost more important function than the reception of stimuli; the protective shield is equipped with its own store of energy and must above all strive to preserve the special forms of conversion of energy operating in it against the effects of the excessive energies at work in the external world, effects which tend toward an equalization of potential and hence toward destruction.' The threat from these energies is one of shocks" (2007, 161).

17. Berlant explains cruel optimism as "a relation of attachment to compromised conditions of possibility. What is cruel about these attachments . . . is that the subjects who have x in their lives might not well endure the loss of their object or scene of desire, even though its presence threatens their well-being, because whatever the content of the attachment, the continuity of the form of it provides something of the continuity of the subject's sense of what it means to keep on living on and to look forward to being in the world. . . . Cruel optimism is the condition of maintaining an attachment to a problematic object in advance of its loss" (2006, 21).

18. Although there are far more ethical ways in which these processes can and should occur.

19. An air-conditioned taxi service.

20. Here I draw on Hannah Arendt to distinguish between work and labor. In *The Human Condition* (1998), Arendt presents a three-part division of human activities, being labor, work, and action (which are associated with the conditions of life, worldliness, and plurality). Arendt is very specific in distinguishing between "labor," which involves impermanent and ceaseless activities connected to the biological process of the body—such as obtaining and cooking food, bearing children, and so forth—and the activities of work, which are connected to the "artificial" world of things (particularly industrial production). While Arendt sees laborers as animal laborans, workers transcend this natural, animallike state and, through their manipulation of the natural world and construction of a semipermanent artificial realm, become human, or homo faber.

21. Perhaps this collision of experience is also the impossible space of the dialectical image? Fragments that can't be, which reveal the mythologies that are not? In *The Arcades Project* Benjamin claims: "It is not that what is past casts its light on what is present, or what is present its light on what is past; rather, an image is that wherein what has been comes together in a flash with the now to form a constellation. In other words: image is dialectics at a standstill. For while the relation of the present to the past is purely temporal, the relation of what-has-been to the now is dialectical: not temporal in nature but figural [*bildlich*]. Only dialectical images are genuinely historical" (1999, [N3, 1] 463).

2. *The Archive of the Worker*

1. I take the term "unvisibility" from China Miéville's novel *The City and the City* (2009). For more on this mode of unseeing, see chapter 1, "The Archive of the Mill."

2. See Gordon 1997, 167.

3. See Petryna 2002.

4. In thinking through how the chemical debris of industrial Southeast Chicago becomes embodied by residents (including herself), Christine Walley writes: "Social theorists generally consider the 'materiality' of class to be expressed in things like bank balances or how one's job fits into an overall field of social relations or economic production. But there is another kind of materiality to class that is less often talked about and that environmental justice advocates gesture toward. Although I may have traveled far away from Southeast Chicago during the course of my life, I am forced to acknowledge that, along with many other current and former residents, I carry the legacy of time spent there in the chemical composition of my body. Just as the industry of Southeast Chicago remains, even after it has left, so too the land, water, and air of the area have become a part of me, even though I no longer live there" (2013, 118). This embodiment of space is critical in understanding how inequality is expressed through the physical and medical repercussions of class and labor. And while Walley draws attention to the force of environmental hazards on the bodies of working-class people, this embodiment of industrial labor is not merely chemical: these traces are also the result of standing with, of moving like, of becoming a machine.

5. On India, see Cohen 1995, 1998; Lamb 1997, 2000, 2002, 2009, 2014; Brijnath 2014. On aging elsewhere, see Myerhoff 1978; Kaufman 1985, 1994; Carsten 2000; Livingston 2003; Kaufman and Morgan 2005; Leibing 2005; Sokolovsky 2009; Lynch 2012; Danely 2014.

6. By drawing on the language of "cyborg" workers, I place myself in conversation with scholars engaging Donna Haraway's "Manifesto for Cyborgs" (1985). While this conversation is critical to current science and technology studies (STS) literature, I am most invested in how it emerges from the intersections of anthropology, queer/gender/disability ("crip") studies, and speculative fiction. In particular, see Downey, Dumit, and Williams's "Cyborg Anthropology" (1995); Balsamo's *Technologies of the Gendered Body: Reading Cyborg Women* (1995); Yuen's "On the Edge of Spaces: 'Blade Runner,' 'Ghost in the Shell,' and Hong Kong's Cityscape" (2000); Allison's "Cyborg Violence: Bursting Borders and Bodies with Queer Machines" (2001); Robertson's "Japan's First Cyborg? Miss Nippon, Eugenics and Wartime Technologies of Beauty, Body and Blood" (2001); Riskin's "The Defecating Duck, Or, The Ambiguous Origins of Artificial Life" (2003); Kafer's "The Cyborg and the Crip: Critical Encounters" (2013); and Ahuja's "Intimate Atmospheres: Queer Theory in a Time of Extinctions" (2015).

7. See Samuel 1977; Nardinelli 1990; Berg 1994; Gray 1996; Honeyman 2007; Humphries 2010.

8. This is an alternative approach—which I argue is critically ethnographic—to

debates raised by Karl Marx in *Capital* (that industrial labor will "transform the worker, from his very childhood, into a part of a specialized machine"; 1990, 547) and labor reformers, arguing that laboring bodies were becoming machines. Instead, I am arguing that laboring bodies—as industrial cyborgs—are *embodying* mechanization through experiences of pain and memories of work. This embodying is the work of archivization.

9. Here I am distancing myself from a historical-materialist critique of industrial labor and instead considering the *affective* dimensions of such a critique (for example, Marx's observation in *Capital*: "The one-sidedness and even the deficiencies of the specialized individual worker become perfections when he is part of the collective worker. The habit of doing only one thing converts him into an organ which operates with the certainty of a force of nature, while his connection with the whole mechanism compels him to work with the regularity of a machine" (1990, 469). And later: "A system of machinery, whether it is based simply on the co-operation of similar machines, as in weaving, or on a combination of different machines, as in spinning, constitutes itself a vast automaton as soon as it is driven by a self-acting prime mover. . . . An organized system of machines to which motion is communicated by the transmitting mechanism from an automatic centre is the most developed form of production by machinery. Here we have, in place of the isolated machine, a mechanical monster whose body fills whole factories, and whose demonic power, at first hidden by the slow and measured motions of its gigantic members, finally bursts forth in the fast and feverish whirl of its countless organs" (502–503).

10. I use the word "retrenchment" because this English word is the term used by workers to describe their forced retirement.

11. Martin Jay explains, "The immediate, passive, fragmented, isolated, and unintegrated inner experience of *Erlebnis* was, Benjamin argued, very different from the cumulative, totalizing accretion of transmittable wisdom, of epic truth, which was *Erfahrung*" (1998, 48–49). According to Benjamin, a symptom of modernity involves a transition from *Erfahrung* to *Erlebnis*: as Dhanraj workers resist this movement through their practice of collective experience, their engagement with time, memory, and history challenges an urban narrative that frames them as archaic and antimodern. The question, of course, is how to simultaneously activate *both Erfahrung and Erlebnis*.

12. Ebron explains:

I use the term *public memory* to signal the process by which a group of people who were once dismissed and never thought of as part of a "public" might become visible to themselves and to others—a public—through their use of memory. I invoke public memory in conversation with more commonly recognized terms, such as *collective memory* and *social memory*. In contrast to the fields these terms evoke, my interest is in the very processes of making communal identity and in the formation of emergent subjectivities. This requires an explicit departure from understandings of memory that assume a basis in personally experienced, remembered events. Rather than evoking actual events of history from which subjects enact their past, public memory directs our attention to the very process of how new publics come into being and the ways in which new subjectivities are formed by public cultural forms and by an ever-circulating set of ideas that turns into an emergent possibility. (2014, 147–148)

13. In writing of narrative memory, Joëlle Bahloul explains that "time is punctuated by the quotidian use of domestic objects and relationships. It is a slow time, interrupted only by imprecise dates." These imprecise dates are punctuated only by "religious rituals or . . . genealogical history," which become the "accents in the rhythm of daily life." But these memories, Bahloul stresses, are measured *outside* of linear, chronological time (1996, 102). At first I was unwilling to let Sushila teach me these lessons about cyclical time. However, her stories felt far more meaningful once I let go of dates and instead looked for context or events that complemented the memories she handed me during such moments of storytelling. Her archive of memory was full of snapshots, and she spread them out for me whenever I asked, as long as I allowed for her own method of organization.

14. See Ferguson 1999.

15. *Erlebnis*, on the other hand, relies on consciousness and is engaged through a deliberate engagement with the world. Benjamin suggests that *Erlebnis* becomes a rupture, which cuts and fragments *Erfahrung*, transforming a collective form of experience into an isolated form of individual experience. At first glance, this rupture seems to devalue *Erfahrung* and endanger the archive of the body through modernity's attachment to *Erlebnis*.

16. In his foreword to *Berlin Childhood around 1900*, Howard Eiland explains Benjamin's textual engagement: "The text as a whole continually superimposes the author's present day on his past, so that everywhere a dead and resurrected world of play is framed in the perspective of exile, and everywhere the man is felt to be prefigured in the child. In this way the text fully realizes the idea of 'intertwined time.' . . . [The child] lives in the antiquity of the everyday. . . . His relationship to things is wholly mimetic" (Benjamin 2006, xiv).

17. For example, in "On the Mimetic Faculty" Benjamin explains how the child plays at being "a windmill and a train" as well as "a shopkeeper and a teacher" (1978, 333).

18. Benjamin explains: "Experience is indeed a matter of tradition, in collective existence as well as private life. It is less the products of facts firmly anchored in memory than of a convergence in memory of accumulated and frequently unconscious data" (2007, 157).

19. In *The Arcades Project*, Benjamin writes: "There is a not-yet-conscious knowledge of what has been: its advancement has the structure of awakening" (1999, [K1,2] 389). If the present moment is that of awakening, then memories lie buried in the realm of sleep and dreams. In this way, recollections appear, disappear, and reappear similarly to the flashes through which a dream is remembered. Familiar, yet strange. Always shifting through the retelling. Benjamin argues that traditionally *Erfahrung* was rooted in the realm of voluntary memory and based in ritual,

storytelling, and other collective forms. This form of experience is famously articulated through Proust's recollection of eating a madeleine in Combray: drawing on this story, Benjamin suggests that what Proust experienced *accidentally* could be harnessed *deliberately* and *collectively* for/in the modern moment. When relying on active memory, a process both fractured and reactive and accessed through the work of his intellect, Proust had failed to clearly remember the town he spent his childhood in. However, it was this pastry, its sensuous properties, that activated his embodied memory and "transported him back to the past."

20. In particular, I am thinking about the critical links made between labor's bodily degradation and medical anthropology's engagement with embodied loss and breakdown. See Scheper-Hughes 1992; Lock 1993b; Martin 1994; Wacquant 2003; Lock and Farquahar 2007; Slavishak 2008; Livingston 2012; Lynch 2012; Jain 2013; Walley 2013; Hankins 2014; Solomon 2016.

21. *Industrial pain*: Joseph D. Hankins's work on "Buraku" leather workers in Japan draws attention to how experiences of work-induced pain are "not a feeling *for* but, rather, a feeling *with*." He explains how such storytelling practices "were a form of self-care, enabled through a connection with others, as well as a form of self-fashioning" (2014, 187). *Dislocation*: Like the lyric poet, Benjamin argues that the storyteller has become an antimodern subject, unrecognizable and illegible in a modern world.

22. Benjamin writes: "We know that in his work Proust did not describe a life as it actually was, but a life as it was remembered by the one who had lived it. And yet even this statement is imprecise and far too crude. For the important thing for the remembering author is not what he experienced, but the weaving of his memory, the Penelope work of recollection. Or should one call it, rather, a Penelope work of forgetting? Is not the involuntary recollection, Proust's *mémoire involuntaire*, much closer to forgetting than what is usually called memory?" (2007, 202). Similarly, Susan Buck-Morss has noted that Benjamin "retained the notion that the Arcades project would present collective history as Proust had presented his own—not 'life as it was,' nor even life remembered, but life as it has been 'forgotten.' Like dream images, urban objects, relics of the past century, were hieroglyphic clues to a forgotten past. Benjamin's goal was to interpret for his own generation these dream fetishes in which, in fossilized form, history's traces had survived" (1999, 39).

23. In 2014, a twenty-four-year-old factory worker and poet named Xu Lizhi committed suicide by jumping out a window in his dormitory at Foxconn, an electronics manufacturer in Shenchen, China. Foxconn manufactures most of the world's iPhones. After his death, fellow factory workers published his poems. "The Last Graveyard" is one of them.

24. This was her age in 2009.

3. The Archive of the Chawl

1. In *Archive Fever*, Derrida claims: "As much as and more than a thing of the past, before such a thing, the archive should call into question the coming of the future. ... It is a question of the future, the question of the future itself, the question of a response, of a promise and of a responsibility for tomorrow. The archive: if we want to know what that will have meant, we will only know in times to come" (1995, 33–36). The archive of the chawl shows, through domestic habitation, how chawl dwellers reconcile their knowledge of the past with their fear of the future, all while occupying an alternative present.

2. I take this call from Carolyn Dinshaw, who writes that the aim of her work on medieval texts and queer time is "not only to explore but also to claim the possibility of a fuller, denser, more crowded *now* that all sorts of theorists tell us is extant but that often eludes our temporal grasp. This means fostering temporalities other than the narrowly sequential. This means taking seriously lives lived in other kinds of time" (2012, 4). I follow this call through the frame of "chawl time."

3. To live in the space of the archive is a bit like living in exile. While none of my informants live in spatial exile, they do live in temporal exile. In writing of war, identity, and home in Sri Lanka, Sharika Thiranagama explains: "Northern Muslims' geographical proximity meant that their past landscape had not disappeared from sensory experience but remained just on the horizon. Furthermore, whenever they could, during ceasefires, they visited their homes and saw the decay over time. They lived close enough to their homes to note the work of time in them, and also too far in time and space to be politically welcomed back into those homes. Both place and people were engaged in simultaneous processes of transforming and becoming, both not entirely of their own volition" (2011, 147). In archiving "loss," I draw awareness to a sense of disappearing/being disappeared, which I watch my informants experience throughout my fieldwork. Like Thiranagama's sense of northern Muslims in Sri Lanka, it is this proximity of space and the distance of time that make this loss all the more tragic.

4. The historian Antoinette Burton, in writing of women's autobiographies and novels in colonial India, asks: "What counts as an archive? Can private memories of home serve as evidence of political history? What do we make of the histories that domestic interiors, once concrete and now perhaps crumbling or even disappeared, have the capacity to yield? And given women's vexed relationship to the kinds of history that archives typically house, what does it mean to say that home can and should be seen not simply as a dwelling-place for women's memory but as one of the foundations of history—history conceived of, that is, as a narrative, a practice, and site of desire?" (2003, 4). In drawing on these intimate renderings of history, Burton argues that such renderings "democratize" the historical archive, revealing it as an "unstable source of history." In drawing on Burton's critical contribution, I push her intervention further: I am not interested in democracy; I am interested in a conceptual revolution as a way of reframing stagnation as survival. While there is nothing revolutionary in "seeing" the chawl or inhabiting its interiors, there *is* revolution in upsetting our obsession with "progress."

5. Shannon Dawdy writes: "Ruins and patinated objects have a special capacity for inducing different temporal states. I am concerned here with understanding the human experience of pastness in two distinct ways, the first a largely slow, structural one (*social stratigraphy*) and the other an effervescent mode that occurs in flashes and uneven tempos (*social relativity of time*). In neither case do these senses of pastness have the linear, teleological character of most historical narratives" (2016, 25).

6. Barbara Voss writes: "Tracing the landscape biography . . . illustrates how experiences of the . . . landscape and the social meanings of structured space are standpoint-dependent" (2008, 170). In writing against the current wave of infrastructure studies in anthropology, I use the standpoint approach of "landscape biography" to widen the recognizable narrative of development in Central Mumbai. Voss continues: "Landscape biography engenders more complicated, nuanced interpretations of the archaeological record. Further, it highlights the ways in which archaeological deposits are interconnected: far from being discrete 'sites,' they represent nodes of social interaction and material practices within a larger social landscape" (2008, 171). In thinking through the habitation of contemporary domestic sites in Central Mumbai, this approach is critical in subverting a narrative overwhelmingly concerned with development and disappearance: by borrowing "landscape biographies" from an archaeologically minded methodology and applying this intervention to ethnography deeply invested in the material world, the archive of the chawl expands what is previously imagined as possible within and across the landscape of Central Mumbai.

7. I draw the term "allochronous" from geologic taxonomy: allochronic segmentation refers to species (or populations) that do not exist at the same time. In referring to "the allochronous space of modernity," I am arguing that chawl dwellers (and mill workers) exist as modern subjects but do not occupy the hegemonic frame of "the modern time."

8. Several ethnographies have helped me conceptualize the archive of the chawl, invested as they are in engaging material life as innovative museums and collections. In particular, this chapter-archive draws on Michael Taussig's ethnographic museum (2004), Jennifer Gabrys's technological fossils (2013), and Gastón R. Gordillo's "nodes of rubble" (2014). These museums, these landfills, these spaces of rubble are all bounded places that, while contained, are simultaneously leaky: history haunts the Gold Museum in Taussig's Bogotá. Electronics become mummified and embalmed, allowing chemicals to linger and perhaps spread beyond Gabrys's mounds of refuse. Crumbling and ruined objects assert a gravitational pull on local communities living among Gordillo's rubble. Similarly, the archive of the chawl is constantly endangered by the encroaching vertical city, but, in the space of "chawl time," residents are able to immerse themselves in this archival space through a temporal disavowal. Like Taussig's museum, the ethnographic archive reveals that which has become lost, forgotten, made seemingly unvisible. Like Gabrys's literal reading of "landfill" (as "a kind of archive, which assembles . . . through a default accumulation of wasted matter tightly packed in airless cells"; 2013, 130), the ethnographic archive

can become metaphorical and air-full when time challenges compression and artifacts and stories are allowed to breathe again. Like Gordillo's framing of "nodes of rubble," the ethnographic archive reveals how what *appears* to be abandoned ruins are also/actually "the constitutive elements of spatial constellations" (2014, 21).

9. A wealth of South Asia–based urban studies literature (Doshi 2013; Ghertner 2014) has grappled with the relationship between tenants, developers, and the state in unregulated spaces. While chawls are legally recognized and legitimate domestic spaces, they have often been framed similarly as and compared to unregulated spaces, particularly through media representations. However, I want to consciously separate my work from scholarship focusing on slums in order to address a very separate set of pressures and struggles experienced by chawl dwellers.

10. For example, on March 15, 2014, seven people were killed and four were injured when a chawl collapsed in the suburban Mumbai neighborhood of Santa Cruz East.

11. While middle-class chawls occasionally defy this stereotype in their seeming stability and structural soundness, complicating the narrative of housing crises and poverty, for the purposes of this chapter, I will limit my discussion of chawls to the housing structures originally designated for working-class migrants employed by the textile industry.

12. For an extended intervention on chawls and chawl life, see Neera Adarkar's edited volume *Galleries of Life: The Chawls of Mumbai* (2011).

13. While the most iconic, these multistoried chawls are not the only forms found throughout Mumbai. Beti chawls, often known as "railway chawls" because they were often used to house railway workers, were single-story structures, and while they usually lacked a courtyard, sometimes they had a wide gallery running up against the side of a neighboring building. Other times, however, they simply opened out onto the street and, at best, had a sidewalk that could be used for washing, cooking, and bathing. While none of my Dhanraj informants lived in beti chawls, many of their friends did, and I spent a considerable amount of time in these alternate forms.

14. In *Futures Past: On the Semantics of Historical Time*, Koselleck establishes the existence of multiple historical times, which are based on different social and political institutions, organizations, and practices. In addition, different social and political groups have different historical times, even if they coexist geographically and chronologically (Koselleck 2004, 2). His work shows how we make use of rules and measurements from "natural" time, but he argues that the coming of modernity (which he defines as beginning with the Enlightenment) brought about new ways of understanding history, which he in turn shows to be tied to notions of "progress." It is an expectation for the future, and a desire to control that future (as well as a belief in the possibility of doing so), that—for Koselleck—marks this modernity. He writes: "In differentiating past and future, or (in anthropological terms) experience and expectation, it is possible to grasp something like historical time" (3).

15. "At once person-specific and interpersonal, expectation also takes place in the today; it is the future made present; it directs itself to the not-yet, to the nonexperienced, to that which is to be revealed. Hope and fear, wishes and desires, cares and

rational analysis, receptive display and curiosity: all enter into expectation and constitute it" (Koselleck 2004, 259).

16. "At first glance, nostalgia is a longing for place, but actually it is a yearning for a different time—the time of our childhood, the slower rhythms of our dreams. In a broader sense, nostalgia is rebellion against the modern idea of time, the time of history and progress. The nostalgic desires to obliterate history and turn it into private or collective mythology, to revisit time like space, refusing to surrender to the irreversibility of time" (Boym 2001, xv). Similarly, Susan Buck-Morss, drawing on Walter Benjamin, notes how children's mimetic improvisation suggests an earlier moment within a lifetime in which existed an "unsevered connection between perception and action" (1999, 263–264)—an insight into the potential for reenchanting the disillusioned modern moment.

17. For Boym (2001), space, in addition to the critical lens of time, is central to any conceptualization of nostalgia, as the word itself is derived from the Greek, longing (*algia*) for home (*nostos*): nostalgia is the longing for a home that no longer exists, or never existed: a foreign country different from the present (Lowenthal 2015).

18. Because textile mills are sites of informalizing labor, such as garment factories and storage warehouses, the continued presence of skeletal textile mills actually enables spaces of unregulated industry.

19. This is not to suggest that such communities are overlooked by structures of power invested in these narratives: however, I am suggesting that, while queer bodies and communities are subject to the regulations of such narratives (which likely result in social and economic exclusion as well as social and legal persecution), they have been simultaneously excluded from benefiting from the protection and rights of full citizenship.

20. Freeman's argument involves a shift in theoretical approaches to "queer": instead of seeing queer theory as avant-garde or progressive, instead of imagining "queer" as located "ahead of actually existing social possibilities," here queer theory is drawn back from this emergent position.

21. See Freeman 2010, 3. I would argue that the notion of "chrononormativity" is also unrealized, perhaps another form of mythology. I am grateful to William Mazzarella for reminding me of this critical point.

22. In *Vibrant Matter: A Political Ecology of Things*, Jane Bennett writes: "These items, they shimmied back and forth between debris and thing—between on the one hand, stuff to ignore, except insofar as it betokened human activity . . . and on the other hand, stuff that commanded attention in its own right, as existents in excess of their association with human meanings, habits, or projects" (2010, 4). In drawing on this framing of materiality, the archive of the chawl engages this vibrant matter with the temporal layering of domestic space.

23. My archival approach to domestic space is greatly influenced by the social archaeologist Victor Buchli's work on the lives of residents in Moscow's Narkomfin Community House. He explains: "I would like to understand how individuals coped with rapidly changing social contingencies by examining their negotiations of domestic architectural space; that space we most directly associate with the most

fundamental structures of human society" (1999, 3). Buchli frames the Narkomfin Community House as an archive and draws attention toward absence and discontinuity (in addition to presence and continuation) in these intimate domestic spaces. In understanding the space of the chawl as an archive, I utilize Buchli's methodology but move beyond material layers in order to address "time" as archival debris, as well as material remains.

24. While each family was supposed to reclaim the redeveloped version of their previous unit, what instead happened was a free-for-all land grab. Prem Kumar tells me: "We didn't fight or anything but what happened was a few of the tenants took three-hundred-square-foot flats that weren't theirs ... there were three or four cases where the owner as well as the tenants both got these big flats. There were about fifteen people who were living here earlier and five more people just barged into their flats ... and the chawl committee decided 'whatever flat you have, stick to what you have now and then take the course of law and fight it out.' And people who entered bigger flats and sat there and living there, and, you know, these other people have accepted the smaller flats and are living there."

When I ask him why this was allowed to continue, he explains there was no proper legal documentation of who should be assigned which flat. When certain tenants sought clarification, "the officials kept saying 'come later, come later,' they kept procrastinating. So some of them [tenants] bribed [the officials] ... and some of them ... were fighting among themselves but then decided 'screw the law, we'll just find our houses and claim them: this is what we want.' So they were better off." I ask him why he didn't fight for a bigger flat, and he tells me: "Our family ... was basically trying to keep everybody happy and we said we'd go according to the law and nothing much happened. When we got smaller houses—because quite a few people got smaller houses—we accepted whatever we got because we wanted to come back here ... our work places were close by ... we didn't want to *not* live here. So we just ... accepted." While the eagerness of the newly formed MHADA *did* result in a new building, the disorganization of the new authority left many tenants in worse situations than they had been in before. As a result, Prem Kumar sees the government as the villains responsible for his current living situation. I think of this story when I talk to tenants who have yet to experience redevelopment, such as Manda and Saraswati: their distrust of the government, and particularly MHADA, is understandable considering the devastating governmental mistakes chawl dwellers like Prem Kumar suffered from.

I ask him if he has any receipts or official documents from this period of redevelopment, but he tells me he is unsure what happened to them. During the strikes, none of the mill workers had the resources to approach a lawyer, so he and eleven of his neighbors handed their paperwork over to a tenant with greater economic resources. When I ask him what came of the case, he tells me that only four out of the eleven were successful in the courts. "And they succeeded because they had made bribes. Because the mills were on strike we didn't have the capacity [for bribes] so we said 'we'll see what happens' and we didn't fight it out." The irony there, of course, is that the post-MHADA intervention, occurring during the authority's infancy, resulted not in transparency and justice but in rising corruption and unfairness.

25. While the earlier chawl, Bhadak Chawl, was a Hindu-only building and primarily Maharashtrian, the redeveloped Shivaraj Bhavan houses people of all religions and regional affiliations. Prem Kumar tells me: "This building has everyone, Hindus, Muslims, Catholics. People from all religions stay here like a family. The riots were near here but they didn't come to this area. Right down the street here is a mosque but there were no issues during the riots. Outsiders try to attack this area but because of our cooperation this was not a problem. You can see here [*points to the street*], children play in the street. We are all like a family." The power of memory plays out through Prem Kumar's sense of community. Most chawls were fairly homogeneous spaces prior to the strike of the early 1980s. However, as many unemployed workers left Mumbai for their ancestral homes during the strike, empty units drew a more diverse tenancy demographic. When chawls entered redevelopment schemes, some tenants chose to sell their claims on their units and move elsewhere, both avoiding the years spent in transit camps and profiting off the downtown real estate market and relocating to the northern suburbs. Such sales helped contribute to an added diversity in the chawls: while I hear stories indicating the preference of selling within "the community" (of Maharashtrian Hindus), the power of the rupee lessened the pull of such sentiments.

26. She never explains the details of her marriage to me, but this union is one of downward mobility for her. In comparison to her new home, the chawl of her childhood was quite spacious, and her family's financial situation felt—at least to a young girl—relatively stable. After marrying, she finds herself living in a 120-square-foot unit with nine other people: her husband, her husband's four sisters and two brothers, her mother-in-law, and her mother-in-law's sister. There wasn't enough room on the floor for everyone to sleep, so they built a platform above their unit, on the roof, where her brothers-in-law could sleep. She tells me, "When I got married I was really scared about the responsibility [of marriage]. But my family members were very supportive and cooperative. They treated me like their own child."

27. Even so, it is close to the Lower Parel train station, and I find myself passing its broken gates quite often. For years I would push past the corrugated gate, waiting for some trace of development on the empty lot. I was continually shocked to find it empty, even as the neighborhood became more and more congested with new buildings. Such abandonment contributed to my sense of haunting, as if the unmarked gate really did lead through the looking glass and into an alternate time/place.

28. This lifestyle proves to be grueling and lonely for teenage Sushila, who remembers: "When I came home from the mill I would engage in household work. I engaged in all my duties and responsibilities and that is why I didn't get any time to make friends. When I was first married I was very scared, but I had to be strong." She continually stresses to me how lucky she was to marry into her husband's family, where everyone was kind to her and treated her as if she were their own daughter or sister. Still, she tells me it took five to six years before she felt comfortable in her

marital home. The stress of poverty, mill work, and domestic responsibilities take a toll. However, five years after her marriage, one of her husband's brothers gets married and leaves the unit. After that she tells me things ease up for her. This is perhaps the combination of one fewer mouth to feed and one fewer body to take up space, or perhaps the accumulation of five years of experience as a chawl wife and mill worker.

29. See Derrida 1988.

30. In mapping out chawl life in the early half of the twentieth century, Rajnarayan Chandavarkar explains: "The extent of overcrowding brought about by high rents, housing shortages and low wages meant that the inhabitants of the chawl spilled over into the courtyard of the wadi and the street. The importance of the street did not derive simply from the fact that men lived on it. Street life imparted its momentum to leisure and politics . . . the working-class actively organized on the streets. . . . The street corner offered a meeting place. . . . Social investigators continue to be bemused that, when asked to give 'an account of their leisure time activities,' the vast majority of workers 'could not be specific and said that they pass time roaming, which they consider a mode of relaxation'" (1998, 103–104).

31. Janaki Abraham's work in Bikaner, Rajasthan, shows how classical distinctions between the "private" and the "public" spheres have prevented "not only a full exploration of how these categories are socially and culturally defined, but also a fuller understanding of the production of space in everyday life, especially in relation to social relationships, hierarchies and power" (2010, 195).

32. In a 2006 article, the widely circulated newspaper *Daily News and Analysis* reported: "Many people choose to keep staying under their crumbling roofs, which may collapse under the monsoon rains. These people are skeptical about the timely redevelopment of their homes by the Maharashtra Housing and Area Development Authority (MHADA). The people are scared that they will have to spend years, perhaps decades, in transit accommodation. Indeed, there have been cases where people have gone to transit camps with their children, and now their grandchildren are growing up there without prospects of shifting back to their redeveloped buildings" (Kelkar 2006).

A 2011 article in the *Hindustan Times* clarified: "Since the 1970s, many residents living in old, dilapidated buildings have moved to MHADA transit camps hoping to return after their premises were redeveloped. However, the redevelopment was disallowed due to various reasons—either the building fell prey to road widening projects or was reserved as a playground or recreation ground or stuck in litigation. The result: Some continued to languish in these transit camps for years, while others sold off their premises" (Kamath 2011). While the second article celebrates a victory for tenants who occupy transit camps for more than two decades (their move "home"), the rise in maintenance costs alone might result in another northern move soon after.

33. Here I am talking about the grammatical structure of ". . ." and drawing on social theorist Lauren Berlant's (2012) emerging work on life in the ellipsis.

34. For more on the question of scale in the global city, see Smith 2002; Sassen 2007; Harvey 2008; Ong 2011.

4. The Archive of the Strike

1. This, in addition to stories about his hatred for Maharashtrian workers and his disdain for women. These two points challenge my ability to trust him, while also pushing me to look beyond his own biases for a deeper story.

2. Initially I wrote: "Kishan is lying to me." But as I worked through what I understood to be transpiring between the two us, I realized that was not the "truth," either.

3. In thinking through Kishan's performance, I am indebted to Aimee Meredith Cox's framing of "shapeshifting," which she defines, within the context of black girls at the Fresh Start Shelter in Detroit, as "a method used to 'find solutions, master concentration, recall, recontextualize ideas, and map out plans'" ([Katherine] Schreiber 2012). The emphasis on memory and mapping is significant because they reflect the ways in which black women mobilize history, whether officially documented or bricolaged through recall and desire, to give new meaning to social contexts that engender cartographic capacities beyond particular physical or ideological sites" (2015, 28).

4. Also see Bleek 1987; McGranahan 2017.

5. My aim throughout this chapter is to explore the ambivalence of "identity" and "belonging" among my North Indian informants. In doing so, I am indebted to a great deal of anthropological scholarship invested in both of these categories.

6. In "After Auschwitz," an essay in *Negative Dialectics*, Adorno writes: "If negative dialectics calls for the self-reflection of thinking, the tangible implication is that if thinking is to be true—if it is to be true today, in any case—it must also be a thinking against itself" (2007, 365). What is critical here is a constant resistance against, a constant refusal to embrace, a framing of the world that empowers the violence of othering through identity, as enabled by a positive dialectic. North Indian workers are aware that their Maharashtrian coworkers are members of the Shiv Sena, a historically violent group invested in ridding Mumbai (and Maharashtra) of "the other." The question this invocation of Adorno and negative dialectics raises here is whether Kishan's position can be imagined as a calling of identity-thinking into question "from within" or whether his North Indianness becomes an identity to be inhabited against the dominant identity. I am arguing for the former, particularly given the ambiguities of Kishan's self-understanding and the ambivalences of his belonging.

7. When Maharashtrian workers speak to me of North Indian migrants, they speak in the language of *desh* (country)—even if India is a nation composed of twenty-nine officially recognized states, I am being told that Maharashtra is a bounded entity and those from outside its borders originate in a foreign country. This suggests the political ambiguity of *desh* vis-à-vis the modern nation-state, as it can stand both for "India" *and* for any number of more locally defined conceptions of homeland.

8. In particular, see Hansen 1999, 2001; Eckert 2003; Upadhyay 2004; A. Sen 2007; M. Menon 2012b.

9. See Morris 1965; van Wersch 1992; D'Monte 2002; Menon and Adarkar 2004; Upadhyay 2004.

10. Here Jennifer Scappettone is specifically referencing her definition of gossip, which she understands as "knowledge that's faulty, that takes the risk of being horribly wrong even as it risks being horribly right about unwanted truths. In this way it's like poetry, for the fault lines of poetry are also the fault lines of possible knowledge: like doubt, they are inventive, damaging, erotic" (2016, 102). I find this particularly helpful in thinking through the meaning behind and within the untruths circulating among North Indian Dhanraj workers.

11. For Muñoz, disidentification is a third form of identification: while identity can be forged through dominant categories (whiteness, straightness, Maharashtrianness, Hindu, etc.) and counteridentification (a seeming rejection of identity through resistance, which still reinscribes identity hierarchies: blackness, queerness, North Indianness, Muslim, etc.), "disidentification" (for Muñoz) is a third category that rejects these two forms of identity construction through emergent possibilities. I argue that North Indian untruths are a practice in this emergence, which rejects linear identity formation and allows for potentially political/radical formations. While Muñoz is framing disidentifications through notions of intersectionality (Crenshaw 1991), I am thinking North Indian relationships with self, history, and time through the ambivalent dialectic between disidentity and nonidentity.

12. Muñoz argues: "The use-value of any narrative of identity that reduces subjectivity to either a social constructivist model or what has been called an essentialist understanding of the self is especially exhausted" (1999, 5). In Dhanraj, the identities of "North Indian" and "Maharashtrian" carry this exhaustion, as they seem to offer simple explanations for animosities that are far more complicated and ambivalent. Instead, I follow Muñoz, who shows how "identity is enacted by minority subjects who must work with/resist the conditions of (im)possibility that dominant culture generates" (6).

13. I want to emphasize that, while my interest in "untruth" as ethnographic material is theoretically invested in a critique of "identity," I am also well aware of the importance of "belonging" through identity categories, particularly in terms of vulnerable, politically unstable groups (like North Indians and other ethnic and religious minorities in Maharashtra). Additionally, I am in no way suggesting that North Indian workers at Dhanraj reject their own identity as North Indian (specifically Bihari or from Uttar Pradesh), Brahmin (as all my North Indian informants are), Hindu, or Hindi speaking. However, I also want to think through how an ambivalent identity—one that is both dynamic and "othered"—can be reconciled.

14. Like my North Indian informants, Adorno was "othered" in his homeland (although unlike my North Indian informants he also became a refugee and a survivor of genocide).

15. Adorno further explains:

> But such dialectics is no longer reconcilable with Hegel. Its motion does not tend to the identity in the difference between each object and its concept; instead, it is suspicious of all identity. Its logic is one of disintegration: of a disintegration of the prepared and objectified form of the concepts which the cognitive sub-

ject faces, primarily and directly. Their identity with the subject is untruth. With this untruth, the subjective pre-formation of the phenomenon moves in front of the nonidentical in the phenomenon, in front of the *individuum ineffabile*. The totality of identical definitions would correspond to the wish-fulfillment picture of traditional philosophy: to the a priori structure and to its archaistic late form, ontology. Yet before any specific content, this structure—as abstractly maintained—is negative in the simplest sense: it is spiritualized coercion. The power of that negativity holds real sway to this day. What would be different has not begun as yet. (2007, 145)

16. Therefore, for Adorno, "a turn towards nonidentity is the hinge of negative dialectics" (2007, 12).

17. This negative dialectic is now a refusal of the dialectic of recognition found within the archive of the mill: for more on this, see chapter 1.

18. Adorno writes: "Identity and contradiction of thought are welded together. Total contradiction is nothing but the manifested untruth of total identification. Contradiction is nonidentity under the rule of a law that affects the nonidentical as well" (2007, 6).

19. This unity is important because the strike is not actually a success, in terms of its seeming economic aims: no resolution was ever reached, and it is, for all intents and purposes, still happening. However, as a political project it is incredibly successful.

20. While my North Indian informants never confess to me they are telling untruths, I have become convinced they do not believe there is ontological truth behind their words. But there *is* affective truth. I can't "prove" this awareness, but I still *believe* it.

21. In asking this question, I draw on scholarship invested in the interpretation of oral history, particularly the work of Luisa Passerini, Alessandro Portelli, and Shahid Amin. Dhanraj testimonies show how "oral sources tell us not just what people did, but what they wanted to do, what they believed they were doing and what they now think they did" (Portelli 2010, 50).

22. Which called into question any possible objective and rationalized link between memory and identity.

23. For more on this relationship between time and imagination, see chapter 3, "The Archive of the Chawl."

24. Indeed, I would argue that this sentiment intersects (negatively) with Adorno's concern over the normalization of memory and history (see Adorno 2005).

25. Most workers lacked contracts and reliable employment before the strike: even though the strike was understood to mark the beginning of the industry's steady decline, it also marked the first moment of truly formalized labor within Mumbai textile mills.

26. For more on Ghati and Konkani culture, see Adarkar 2011.

27. When speaking of his children, Kishan always refers to them as his wife's children.

28. *Kalyug* is the "age of Kali" and the last of the four stages of the world's temporal cycle.

29. For an excellent account of both the strike and Datta Samant's involvement, see Hugo van Wersch's 1992 study, *Bombay Textile Strike 1982–1983*.

30. Samant's political persona is rocky from the start. He is then elected to the Maharashtra Vidhan Sabha (legislative assembly) as a Congress Party candidate and serves briefly as a legislator. For twenty-one months, between June 1975 and March 1977, India is declared to be in a state of emergency, allowing Prime Minister Indira Gandhi the power to rule by decree. "The Emergency," as it is popularly known, suspends elections and civil liberties, resulting in mass arrests, censorship, and intimidation. Because of his reputation as a "militant unionist," Samant is arrested in 1975, despite belonging to the Congress Party (which Prime Minister Gandhi represented). After two years in prison, his popularity increases dramatically after his release in 1977.

31. Hemant Babu writes: "On October 23, hundreds of workers from the Standard mills marched for several kilometers to the residence of militant trade union leader Dr Datta Samant, asking him to take over the leadership of their struggle. Reluctant Dr Samant finally agreed to lead the textile workers and struck an immediate rapport with thousands of workers by lashing out at the monopoly RMMS union in the first gate meeting outside Standard mills. In a matter of days workers from mill after another [*sic*] flocked behind Dr Samant and he emerged to be the undisputed leader of the textile workers in Mumbai" (2002, 3).

32. Even as many workers, including a large number of North Indian workers, continue to work throughout the strike: a ghostly prequel to Dhanraj workers working when the mills "no longer exist."

33. Samant's position is also anomalous vis-à-vis the hardening "economy of stances" (see Hansen 1999).

34. In order to understand the reach and mobilization of the Shiv Sena, it is critical to begin with the Samyukta Maharashtra Samiti (SMS, or United Maharashtra Committee) movement of the 1940s and 1950s, which fought for an independent Marathi-speaking state. The SMS galvanized Maharashtrians across caste lines, as these antagonisms grew out of the anti-Brahmin movements of the 1920s and 1930s. The targets of the anti-Brahmin movement were the non-Marathi-speaking Shetji (rich person) and the Marathi-speaking Bhatji (Brahmin priest). Emerging from the activism of Jotirao Phule in the middle to late nineteenth century, the Maharashtrian anti-Brahmin movement reacted to the tiny minority of Brahmin elite, estimated by G. S. Gore to constitute only 3 to 5 percent of the population. While many Gujarati Parsis (a merchant class) moved to Bombay toward the end of the nineteenth century, Pune remained the cultural center of Maharashtra, and it remained socially, politically, and economically a Brahman-dominated city. While this demographic makeup fostered a sense of caste-based resentment, the SMS dropped the anti-Bhatji aspect of the movement in favor of a more distant enemy: the foreign industrialists and business class from outside of Maharashtra. While the SMS was originally formed in 1946 as the Samyukta Maharashtra Sabha, it was unified on February 6,

1956, under the leadership of Keshavrao Jedhe in Pune. The second-largest city in Maharashtra, and the former center of the Maratha Empire, Pune lies 180 kilometers southeast of Mumbai. This originating location is quite important in understanding the development of SMS ideology, particularly in contrast to the Mumbai-based Shiv Sena. The historian Y. D. Phadke wrote: "Invariably, the struggle for Samyukta Maharashtra was described as basically a struggle between the capitalists and the masses whose legitimate aspirations were throttled by the decision-makers amenable to the pressure exerted by the industrialists and business men" (1979, xxi). The Shiv Sena draws strength from many former SMS supporters, most notably Bal Thackeray's father, former Samyukta leader Keshav Sitaram Thackeray. However, the Sena differed in its political positioning in at least one significant way. While the SMS—centered in Pune and understood to exist in opposition to the industrial class of its coastal urban neighbor—forged alliances with communist organizers and understood its role in terms of worker agitation, the Shiv Sena emerged within a class of white-collar Bombay workers (most centrally, Thackeray), who saw their most obvious and immediate enemy to be educated South Indian migrants (Gupta 1982, 61). Unlike the SMS, Thackeray had no issue with the industrial elite of Bombay and instead embraced capitalism as the ideology of nationalism, just as he virulently opposed communism as its antithesis.

35. It cannot be accidental that Bal Thackeray inaugurated the Shiv Sena ten years after the Battle of Bombay and trafficked in the legacy left behind by the disillusioned Marathi-speaking middle class.

36. Gupta goes on to explain: "The Shiv Sena . . . appeals to the regional and linguistic sentiments of the Maharashtrians much as the Samayukta Maharashtra Samithi had done earlier. It also invokes the glorious days of Shivaji Maharaj, of the Maratha Empire and the Hindu *pad padshahi* (Shivaji's Hindu Empire). The Shiv Sena thrives on the belief that Maharashtrians, who are a superior community with an exemplary history and culture, are the underdogs in Bombay, as they are exploited by migrants from other states. The hortatory message of the Shiv Sena is almost exclusively based on this point" (1982, 49). Gupta stresses, however, that the Sena cannot be understood as a continuation of the SMS. Unlike the SMS, the Sena was a very urban phenomenon, emerging within Bombay and remaining most present within the Bombay-Thane industrial belt. While the contemporary face of the Shiv Sena stretches across rural Maharashtra and throughout much of India, the Sena's early reach and focus were very Bombay-centric and did not engage with Pune city at all. However, similar anxieties concerning cultural and economic marginalization due to migration still lent power to the movement.

37. While the SMS concentrates on the geopolitical stakes of Maharashtrian identity, the Sena originates as an antipolitical movement of direct action: a Robin Hood figure operating primarily outside of the law. Each act of violence performed by the Sena has managed to strengthen its platform, revealing the limits and precariousness of state sovereignty (Katzenstein 1973; Hansen 1999, 2001, 2008; N. Menon and Adarkar 2004).

38. However, Ram Joshi reveals the contradictions inherent within this descrip-

tion when he explains: "The definition thus has the effect of dividing the residents of Bombay into three mutually exclusive categories of (1) sons of the soil, (2) those who look upon Maharashtra as their home-land, and (3) 'outsiders,' and implies that the term 'Maharashtrian' extends to the first two categories. The Shiv Sena, however, has not always been consistent in its use of the term. In its survey concerning executive positions referred to above, for example, among the 75 'Maharashtrian' executive officers not a single Parsee, Christian, Muslim, Sindhi or Gujarati is included. On the other hand, Marathi-speaking people resident in other states for decades are still regarded as Maharashtrians. Thus, it appears that for the Shiv Sena the terms 'Maharashtrians' and 'Marathi-speaking persons' are interchangeable. This suggests purposeful ambivalence on a vital point" (Joshi 1970, 967–978).

39. In his history of the industry's decline, Daryl D'Monte writes: "[Datta Samant] undoubtedly had the support of the majority of the workers. . . . As we can see from his election to the Lok Sabha (a year after the 18 month strike) and the presence of thousands of people for his funeral in 1997 . . . whatever industrialists, the state and the elite thought of Samant's militant tactics, the working-class revered him" (2002, 88, 164). Similarly, Hugo van Wersch writes: "The very attitude which caused so much suffering to the workers, namely his refusal to call off the strike, has helped him retain his image as an incorruptible leader. His popularity today in the sympathy that tens of thousands of textile workers feel for him in spite of the collapse of the strike" (1992, 257).

40. It is such sentiments that allow Samant to emerge as the heroic symbol of Mumbai's tragic deindustrialization. His iconic status seems absolute and long-lasting: a revolutionary who fought and died for the common man. On October 10, 2010, a group of students create a community Facebook page in honor of Datta Samant, which is full of smiling pictures of "Doctorsaheb" and comments of love and support (from 109 "followers"). One "fan" wrote that he was "the uncrowned king of labour movement across the world."

41. As part of a push to reclaim the city as a locus of Marathi identity and as a central space for Maharashtrians, the Shiv Sena officially changed the name "Bombay" to "Mumbai" in 1995 (for a detailed social and political history, see Hansen 2001).

42. The Shiv Sena cannot claim such an ambition.

43. The lost object: an object that never in fact existed (Lacan 1994).

44. While Samant still planned a massive strike through his Maharashtra Girni Kamghar Union (MGKU), Sudarshan explains: "Prime Minister Indira Gandhi did not support the strike and she did a lot of things to prevent the strike from being successful. She asked the police and the local authorities to help the workers come and go to the mills, for the workers who wanted to keep working."

45. I continue to ask Mr. Lal for these records throughout the entirety of my fieldwork: for a year he promises to get them for me but puts me off each time I remind him. Then, in November 2009, he claims they were destroyed in the fire (for more on this, see chapter 5, "The Archive of the Fire"). I still have no idea why he wouldn't share the employee records with me, and it seems he's now taken that answer to the grave with him.

46. Eve Kosofsky Sedgwick asks how do we "open a space for moving from the rather fixated question Is a particular piece of knowledge true, and how can we know? to the further question: What does knowledge *do*—the pursuit of it, the having and exposing of it, the receiving again of knowledge of what one already knows? *How*, in short, is knowledge performative, and how best does one move among its causes and effects?" (2002, 124).

47. Judith Butler shows how performative acts express "*fabrications* manufactured and sustained through corporeal signs and other discursive means" and that such performative acts have "no ontological status apart from the various acts which constitute [their] reality" (1990, 136).

48. By drawing on Veena Das's work, I understand the 1982 strike as a "critical event," one in which the aftermath of the strike provides a space through which "new modes of action come into being" and new forms of identity and memory work are "acquired by a variety of political actors" (1995, 6).

49. Derrida argues: "'Archive' is only a *notion*, an impression associated with a word and for which, together with Freud, we do not have a concept. We have only an impression, an insistent impression through the unstable feeling of a shifting figure, of a schema, or of an in-finite or indefinite process" (1995, 29). Derrida's "Freudian Impression" is the tension between the archive as preserver of history and memory and the death drive's need for its destruction and forgetting.

50. *Bhaiyyas* translates literally as "little brother" but is used (often derogatorily) to refer to North Indian Hindi speakers.

51. Even as Maharashtrians accuse North Indians of being archaic in their attachments to caste, North Indians also leverage this narrative, as Kishan shows how the accusation of casteism can be thrown back in the other direction.

52. This is especially true if that worker is unemployed: for more on this, see chapter 2, "The Archive of the Worker."

5. The Archive of the Fire

1. In her poetic archaeology of hazardous-waste sites, *The Republic of Exit 43: Outtakes and Scores from an Archaeology and Pop-Up Opera of the Corporate Dump*, Jennifer Scappettone writes: "Rumor ekes out of the infrastructure of managed landscape. When regulations arrive decades late and impact reports prove inconclusive, it is gossip that helps us divine that the infrastructure of tragedy turns out to be one and the same as the infrastructure of abundance, in both material and aesthetic senses: it suggests that the infrastructure of cancerous byproducts may trail the infrastructure of planned obsolescence" (2016, 103).

2. See Smith 2002; Atkinson and Bridge 2005.

3. Here I distinguish these large-scale fires, visible within a declining industry, from the banality of mill fires occurring at the height of industrial production. Within a highly operational mill, fire was common and, although occasionally destructive, small in scale. Before the strike, Mumbai mills were run around the clock, staffed in three rotational shifts (including a night shift). I was told accidental fires

were not uncommon, and the high volume of workers present twenty-four hours a day allowed for early detection and immediate action. It is only after the strike and the subsequent reopening of many mills that the "mysterious night fires" are equated with arson and extra-legal development efforts.

4. Neil Smith writes: "The revanchist city is, to be sure, a dual and divided city of wealth and poverty. . . . But it is more. It is a divided city where the victors are increasingly defensive of their privilege, such as it is, and increasingly vicious defending it. . . . The benign neglect of 'the other half,' so dominant in the liberal rhetoric of the 1950s and 1960s, has been superseded by a more active viciousness that attempts to criminalize a whole range of 'behavior,' individually defined, and to blame the failure of post-1968 urban policy on the populations it was supposed to assist" (1996, 227). Also see MacLeod 2002; Manley 2005.

5. By "gentrification," I am loosely referring to class-based population displacement resulting from an increased cost of living. For an excellent challenge to gentrification in the Indian city, see Ghertner 2014.

6. On Mumbai being understood as postindustrial, see Mehrotra 2008; Mhaskar 2012.

7. In fact, all the mill records were stored in a downtown office, far from the mill itself. I had been aware of this for months.

8. In 2006, fourteen out of the fifty-eight original mills were still operating in some capacity. Of those fourteen, the National Textile Corporation controls ten, and four remain in the private sphere. But this number has been shrinking steadily. As of 2012, only six of those ten NTC mills were still operating. Within the private sphere, three of the four remained semioperational. Most of these mills stopped processing raw cotton and retained only spinning and weaving operations.

9. For more on this, see D'Monte 2002.

Epilogue

1. Drawing again on Benjamin, Peter Fenves writes: "Messianic time is not another time; it is just time—time and nothing but 'plastic' time. The paradisal character of space, toward which the painterly plane tends, accords with the messianic character of time, which is thus charged with tension and can be called 'full' because every stretch of time contains all of time. In 'World and Time' Benjamin says of the first category: 'there is nothing continuous' (6:99); the opposite condition characterizes the other concept under consideration, namely time—'turned' by 'now'—is the coming world" (2011, 244). Here Fenves, through Benjamin, argues that "plastic" time—messianic time—reflects the natural progression of the world, which, through language, people attempt to control and manipulate.

2. In the introduction to their translation of Walter Benjamin's *The Arcades Project*, Howard Eiland and Kevin McLaughlin write: "Welcomed into a present moment that seems to be waiting just for it—'actualized,' as Benjamin likes to say—the moment from the past comes alive as never before. In this way the 'now' is itself experienced as preformed in the 'then,' as its distillation" (1999, xii).

3. Later Hanssen clarifies: "'Natural history' referred to the mutual imbrication of nature and history, for both converged in the moment of transience that befell both. As such, Benjamin's novel conception of this old term put to shame all philosophical claims to foundationalism, including the traces of essentialism that seemingly still beleaguered his own conception of ur-history (*Urgeschichte*)" (1998, 16).

4. In unraveling the potentiality of natural history, Hanssen reveals how Benjamin's interpretation of the concept also liberates "allegory" (and allegory's dialectical potential is: the meaning of allegory is not fixed, but constantly changing/open to revision and reformulation) from the limits of representation and instead reframes it as a "thanatological mode of interpretation" (1998, 33) invested in the "debris of human history" (15). I find this helpful in framing Dhanraj as a prophetic space: meanings are emergent, they are about becoming, and they are constantly shifting through the process of decay. The only way to experience this is to live through it.

References

Abel, Emily, and Margaret Nelson, eds. 1990. *Circles of Care: Work and Identity in Women's Lives*. Albany: State University of New York Press.

Abraham, Janaki. 2010. "Veiling and the Production of Gender and Space in a Town in North India: A Critique of the Public/Private Dichotomy." *Indian Journal of Gender Studies* 17 (2): 191–222.

Adarkar, Neera, ed. 2011. *The Chawls of Mumbai: Galleries of Life*. Delhi: Imprint-One.

Adarkar, Neera, and V. K. Phatak. 2005. "Recycling Mill Land." *Economic and Political Weekly* 40 (51): 5365–5368.

Adorno, Theodor W. 1991. *Notes to Literature*, vol. 1. Translated by Shierry Weber Nicholsen. New York: Columbia University Press.

Adorno, Theodor W. 2005. "The Meaning of Working Through the Past." In *Critical Models: Interventions and Catchwords*, trans. Henry W. Pickford. New York: Columbia University Press.

Adorno, Theodor W. 2007. *Negative Dialectics*. New York: Continuum.

Ahmed, Sara. 2004. *The Cultural Politics of Emotion*. New York: Routledge.

Ahuja, Neel. 2015. "Intimate Atmospheres: Queer Theory in a Time of Extinctions." *GLQ* 21 (2–3): 365–385.

Alcalá, Rosa. 2012. "Inflection." In *The Lust of Unsentimental Waters*, 17. Bristol: Shearsman Books.

Allison, Anne. 2001. "Cyborg Violence: Bursting Borders and Bodies with Queer Machines." *Cultural Anthropology* 16 (2): 237–265.

Ameeriar, Lalaie. 2017. *Downwardly Global: Women, Work, and Citizenship in the Pakistani Diaspora*. Durham, NC: Duke University Press.

Amin, Shahid. 1995. *Event, Metaphor, Memory: Chauri Chaura, 1922–1992*. Berkeley: University of California Press.

Anand, Nikhil. 2011. "Pressure: The Polytechnics of Water Supply in Mumbai." *Cultural Anthropology* 26 (4): 542–563.

Anand, Nikhil. 2012. "Municipal Disconnect: On Abject Water and Its Urban Infrastructures." *Ethnography* 13 (4): 487–509.

Anand, Nikhil. 2015. "Leaky States: Water Audits, Ignorance and the Politics of Infrastructure." *Public Culture* 27 (2): 305–330.

Anand, Nikhil. 2016. "Hydraulic Publics." Special issue on Public Infrastructures/Infrastructural Publics, *Limn* 7: 97–100.

Anand, Nikhil. 2017. *Hydraulic City: Water and the Infrastructures of Citizenship in Mumbai*. Durham, NC: Duke University Press.

Anand, Nikhil, and Anne Rademacher. 2011. "Housing in the Urban Age: Inequality and Aspiration in Mumbai." *Antipode* 43: 1748–1772.

Anjaria, Jonathan Shapiro. 2006. "Street Hawkers and Public Space in Mumbai." *Economic and Political Weekly* 41 (6): 2140–2146.

Anjaria, Jonathan Shapiro. 2009. "Guardians of the Bourgeois City: Citizenship, Public Space, and Middle-Class Activism in Mumbai." *Cities and Community* 8 (4): 391–406.

Appel, Hannah. 2012. "Walls and White Elephants: Oil Extraction, Responsibility, and Infrastructural Violence in Equatorial Guinea." Special issue on Infrastructural Violence, *Ethnography* 13 (4): 439–465.

Appel, Hannah, Nikhil Anand, and Akhil Gupta. 2015. "The Infrastructure Toolbox." Theorizing the Contemporary, *Cultural Anthropology* website, September 24. https://culanth.org/fieldsights/725-the-infrastructure-toolbox.

Arendt, Hannah. 1978. *Between Past and Future: Eight Exercises in Political Thought*. New York: Penguin Books.

Arendt, Hannah. 1990. *On Revolution*. London: Penguin Books.

Arendt, Hannah. 1998. *The Human Condition*. Chicago: University of Chicago Press.

Arendt, Hannah. 2004. *The Origins of Totalitarianism*. New York: Schocken Books.

Arondekar, Anjali. 2009. *For the Record: On Sexuality and the Colonial Archive in India*. Durham, NC: Duke University Press.

Arthur, Chris. 1983. "Hegel's Master-Slave Dialectic and a Myth of Marxology." *New Left Review* 9: 67–75.

Ashraf, Syed Firdaus. 1996. "India Has No Future. Sometimes I Feel My Life Is a Failure" (interview with Dr. Datta Samant). *Rediff*. http://www.rediff.com/news/1996/16datta.htm.

Atkinson, Rowland, and Gary Bridge. 2005. *Gentrification in a Global Context: The New Urban Colonialism*. New York: Routledge.

Babu, Hemant. 2002. *Death in an Industrial City: Testimonies of Life around Bombay Textile Strike of 1982*. Noida: V. V. Giri National Labour Institute.

Bachelard, Gaston. 1968. *The Psychoanalysis of Fire*. Boston: Beacon Press.

Bachelard, Gaston. 1994. *The Poetics of Space*. Boston: Beacon Press.

Bahloul, Joëlle. 1996. *The Architecture of Memory: A Jewish-Muslim Household in Colonial Algeria, 1937–1962*. New York: Cambridge University Press.

Baines, Edward. 1835. *History of the Cotton Manufacture in Great Britain*. London: Fisher, Fisher, and Jackson.

Bakhtin, M. M. 1981. *The Dialogic Imagination: Four Essays*. Translated by Caryl Emerson and Michael Holquist. Austin: University of Texas Press.

Balsamo, Anne. 1995. *Technologies of the Gendered Body: Reading Cyborg Women.* Durham, NC: Duke University Press.

Barndt, Kerstin. 2010. "Layers of Time: Industrial Ruins and Exhibitionary Temporalities." *PMLA* 125 (1): 134–141.

Baron, Ava, and Eileen Boris. 2007. "'The Body' as a Useful Category for Working-Class History." *Labor: Studies in Working-Class History of the Americas* 4 (2): 23–43.

Barthes, Roland. 1972. *Mythologies.* New York: Hill and Wang.

Barthes, Roland. 1975. "On Leaving the Cinema." In *The Rustle of Language*, 345–349. Translated by Richard Howard. New York: Hill and Wang.

Bear, Laura. 2007. "Ruins and Ghosts: The Domestic Uncanny and the Materialization of Anglo-Indian Genealogies in Kharagpur." In *Ghosts of Memory: Essays on Remembrance and Relatedness*, edited by J. Carsten, 36–57. Malden, MA: Blackwell.

Beckert, Sven. 2014. *Empire of Cotton: A Global History.* New York: Vintage Books.

Benjamin, Walter. 1978. *Reflections: Essays, Aphorisms, Autobiographical Writings.* New York: Schocken Books.

Benjamin, Walter. 1999. *The Arcades Project.* Cambridge, MA: Belknap Press of Harvard University Press.

Benjamin, Walter. 2005. *Walter Benjamin: Selected Writings.* Vol. 2, pt. 2, *1931–1934.* Edited by Michael W. Jenkins. Cambridge, MA: Harvard University Press.

Benjamin, Walter. 2006. *Berlin Childhood around 1900.* Cambridge, MA: Belknap Press of Harvard University Press.

Benjamin, Walter. 2007. *Illuminations: Essays and Reflections.* New York: Schocken Books.

Benjamin, Walter. 2009. *The Origin of German Tragic Drama.* Translated by John Osborne. Brooklyn, NY: Verso.

Bennett, Jane. 2010. *Vibrant Matter: A Political Ecology of Things.* Durham, NC: Duke University Press.

Berg, Maxine. 1991. "On the Origins of Capitalist Hierarchy." In *Power and Economic Institutions: Reinterpretations in Economic History*, edited by Bo Gustafsson, 173–194. Aldershot, UK: Edward Elgar.

Berg, Maxine. 1994. *The Age of Manufactures: Industry, Innovation, and Work in Britain, 1700–1820.* 2nd ed. New York: Routledge.

Bergvall, Caroline. 2014. *Drift.* New York: Nightboat Books.

Berlant, Lauren. 2006. "Cruel Optimism." *differences: A Journal of Feminist Cultural Studies* 17 (3): 20–36.

Berlant, Lauren. 2007. "Nearly Utopian, Nearly Normal: Post-Fordist Affect in *La Promesse* and *Rosetta*." *Public Culture* 19 (2): 273–301.

Berlant, Lauren. 2011. *Cruel Optimism.* Durham, NC: Duke University Press.

Berlant, Lauren. 2012. "Culture@Large: On Biopolitics and the Attachment to Life." Panel discussion at the annual conference of the American Anthropological Association. San Francisco, November 17.

Berlant, Lauren. 2016. "The Commons: Infrastructures for Troubling Times." *Environment and Planning D: Society and Space* 34 (3): 393–419.

Berry, Wendell. 1994. "Enemies." In *Entries: Poems*, 38. New York: Random House.

Béteille, André. 1990. "Race, Caste and Gender." *Man*, New Series, 25 (3): 489–504.

Bhabha, Homi. 2012. *The Location of Culture*. New York: Routledge.

Bhambra, Gurminder K. 2007. *Rethinking Modernity: Postcolonialism and the Sociological Imagination*. Basingstoke: Palgrave Macmillan.

Bhattacharya, Sourish. 2009. "Kaminey and the Pao of Politics." *India Today*, August 15, 2009.

Bhattacherjee, Debashish. 1999. "Organized Labour and Economic Liberalization, India: Past, Present and Future." In *Labour and Society Program: Discussion Paper*. Geneva: International Institute for Labour Studies. Discussion Series no. 105.

Bhomik, Sharit K. 2006. "Contesting Urban Space in Mumbai: 'Citizens' versus 'Slum Dwellers.'" In *Contested Transformations: Changing Economies and Identities in Contemporary India*, edited by M. E. John, P. K. Jha, and S. S. Jodhka, 147–164. New Delhi: Tulika Books.

Bjorkman, Lisa. 2014. "Un/known Waters: Hedging Everyday Risks of Infrastructural Breakdown in Mumbai." *Comparative Studies of South Asia, Africa and the Middle East* 34 (3): 497–517.

Bjorkman, Lisa. 2015. *Pipe Politics, Contested Waters: Embedded Infrastructures of Millennial Mumbai*. Durham, NC: Duke University Press.

Bleek, Wolf. 1987. "Lying Informants: A Fieldwork Experience from Ghana." *Population and Development Review* 13 (2): 314–322.

Bonhomme, Julien. 2012. "The Dangers of Anonymity: Witchcraft, Rumor, and Modernity in Africa." *HAU: Journal of Ethnographic Theory* 2 (2): 205–33.

Bose, Sugata, and Ayesha Jalal. 1997. *Nationalism, Democracy, and Development: State and Politics in India*. New Delhi: Oxford University Press.

Boym, Svetlana. 1994. *Common Places: Mythologies of Everyday Life in Russia*. Cambridge, MA: Harvard University Press.

Boym, Svetlana. 2001. *The Future of Nostalgia*. New York: Basic Books.

Boym, Svetlana. 2008a. "Ruinophilia: Appreciation of Ruins." *Atlas of Transformation*. http://monumenttotransformation.org/atlas-of-transformation/html/r /ruinophilia/ruinophilia-appreciation-of-ruins-svetlana-boym.html.

Boym, Svetlana. 2008b. "Tatlin, or, Ruinophilia." *Cabinet Magazine*, no. 28 ("Bones"). Adapted from *Architecture of the Off-Modern*, a FORuM Project Publication of the Temple Hoyne Buell Center for the Study of American Architecture at Columbia University.

Brass, Paul R. 1997. *Theft of an Idol: Text and Context in the Representation of Collective Violence*. Princeton, NJ: Princeton University Press.

Braverman, Harry. 1974. *Labor and Monopoly Capital: The Degradation of Work in the Twentieth Century*. New York: Monthly Review Press.

Breman, Jan. 1996. *Footloose Labour: Working in India's Informal Economy*. Cambridge: Cambridge University Press.

Breman, Jan. 1999. "The Study of Industrial Labour in Post-colonial India—the

Formal Sector: An Introductory Review." In *The Worlds of Industrial Labour*, edited by Jonathan P. Parry, Jan Breman, and Karin Kapadia, 1–42. New Delhi: Sage.

Brijnath, Bianca. 2014. *Unforgotten: Love and the Culture of Dementia Care in India*. Oxford: Berghahn.

Brockmeir, Jess. 2010. "After the Archive: Remapping Memory." *Culture and Psychology* 16 (1): 5–35.

Buchli, Victor. 1999. *An Archaeology of Socialism*. Oxford: Berg.

Buchli, Victor, and Gavin Lucas, eds. 2001. *Archaeologies of the Contemporary Past*. London: Routledge.

Buck-Morss, Susan. 1977. *The Origins of Negative Dialectics: Theodor W. Adorno, Walter Benjamin, and the Frankfurt Institute*. New York: Free Press.

Buck-Morss, Susan. 1999. *The Dialectics of Seeing: Walter Benjamin and the Arcades Project*. Cambridge, MA: MIT Press.

Burawoy, Michael. 1979. *Manufacturing Consent: Changes in the Labor Process under Monopoly Capitalism*. Chicago: University of Chicago Press.

Burnett-Hurst, A. R. 1925. "Labour and Housing in Bombay: A Study in the Economic Conditions of the Wage-Earning Classes in Bombay." Master's thesis, University of London.

Burra, Sundar. 2000. *A Journey towards Citizenship: The Byculla Area Resource Center, Mumbai*. Mumbai: SPARC.

Burton, Antoinette. 2003. *Dwelling in the Archive: Women Writing House, Home, and History in Late Colonial India*. New York: Oxford University Press.

Butler, Judith. 1990. *Gender Trouble*. London: Routledge.

Butler, Judith. 1997. *The Psychic Life of Power: Theories in Subjection*. Stanford, CA: Stanford University Press.

Byler, Darren. 2012. "Walking Around in Lauren Berlant's 'Elliptical Life.'" Fieldsights, Anthro Happenings, *Cultural Anthropology* online, December 10. https://culanth.org/fieldsights/32-walking-around-in-lauren-berlant-s-elliptical-life.

Byrne, Denis. 2007. *Surface Collection: Archaeological Travels in Southeast Asia*. Lanham, MD: AltaMira Press.

Callard, Felicity J. 1998. "The Body in Theory." *Environment and Planning D: Society and Space* 16: 387–400.

Calvino, Italo. 1972. *Invisible Cities*. Translated by William Weaver. San Diego: Harcourt.

Canetti, Elias. 1984. *Crowds and Power*. New York: Farrar, Straus and Giroux.

Canning, Kathleen. 1999. "The Body as Method? Reflections on the Place of the Body in Gender History." *Gender and History* 11 (3): 499–513.

Carney, Judith A. 2001. *Black Rice: The African Origins of Rice Cultivation in the Americas*. Cambridge, MA: Harvard University Press.

Carrithers, Michael, Steven Collins, and Steven Lukes. 1985. *The Category of the Person: Anthropology, Philosophy, History*. Cambridge: Cambridge University Press.

Carsten, Janet. 2000. "Introduction: Cultures of Relatedness." In *Cultures of Re-*

latedness: New Approaches to the Study of Kinship, edited by J. Carsten, 1–36. Cambridge: Cambridge University Press.

Carsten, Janet. 2004. *After Kinship*. Cambridge: Cambridge University Press.

Carsten, Janet. 2007. *Ghosts of Memory: Essays on Remembrance and Relatedness*. Malden, MA: Blackwell.

Caru, Vanessa. 2011. "The Making of a Working-Class Area: The Worli BDD Chawls (1920–40)." In *The Chawls of Mumbai: Galleries of Life*, edited by N. Adarkar, 26–36. Delhi: ImprintOne.

Chakrabarty, Dipesh. 1989. *Rethinking Working-Class History: Bengal, 1890–1940*. Princeton, NJ: Princeton University Press.

Chandavarkar, Rajnarayan. 1994. *The Origins of Industrial Capitalism in India: Business Strategies and the Working Classes in Bombay, 1900–1940*. Cambridge: Cambridge University Press.

Chandavarkar, Rajnarayan. 1998. *Imperial Power and Popular Politics: Class, Resistance and the State in India, c. 1850–1950*. New York: Cambridge University Press.

Chandavarkar, Rajnarayan. 1999. "Questions of Class: The General Strikes in Bombay, 1928–29." In *The Worlds of Indian Industrial Labour*, edited by J. P. Parry, J. Breman, and K. Kapadia, 205–238. New Delhi: Sage.

Chandavarkar, Rajnarayan. 2004. "From Neighbourhood to Nation: The Rise and Fall of the Left in Bombay's Girangaon in the Twentieth Century." Introductory essay in Meena Menon and Neera Adarkar, *One Hundred Years, One Hundred Voices: The Mill Workers of Girangaon: An Oral History*, 7–80. Calcutta: Seagull Books.

Chandavarkar, Rajnarayan. 2009a. *History, Culture and the Indian City: Essays*. Cambridge: Cambridge University Press.

Chandavarkar, Rajnarayan. 2009b. "Perspectives on the Politics of Class." In *Industrial Work and Life: An Anthropological Reader*, edited by J. P. Parry, M. Mollona, and G. de Neve, 405–414. Oxford: Berg.

Channel, David F. 1991. *The Vital Machine: A Study of Technology and Organic Life*. Oxford: Oxford University Press.

Chatterjee, Indrani. 2004. *Unfamiliar Relations: Family and History in South Asia*. New Brunswick, NJ: Rutgers University Press.

Chatterjee, Partha. 2004. *The Politics of the Governed: Reflections on Popular Politics in Most of the World*. New York: Columbia University Press.

Chu, Julie. 2014. "When Infrastructures Attack: The Workings of Disrepair in China." *American Ethnologist* 41 (2): 351–367.

Cohen, Lawrence. 1995. "Toward an Anthropology of Senility: Anger, Weakness and Alzheimer's in Banaras, India." *Medical Anthropology Quarterly* 9: 314–334.

Cohen, Lawrence. 1998. *No Aging in India: Alzheimer's, the Bad Family, and Other Modern Things*. Berkeley: University of California Press.

Confino, Alon. 1997. "Collective Memory and Cultural History: Problems of Method." *American Historical Review* 102 (5): 1386–1403.

Cornish, Mary. 2007. "Numbers." In *Red Studio*, 50–51. Oberlin: Oberlin College Press.

Cox, Aimee Meredith. 2015. *Shapeshifters: Black Girls and the Choreography of Citizenship*. Durham, NC: Duke University Press.

Crenshaw, Kimberlé. 1991. "Mapping the Margins: Intersectionality, Identity Politics, and Violence against Women of Color." *Stanford Law Review* 43 (6): 1241–1299.

Csordas, Thomas. 1990. "Embodiment as a Paradigm for Anthropology." *Ethos* 18: 5–47.

Cvetkovich, Ann. 1992. *Mixed Feelings: Feminism, Mass Culture, and Victorian Sensationalism*. New Brunswick, NJ: Rutgers University Press.

Danely, J. 2014. *Aging and Loss: Mourning and Maturity in Contemporary Japan*. New Brunswick, NJ: Rutgers University Press.

Das, Veena. 1995. *Critical Events: An Anthropological Perspective on Contemporary India*. Delhi: Oxford University Press.

Dave, Naisargi. 2012. *Queer Activism in India: A Story in the Anthropology of Ethics*. Durham, NC: Duke University Press.

Dawdy, Shannon Lee. 2016. *Patina: A Profane Archaeology*. Chicago: University of Chicago Press.

de Certeau, Michel. 1984. *The Practice of Everyday Life*. Berkeley: University of California Press.

DeHaan, Arjan. 1999. "The Badli System in Industrial Labour Recruitment: Managers' and Workers' Strategies in Calcutta's Jute Industry." In *The Worlds of Indian Industrial Labour*, edited by J. P. Parry, J. Breman, and K. Kapadia, 271–302. New Delhi: Sage.

De Kosnik, Abigail. 2016. *Rogue Archives: Digital Cultural Memory and Media Fandom*. Cambridge, MA: MIT Press.

De Neve, Geert. 1999. "Asking For and Giving Baki: Neo-Bondage, or the Interplay of Bondage and Resistance in the Tamilnadu Power-Loom Industry." In *Industrial Work and Life: An Anthropological Reader*, edited by J. P. Parry, M. Mollona, and G. de Neve, 363–386. Oxford: Berg.

De Neve, Geert. 2005. *The Everyday Politics of Labour: Working Lives in India's Informal Economy*. New Delhi: Social Science Press.

De Neve, Geert, and Henrike Donner. 2006. *The Meaning of the Local: Politics of Place in Urban India*. London: Routledge.

Derrida, Jacques. 1988. "Signature Event Context." In *Limited Inc.*, 1–34. Evanston, IL: Northwestern University Press.

Derrida, Jacques. 1995. *Archive Fever: A Freudian Impression*. Translated by Eric Prenowitz. Chicago: University of Chicago Press.

DeSilvey, C. 2006. "Observed Decay: Telling Stories with Mutable Things." *Journal of Material Culture* 11 (3): 318–338.

Desjarlais, Robert. 1992. *Body and Emotion: The Aesthetics of Healing in the Nepal Himalayas*. Philadelphia: University of Pennsylvania Press.

Desjarlais, Robert. 1997. *Shelter Blues: Sanity and Selfhood among the Homeless*. Philadelphia: University of Pennsylvania Press.

Desjarlais, Robert. 2003. *Sensory Biographies: Lives and Deaths among Nepal's Yolmo Buddhists*. Berkeley: University of California Press.

Dick, P. K. [1968] 2017. *Do Androids Dream of Electric Sheep?* New York: Del Ray.

Dinshaw, Carolyn. 2012. *How Soon Is Now? Medieval Texts, Amateur Readers, and the Queerness of Time*. Durham, NC: Duke University Press.

D'Monte, Darryl. 2002. *Ripping the Fabric: The Decline of Mumbai and Its Mills*. Delhi: Oxford University Press.

D'Monte, Darryl. 2006. *Mills for Sale: The Way Ahead*. Mumbai: Marg Publications on behalf of the National Centre for the Performing Arts.

Dolar, Mladen. 1991. "'I Shall Be with You on Your Wedding-Night': Lacan and the Uncanny." *Rendering the Real* 58: 5–23.

Doshi, Sapana. 2013. "The Politics of the Evicted: Redevelopment, Subjectivity, and Difference in Mumbai's Slum Frontier." *Antipode: A Radical Journal of Geography* 45 (4): 844–865.

Doshi, Sapana. 2014. "Imperial Water, Urban Crisis: A Political Ecology of Colonial State Formation in Bombay, 1850–1890." *Review: Journal of the Fernand Braudel Center* 37 (3/4): 173–218.

Doshi, Sapana. 2017. "Embodied Urban Political Ecology: Five Propositions." *Area* 49 (1): 125–128.

Doshi, Sapana, and Ranganathan Malinin. 2017. "Contesting the Unethical City: Land Dispossession and Corruption Narratives in Urban India." *Annals of the American Association of Geographers* 107 (1): 183–199.

Dossal, Mariam. 1996. *Imperial Designs and Indian Realities: The Planning of Bombay City, 1845–1875*. Delhi: Oxford University Press.

Downey, Gary Lee, Joseph Dumit, and Sarah Williams. 1995. "Cyborg Anthropology." *Cultural Anthropology* 10 (2): 264–269.

Dudley, Kathryn Marie. 1994. *The End of the Line: Lost Jobs, New Lives in Postindustrial America*. Chicago: University of Chicago Press.

Eagleton, Terry. 1991. *Ideology: An Introduction*. London: Verso.

Easterling, Keller. 2014. *Extrastatecraft: The Power of Infrastructure Space*. London: Verso.

Ebron, Paulla. 2014. "Slavery and Transnational Memory: The Making of New Publics." In *Transnational Memory: Circulation, Articulation, Scales*, edited by Chiara De Cesari and Ann Rigney, 147–168. Berlin: Walter de DeGruyter.

Ebron, Paulla. 2015. "Which Memory." In *Transatlantic Memories of Slavery*, edited by Elisa Bordin and Anna Scacchi, 133–160. Amherst, NY: Cambria Press.

Eckert, Julia M. 2003. *The Charisma of Direct Action: Power, Politics, and the Shiv Sena*. New Delhi: Oxford University Press.

Edensor, T. 2005. *Industrial Ruins: Space, Aesthetics and Materiality*. Oxford: Berg.

Edwards, Richard. 1979. *Contested Terrain: The Transformation of the Workplace in the Twentieth Century*. New York: Basic Books.

Ellison, Ralph. [1952] 1995. *Invisible Man*. New York: Vintage Books.

Elyachar, Julia. 2005. *Markets of Dispossession: NGOs, Economic Development, and the State in Cairo*. Durham, NC: Duke University Press.

Elyachar, Julia. 2012. "Next Practices: Infrastructure, Public Goods, and the State from the Bottom of the Pyramid." *Public Culture* 24 (1): 109–129.

Elyachar, Julia. 2014. "Upending Infrastructure: Tamarod, Resistance, and Agency after the January 25th Revolution in Egypt." *History and Anthropology* 25 (4): 452–471.

Eng, David L., with J. Halberstam and José Esteban Muñoz. 2005. "Introduction: What's Queer about Queer Studies Now?" *Social Text* 23 (3–4): 1–17.

Engels, Friedrich. [1844] 1987. *The Condition of the Working Class in England*. London: Penguin Books.

Entrikin, Nicholas. 1991. *The Betweenness of Place: Towards a Geography of Modernity*. Basingstoke: Macmillan.

Evenson, Norma. 1995. "An Architectural Hybrid." In BOMBAY: *Mosaic of Modern Culture*, edited by S. Patel and A. Thorner, 165–174. New Delhi: Oxford University Press.

Favret-Saada, Jeanne. 1977. *Deadly Words: Witchcraft in the Bocage*. Cambridge: Cambridge University Press.

Favret-Saada, Jeanne. 2012. "Being Affected." HAU: *Journal of Ethnographic Theory* 2 (1): 435–445.

Fenves, Peter. 2011. *The Messianic Reduction: Walter Benjamin and the Shape of Time*. Stanford, CA: Stanford University Press.

Ferguson, James. 1999. *Expectations of Modernity: Myths and Meanings of Urban Life on the Zambian Copperbelt*. Berkeley: University of California Press.

Fernandes, Leela. 1997. *Producing Workers: The Politics of Gender, Class, and Culture in the Calcutta Jute Mills*. Philadelphia: University of Pennsylvania Press.

Fernandes, Leela. 2004. "The Politics of Forgetting: Class Politics, State Power and the Restructuring of Urban Space in India." *Urban Studies* 41 (12): 2415–2430.

Finkelstein, Maura. 2011. "The Chronotope of the Chawl: A Ghost Story in Three Acts." In *The Chawls of Mumbai: Galleries of Life*, edited by N. Adarkar, 49–57. Delhi: ImprintOne.

Finkelstein, Maura. 2015. "Landscapes of Invisibility: Anachronistic Subjects and Allochronous Spaces in Mill Land Mumbai." *City and Society* 27 (3): 250–271.

Fortes, Meyer, and Jack Goody. 1987. *Religion, Morality, and the Person: Essays on Tallensi Religion*. Cambridge: Cambridge University Press.

Foucault, Michel. 1972. *The Archaeology of Knowledge and the Discourse of Language*. New York: Pantheon Books.

Foucault, Michel. 1991. "Governmentality." In *The Foucault Effect: Studies in Governmentality*, edited by G. Burchell, C. Gordon, and P. Miller, 87–104. London: Harvester Wheatsheaf.

Foucault, Michel. 2008. *The Birth of Biopolitics: Lectures at the Collège de France 1978–1979*. Edited by Michel Sennelart, translated by Graham Burchell. Basingstoke: Palgrave.

Freeman, Elizabeth. 2010. *Time Binds: Queer Temporalities, Queer Histories*. Durham, NC: Duke University Press.

Fujii, Lee Ann. 2010. "Shades of Truth and Lies: Interpreting Testimonies of War and Violence." *Journal of Peace Research* 47 (2): 231–241.

Gabrys, Jennifer. 2013. *Digital Rubbish: A Natural History of Electronics*. Ann Arbor: University of Michigan Press.

Gallagher, John, Gordon Johnson, and Anil Seal. 1973. *Locality, Province, and Nation: Essays on Indian Politics 1870 to 1940*. Cambridge: Cambridge University Press.

Garcia, Angela. 2016. "The Blue Years: An Ethnography of a Prison Archive." *Cultural Anthropology* 31 (4): 571–594.

Geddes, Patrick. 1904. *City Development, a Study of Parks, Gardens, and Culture-Institutes: A Report to the Carnegie Dunfermline Trust*. Edinburgh: Geddes and Company.

Geertz, Clifford. 1973. *The Interpretation of Cultures*. New York: Basic Books.

Ghertner, D. Asher. 2014. "India's Urban Revolution: Geographies of Displacement beyond Gentrification." *Environment and Planning A* 46: 1554–1571.

Ghosh, Amitav. 1988. *The Shadow Lines*. Boston: Houghton Mifflin.

Gibson-Graham, J. K. 2008. "Diverse Economies: Performative Practices for 'Other Worlds.'" *Progress in Human Geography* 32 (5): 613–632.

Gladman, Renee. 2003. *The Activist*. Berkeley: Krupskaya.

Gladman, Renee. 2010. *Event Factory*. St. Louis, MO: Dorothy Project.

Gladman, Renee. 2011. *The Ravickians*. St. Louis, MO: Dorothy Project.

Gladman, Renee. 2013. *Ana Patova Crosses a Bridge*. St. Louis, MO: Dorothy Project.

Gladman, Renee. 2017. *Houses of Ravicka*. St. Louis, MO: Dorothy Project.

Good, Byron. 1994. *Medicine, Rationality, and Experience: An Anthropological Perspective*. Cambridge: Cambridge University Press.

Gordillo, Gastón R. 2014. *Rubble: The Afterlife of Destruction*. Durham, NC: Duke University Press.

Gordon, Avery. 1997. *Ghostly Matters: Haunting and the Sociological Imagination*. Minneapolis: University of Minnesota Press.

Gray, Robert. 1996. *The Factory Question and Industrial England, 1830–1860*. New York: Cambridge University Press.

Gupta, Dipankar. 1982. *Nativism in a Metropolis: The Shiv Sena in Bombay*. New Delhi: Manohar.

Gupta, Dipankar. 2000. *Culture, Space, and the Nation-State: From Sentiment to Structure*. New Delhi: Sage.

Halberstam, Judith. 2005. *In a Queer Time and Place: Transgender Bodies, Subcultural Lives*. New York: New York University Press.

Hankins, Joseph D. 2014. *Working Skin: Making Leather, Making a Multicultural Japan*. Berkeley: University of California Press.

Hansen, Thomas Blom. 1999. *The Saffron Wave: Democracy and Hindu Nationalism in Modern India*. Princeton, NJ: Princeton University Press.

Hansen, Thomas Blom. 2001. *Wages of Violence: Naming and Identity in Postcolonial Bombay*. Princeton, NJ: Princeton University Press.

Hansen, Thomas Blom. 2008. "The Political Theology of Violence in Contemporary India." *South Asia Multidisciplinary Academic Journal* 2 ("Outraged Communities"). https://journals.openedition.org/samaj/1872.

Hansen, Thomas Blom. 2012. *Melancholia of Freedom: Anxiety, Race and Everyday Life in a South African Township*. Princeton, NJ: Princeton University Press.

Hanssen, Beatrice. 1998. *Walter Benjamin's Other History: Of Stones, Animals, Human Beings, and Angels*. Berkeley: University of California Press.

Haraway, Donna. 1985. "Manifesto for Cyborgs: Science, Technology, and Socialist Feminism in the 1980s." *Socialist Review* 80: 65–108.

Haraway, Donna. 1991. "A Cyborg Manifesto: Science, Technology, and Socialist-Feminism in the Late Twentieth Century." In *Simians, Cyborgs, and Women: The Reinvention of Nature*, 149–182. New York: Routledge.

Harms, Erik. 2011. *Saigon's Edge: On the Margins of Ho Chi Minh City*. Minneapolis: University of Minnesota Press.

Harris, Andrew. 2012. "The Metonymic Urbanism of Twenty-First-Century Mumbai." *Urban Studies* 49 (13): 2955–2973.

Harris, Nigel. 1995. "Bombay in the Global Economy." In *Bombay: Metaphor for Modern India*, edited by S. Patel and A. Thorner, 47–63. Bombay: Oxford University Press.

Harrison, R., and J. Schofield. 2001. *Wages of Violence: Naming and Identity in Postcolonial Bombay*. Princeton, NJ: Princeton University Press.

Harrison, R., and J. Schofield. 2010. *After Modernity: Archaeological Approaches to the Contemporary Past*. New York: Oxford University Press.

Harriss-White, Barbara. 2003. *India Working: Essays on Society and Economy*. Cambridge: Cambridge University Press.

Hartman, Saidiya. 2008. "Venus in Two Acts." *Small Axe* 12 (2): 1–14.

Harvey, David. 2000. *Spaces of Hope*. Berkeley: University of California Press.

Harvey, David. 2005. *A Brief History of Neoliberalism*. Oxford: Oxford University Press.

Harvey, David. 2006. *The Limits to Capital*. New edition. London: Verso Books.

Harvey, David. 2008. "The Right to the City." *New Left Review* 53: 23–40.

Hazareesingh, Sandip. 2007. *The Colonial City and the Challenge of Modernity: Urban Hegemonies and Civic Contestations in Bombay City, 1900–1925*. Hyderabad: Orient Longman.

Hecht, Tobias. 2007. *Afterlife*. Durham, NC: Duke University Press.

Hell, J., and A. Schönle. 2010. *Ruins of Modernity*. Durham, NC: Duke University Press.

Herzfeld, Michael. 1991. *A Place in History: Monumental and Social Time in a Cretan Town*. Princeton, NJ: Princeton University Press.

Honeyman, Katherine. 2007. *Child Workers in England, 1780–1820: Parish Apprentices and the Making of the Early Industrial Labour Force*. New York: Routledge.

Hoskins, Janet. 1998. *Biographical Objects: How Things Tell the Stories of People's Lives*. New York: Routledge.

Humphries, Jane. 2010. *Childhood and Child Labour in the British Industrial Revolution*. New York: Cambridge University Press.

Hunt, Nancy Rose. 2016. *A Nervous State: Violence, Remedies, and Reverie in Colonial Congo*. Durham, NC: Duke University Press.

Husserl, Edmund. 1970. *The Crisis of European Sciences and Transcendental Phenomenology: An Introduction to Phenomenological Philosophy*. Evanston, IL: Northwestern University Press.

Huyssen, Andreas. 2003. *Present Pasts: Urban Palimpsests and the Politics of Memory*. Stanford, CA: Stanford University Press.

Huyssen, Andreas. 2006. "Nostalgia for Ruins." *Grey Room* 23 (Spring): 6–21.

Ingold, Tim. 2000. *The Perception of the Environment: Essays on Livelihood, Dwelling, and Skill*. London: Routledge.

Jackson, Michael. 1983. "Thinking through the Body: An Essay on Understanding Metaphor." *Social Analysis* 14: 127–148.

Jain, S. Lochlann. 2013. *Malignant: How Cancer Becomes Us*. Berkeley: University of California Press.

Jakobson, Roman. 1956. "Two Types of Language and Two Types of Aphasic Disturbances." In *Fundamentals of Language*, 55–82. Gravenhage: Mouton.

Jakobson, Roman, and Morris Halle. 1956. *Fundamentals of Language*. Gravenhage: Mouton.

Jay, Martin. 1998. *Cultural Semantics: Keywords of Our Time*. Amherst: University of Massachusetts Press.

Jessop, R. D., N. Benner, M. Jones, and G. MacLeod. 2003. "State Space in Question." In *State/Space: A Reader*, edited by R. D. Jessop, N. Benner, M. Jones, and G. MacLeod, 1–26. Oxford: Blackwell.

Jha, Manisha. 2013. "Bombay Dyeing Yet to Give Up Prime Mumbai Land to Govt." *Hindu Business Line*, February 10, 2013. https://www.thehindubusinessline.com /companies/bombay-dyeing-yet-to-give-up-prime-mumbai-land-to-govt /article20576541.ece1.

Joshi, Chitra. 2003. *Lost Worlds: Indian Labour and Its Forgotten Histories*. Delhi: Permanent Black.

Joshi, Chitra. 2009. "Despair: The Decline of the Kanpur Textile Mills." In *Industrial Work and Life: An Anthropological Reader*, edited by J. P. Parry, M. Mollona, and G. de Neve, 331–340. New York: Berg.

Joshi, Ram. 1970. "The Shiv Sena: A Movement in Search of Legitimacy." *Asian Survey* 10 (11): 967–978.

Kaatinen, Timo. 2010. *Songs of Travel, Stories of Place: Poetics of Absence in an Eastern Indonesian Society*. Helsinki: Suomalainen Tiedeakatemia Academia Scientiarum Fennica.

Kafer, Alison. 2013. "The Cyborg and the Crip: Critical Encounters." In *Feminist, Queer, Crip*, 103–128. Bloomington: Indiana University Press.

Kalyvas, Andreas. 2008. *Democracy and the Politics of the Extraordinary: Max Weber, Carl Schmitt, and Hannah Arendt*. Cambridge: Cambridge University Press.

Kamath, Naresh. 2011. "5,000 Transit Camp Residents Will Get Houses." *Hindustan Times*, January 29, 2011. https://www.hindustantimes.com/mumbai/5-000-transit -camp-residents-will-get-houses/story-YbxIUpVlAsvE7YsS9wqBlK.htmlharon.

Kammen, Michael. 1991. *Mystic Chords of Memory: The Transformation of Tradition in American Culture*. New York: Knopf.

Kang, Chloe Taft. 2016. *From Steel to Slots: Casino Capitalism in the Postindustrial City*. Cambridge, MA: Harvard University Press.

Kang, Minsoo. 2011. *Sublime Dreams of Living Machines: The Automaton in the European Imagination*. Cambridge, MA: Harvard University Press.

Katzenstein, Mary F. 1973. "Origins of Nativism: The Emergence of the Shiv Sena in Bombay." *Asian Survey* 13 (4): 386–399.

Kaufman, Sharon R. 1985. *The Ageless Self: Sources of Meaning in Late Life*. Madison: University of Wisconsin Press.

Kaufman, Sharon R. 1994. "The Social Construction of Frailty: An Anthropological Perspective." *Journal of Aging Studies* 8: 45–58.

Kaufman, Sharon R., and L. M. Morgan. 2005. "The Anthropology of the Beginnings and Ends of Life." *Annual Review of Anthropology* 34: 317–341.

Kelkar, Suhit. 2006. "Transit Camps Far from Promised Land." *Daily News and Analysis*, May 29, 2006. http://www.dnaindia.com/mumbai/report-transit-camps -far-from-promised-land-1032195.

Ketabgian, Tamara. 2011. *The Lives of Machines: The Industrial Imaginary in Victorian Literature and Culture*. Ann Arbor: University of Michigan Press.

Khan, Naveeda. 2006. "Flaws in the Flow: Roads and Their Modernity in Pakistan." *Social Text* 89 (4): 87–113.

Kojève, Alexandre. 1980. *Introduction to the Reading of Hegel*. Ithaca, NY: Cornell University Press.

Koppikar, Smruti. 2010. "Inner Spaces, Women's Voices." In *The Chawls of Mumbai: Galleries of Life*, edited by N. Adarkar, 119–128. Delhi: ImprintOne.

Koselleck, Reinhart. 2004. *Futures Past: On the Semantics of Historical Time*. New York: Columbia University Press.

Krishnan, Shekhar. 2000. *The Murder of Phoenix Mills*. Pamphlet. Mumbai: Girni Kamgar Sangharsh Samiti (GKSS), Girangaon Bachao Andolan, and Lokshahi Hakk Sanghatana.

Lacan, Jacques. 1991. *The Ego in Freud's Theory and in the Technique of Psychoanalysis, 1954–1955*. Translated by Sylvana Tomaselli. New York: W. W. Norton.

Lacan, Jacques. 1994. *The Four Fundamental Concepts of Psycho-analysis*. Edited by Jacques-Alain Miller, translated by Alan Sheridan. London: Penguin Books.

Lamb, S. 1997. "The Making and Unmaking of Persons: Notes on Aging and Gender in North India." *Ethnos* 25: 279–302.

Lamb, S. 2000. *White Saris and Sweet Mangoes: Aging, Gender, and Body in North India*. Berkeley: University of California Press.

Lamb, S. 2002. "Intimacy in a Transnational Era: The Remaking of Aging among Indian Americans." *Diaspora* 11: 299–330.

Lamb, S. 2009. *Aging and the Indian Diaspora: Cosmopolitan Families in India and Abroad*. Bloomington: Indiana University Press.

Lamb, S. 2014. "Permanent Personhood or Meaningful Decline? Toward a Critical Anthropology of Successful Aging." *Journal of Aging Studies* 29: 41–52.

Larkin, Brian. 2013. "The Politics and Poetics of Infrastructure." *Annual Review of Anthropology* 42: 327–343.

Lavie, Smadar, Kirin Narayan, and Renato Rosaldo. 1993. *Creativity/Anthropology*. Ithaca, NY: Cornell University Press.

Lear, Jonathan. 2006. *Radical Hope: Ethics in the Face of Cultural Devastation*. Cambridge, MA: Harvard University Press.

Lefebvre, Henri. 1991. *The Production of Space*. Translated by Donald Nicholson-Smith. Oxford: Blackwell.

Lefebvre, Henri. 2003. *The Urban Revolution*. Minneapolis: University of Minnesota Press.

Leibing, A. 2005. "The Old Lady from Ipanema: Changing Notions of Old Age in Brazil." *Journal of Aging Studies* 19: 15–31.

Lepselter, Susan. 2016. *The Resonance of Unseen Things: Poetics, Power, Captivity, and UFOs in the American Uncanny*. Ann Arbor: University of Michigan Press.

Linkon, Sherry Lee, and John Russo. 1994. *Steeltown USA: Work and Memory in Youngstown*. Lawrence: University Press of Kansas.

Livingston, Julie. 2003. "Reconfiguring Old Age: Elderly Women and Concerns over Care in Southeastern Botswana." *Medical Anthropology Cross Cultural Studies of Health and Illness* 22: 205–231.

Livingston, Julie. 2012. *Improvising Medicine: An African Oncology Ward in an Emerging Cancer Epidemic*. Durham, NC: Duke University Press.

Lizhi, Xu. 2011. "The Last Graveyard." Libcom.org. https://libcom.org/blog/xulizhi -foxconn-suicide-poetry.

Lock, Margaret. 1993a. "Cultivating the Body: Anthropology and Epistemologies of Bodily Practice and Knowledge." *Annual Review of Anthropology* 22: 133–155.

Lock, Margaret. 1993b. *Encounters with Aging: Mythologies of Menopause in Japan and North America*. Berkeley: University of California Press.

Lock, Margaret, and Judith Farquhar, eds. 2007. *Beyond the Body Proper: Reading the Anthropology of Material Life*. Durham, NC: Duke University Press.

Lockrem, Jessica, and Adonia Lugo. 2012. Editorial Introduction, *Infrastructure*. Online curated collection, *Cultural Anthropology*. http://culanth.org/curated _collections/11-infrastructure.

Longhurst, Robyn. 1997. "(Dis)embodied Geographies." *Progress in Human Geography* 21 (4): 486–501.

Love, Heather. 2007. *Feeling Backward: Loss and the Politics of Queer History*. Cambridge, MA: Harvard University Press.

Low, Setha M., and Neil Smith. 2006. *The Politics of Public Space*. New York: Routledge.

Lowenthal, David. 2015. *The Past Is a Foreign Country Revisited*. Cambridge: Cambridge University Press.

Lukács, Georg. 1971. *History and Class Consciousness: Studies in Marxist Dialectics*. Translated by Rodney Livingstone. Cambridge, MA: MIT Press.

Lynch, Caitrin. 2012. *Retirement on the Line: Age, Work, and Value in an American Factory*. Ithaca, NY: Cornell University Press.

MacKenzie, Donald A. 1996. *Knowing Machines: Essays on Technical Change*. Cambridge, MA: MIT Press.

MacLeod, Gordon. 2002. "From Urban Entrepreneurialism to a 'Revanchist City'? On the Spatial Injustices of Glasgow's Renaissance." *Antipode* 34 (3): 602–624.

Mani, Lata. 1998. *Contentious Traditions: The Debate on Sati in Colonial India*. Berkeley: University of California Press.

Manley, Theodoric. 2005. "The Revanchist City: Downtown Chicago and the Rhetoric of Redevelopment in Bronzeville." Paper presented at the annual meeting of the American Sociological Association, Philadelphia, PA, August 13–16.

Marcus, Sharon. 1999. *Apartment Stories: City and Home in Nineteenth-Century Paris and London*. Berkeley: University of California Press.

Markovits, Claude. 1995. "Bombay as a Business Centre in the Colonial Period: A Comparison with Calcutta." In *Bombay: Metaphor for Modern India*, edited by S. Patel and A. Thorner, 26–46. Bombay: Oxford University Press.

Marriott, McKim. 1965. *Caste Ranking and Community Structure in Five Regions of India and Pakistan*. Poona: Deccan College Postgraduate and Research Institute.

Marriott, McKim. 1990. *India through Hindu Categories*. New Delhi: Sage.

Martin, Emily. 1994. *Flexible Bodies: Tracking Immunity in American Culture from the Days of Polio to the Age of AIDS*. Boston: Beacon Press.

Marx, Karl. 1990. *Capital: A Critique of Political Economy*. 3 vols. Translated by B. Fowkes. London: Penguin Classics.

Massey, Doreen. 1994. *Space, Place, and Gender*. Minneapolis: University of Minnesota Press.

Massumi, Brian. 2002. *Parables for the Virtual: Movement, Affect, Sensation*. Durham, NC: Duke University Press.

Mazzarella, William. 2009. "Affect: What Is It Good For?" In *Enchantments of Modernity: Empire, Nation, Globalization*, edited by Saurabh Dube, 291–309. London: Routledge.

Mazzarella, William. 2017. *The Mana of Mass Society*. Chicago: University of Chicago Press.

McCarthy, Tom. 2005. *Remainder*. New York: Vintage Books.

McGranahan, Carole. 2017. "An Anthropology of Lying: Trump and the Political Sociality of Moral Outrage." *American Ethnologist* 44 (2): 243–248.

Mehrotra, Rahul. 2008. "Negotiating the Static and Kinetic Cities: The Emergent Urbanism of Mumbai." In *Other Cities, Other Worlds: Urban Imaginaries in a Globalizing Age*, edited by A. Huyssen, 205–218. Durham, NC: Duke University Press.

Mehrotra, Rahul, and Sharada Dwiwedi, eds. 2001. *Bombay: The Cities Within*. Bombay: Eminence Designs.

Mehta, Kaiwan. 2009. *Alice in Bhuleshwar: Navigating a Mumbai Neighbourhood*. Bombay: Yoda Press.

Menon, Meena. 2012a. "Mumbai's Mill Workers: A Small but Significant Victory." *NewsClick*, 14 June. https://www.newsclick.in/india/mumbai%E2%80%99s-mill -workers-small-significant-victory.

Menon, Meena. 2012b. *Riots and After in Mumbai: Chronicles of Truth and Reconciliation*. New Delhi: Sage.

Menon, Meena, and Neera Adarkar. 2004. *One Hundred Years, One Hundred Voices: The Millworkers of Girangaon: An Oral History*. Calcutta: Seagull Books.

Menon, Nivedita, and Aditya Nigam. 2007. *Power and Contestation: India since 1989*. New York: Fernwood.

Merleau-Ponty, Maurice. 2002. *Phenomenology of Perception*. London: Routledge and Kegan Paul.

Merrifield, Andrew. 1993. "Place and Space: A Lefebvrian Reconciliation." *Transactions of the Institute of British Geographers* 18 (4): 516–531.

Mhaskar, Sumeet. 2012. "The Unmaking of the Worker-Self in Post-industrial Mumbai: A Study of Ex-Millworkers' Responses to the Closure of Textile Mills in Girangaon." PhD diss., University of Oxford.

Miéville, China. 2009. *The City and the City*. New York: Random House.

Miller, Daniel. 2008. *The Comfort of Things*. Cambridge: Polity.

Moore, Niamh, and Yvonne Whelan, eds. 2007. *Heritage, Memory and the Politics of Identity: New Perspectives on the Cultural Landscapes*. Farnham, UK: Ashgate.

Morgan, Jennifer L. 2004. *Laboring Women: Gender and Reproduction in New World Slavery*. Philadelphia: University of Pennsylvania Press.

Morris, Morris David. 1965. *The Emergence of an Industrial Labor Force in India: A Study of the Bombay Cotton Mills, 1854–1947*. Berkeley: University of California Press.

Muñoz, José Esteban. 1999. *Disidentifications: Queers of Color and the Performance of Politics*. Minneapolis: University of Minnesota Press.

Muri, Allison. 2007. *The Enlightenment Cyborg: A History of Communications and Control in the Human Machine, 1660–1830*. Toronto: University of Toronto Press.

Myerhoff, Barbara. 1978. *Number Our Days*. New York: Simon and Schuster.

Nagarkar, Kiran. 1995. *Ravan & Eddie*. New Delhi: Viking.

Nandy, Ashis. 2001. *An Ambiguous Journey to the City: The Village and Other Odd Ruins of the Self in the Indian Imagination*. New Delhi: Oxford University Press.

Narayan, Kirin. 1989. *Storytellers, Saints, and Scoundrels: Folk Narrative in Hindu Religious Teaching*. Philadelphia: University of Pennsylvania Press.

Narayan, Kirin. 2007. "Ethnography and Fiction: Where Is the Border?" *Anthropology and Humanism* 24 (2): 134–147.

Nardinelli, Clark. 1990. *Child Labour and the Industrial Revolution*. Bloomington: Indiana University Press.

Navaro-Yashin, Yael. 2009. "Affective Space, Melancholic Objects: Ruination and the Production of Anthropological Knowledge." *Journal of the Royal Anthropological Institute* 15: 1–18.

O'Connor, Erin. 2000. *Raw Material: Producing Pathology in Victorian Culture*. Durham, NC: Duke University Press.

Orzeck, Reecia. 2007. "What Does Not Kill You: Historical Materialism and the Body." *Environment and Planning D: Society and Space* 25: 496–514.

Oswin, Natalie. 2014. "Queer Time in Global City Singapore: Neoliberal Futures and the 'Freedom to Love.'" *Sexualities* 17 (4): 412–433.

Ozeki, Ruth. 2013. *A Tale for the Time Being*. New York: Penguin Books.

Pamuk, Orhan. 2009. *The Museum of Innocence*. New York: Vintage International.

Pandey, Gyanendra. 1990. *The Construction of Communalism in Colonial North India*. Delhi: Oxford University Press.

Pandian, Anand. 2009. *Crooked Stalks: Cultivating Virtue in South India*. Durham, NC: Duke University Press.

Papalias, Penelope. 2005. *Genres of Recollection: Archival Poetics and Modern Greece*. New York: Palgrave Macmillan.

Parish, Steven M. 1994. *Moral Knowing in a Hindu Sacred City: An Exploration of Mind, Emotion, and Self*. New York: Columbia University Press.

Parry, Jonathan P. 1999. "Lords of Labour: Working and Shirking in Bhilai." *Contributions to Indian Sociology* 33: 107–140.

Parry, Jonathan P. 2008. "The Sacrifices of Modernity in a Soviet-Built Steel Town in Central India." In *On the Margins of Religion*, edited by Frances Pine and João de Pina-Cabral, 233–262. Oxford: Berghahn.

Parry, Jonathan P. 2009. "Satanic Fields, Pleasant Mills: Work in an Indian Steel Plant." In *Industrial Work and Life: An Anthropological Reader*, edited by J. P. Parry, M. Mollona, and G. de Neve, 65–82. Oxford: Berg.

Parry, Jonathan P., Massimiliano Mollona, and Geert de Neve, eds. 2009. *Industrial Work and Life: An Anthropological Reader*. Oxford: Berg.

Pendse, Sandeep, Neera Adarkar, and Maura Finkelstein. 2011. "Overview." In *The Chawls of Mumbai: Galleries of Life*, edited by N. Adarkar, 1–12. Delhi: ImprintOne.

Personal Narratives Group. 1989. *Interpreting Women's Lives: Feminist Theory and Personal Narratives*. Bloomington: Indiana University Press.

Petryna, Adriana. 2002. *Life Exposed: Biological Citizens after Chernobyl*. Princeton, NJ: Princeton University Press.

Phadke, Y. D. 1979. *Politics and Language*. Bombay: Himalaya Publishing House.

Phelan, Craig, Aditya Nigam, Sonia McKay, Jan Breman, and Rohini Hensman. 2011. "Labor History Symposium: Rohini Hensman, Workers, Unions and Global Capitalism: Lessons from India." *Labor History* 52 (4): 535–562.

Pine, Jason. 2016. "Last Chance Incorporated." *Cultural Anthropology* 31 (2): 297–318.

Pinto, Sarah. 2008. *Where There Is No Midwife: Birth and Loss in Rural India*. Oxford: Berghahn Books.

Portelli, Alessandro. 1991. *The Death of Luigi Trastulli and Other Stories: Form and Meaning in Oral History*. Albany: State University of New York Press.

Povinelli, Elizabeth. 2011. "The Woman on the Other Side of the Wall: Archiving the Otherwise in Postcolonial Digital Archives." *differences: A Journal of Feminist Cultural Studies* 22 (1): 146–171.

Prakash, Gyan. 2011. *Mumbai Fables*. Princeton, NJ: Princeton University Press.

Proust, Marcel. 2002. *Swann's Way*. Translated by Lydia Davis. New York: Penguin Books.

Puar, Jasbir. 2005. "Queer Times, Queer Assemblages." *Social Text* 23 (3–4): 121–139.

Pyne, Stephen. 2001. *Fire: A Brief History*. Seattle: University of Washington Press.

Radcliffe-Brown, A. R. 1952. *Structure and Function in Primitive Society: Essays and Addresses*. Glencoe, IL: Free Press.

Rao, Nikhil. 2012. *House, but No Garden: Apartment Living in Bombay's Suburbs, 1898–1964*. Minneapolis: University of Minnesota Press.

Ray, Bharati. 1995. *From the Seams of History: Essays on Indian Women*. Delhi: Oxford University Press.

Riello, Giorgio. 2013. *Cotton: The Fabric That Made the Modern World*. Cambridge: Cambridge University Press.

Riley, Patrick. 1981. "Introduction to the Reading of Alexander Kojève." *Political Theory* 9 (1): 5–48.

Riskin, Jessica. 2003. "The Defecating Duck, Or, The Ambiguous Origins of Artificial Life." *Critical Inquiry* 29 (4): 599–633.

Riskin, Jessica. 2007. *Genesis Redux: Essays in the History and Philosophy of Artificial Life*. Chicago: University of Chicago Press.

Robertson, Jennifer. 2001. "Japan's First Cyborg? Miss Nippon, Eugenics and Wartime Technologies of Beauty, Body and Blood." *Body and Society* 7 (1): 1–34.

Rofel, Lisa. 2009. "The Poetics of Productivity." In *Industrial Work and Life: An Anthropological Reader*, edited by J. P. Parry, M. Mollona, and G. de Neve, 341–362. Oxford: Berg.

Rose, Sarah F. 2005. "'Crippled' Hands: Disability in Labor and Working-Class History." *Labor: Studies in Working-Class History of the Americas* 2 (1): 27–54.

Rosenthal, Donald B. 1977. *The Expansive Elite: District Politics and State Policy-Making in India*. Berkeley: University of California Press.

Roy, Ananya, and Aihwa Ong, eds. 2011. *Worlding Cities: Asian Experiments and the Art of Being Global*. Malden MA, Oxford: Wiley-Blackwell.

Rudolph, Lloyd I., and Susanne Hoeber Rudolph. 1967. *The Modernity of Tradition: Political Development in India*. Chicago: University of Chicago Press.

Said, Edward. 1984. "Reflections on Exile." *Granta* 13: 159–172.

Samuel, Raphael. 1977. "Workshop of the World: Steam Power and Hand Technology in Mid-Victorian Britain." *History Workshop Journal* 3 (1): 6–72.

Sassen, Saskia, ed. 2007. *Deciphering the Global: Its Scales, Spaces and Subjects*. New York: Routledge.

Scappettone, Jennifer. 2016. *The Republic of Exit 43: Outtakes and Scores from an Archaeology and Pop-Up Opera of the Corporate Dump*. Berkeley: Atelos.

Scarry, Elaine. 1985. *The Body in Pain: The Making and Unmaking of the World*. Oxford: Oxford University Press.

Scheper-Hughes, Nancy. 1992. *Death without Weeping: The Violence of Everyday Life in Brazil*. Durham, NC: Duke University Press.

Schwalm, Leslie A. 1997. *A Hard Fight for We: Women's Transition from Slavery to Freedom in South Carolina*. Champaign: University of Illinois Press.

Scott, James C. 1987. *Weapons of the Weak: Everyday Forms of Peasant Resistance*. New Haven, CT: Yale University Press.

Scott, Joan. 1991. "The Evidence of Experience." *Critical Inquiry* 17 (4): 773–797.

Seal, Anil. 1968. *The Emergence of Indian Nationalism: Competition and Collaboration in the Later Nineteenth Century*. Cambridge: Cambridge University Press.

Sedgwick, Eve Kosofsky. 2002. *Touching Feeling: Affect, Pedagogy, Performativity*. Durham, NC: Duke University Press.

Sen, Atreyee. 2007. *Shiv Sena Women: Violence and Communalism in a Bombay Slum*. Bloomington: Indiana University Press.

Sen, Samita. 1999. "At the Margins: Women Workers in the Bengal Jute Industry." In *The Worlds of Indian Industrial Labour*, edited by J. P. Parry, J. Breman, and K. Kapadia, 239–270. New Delhi: Sage.

Shackel, Paul S., and Mathew Palus. 2006. "Remembering an Industrial Landscape." *International Journal of Historical Archaeology* 10 (1): 49–71.

Sharp, Leslie. 2000. "The Commodification of the Body and Its Parts." *Annual Review of Anthropology* 29: 287–328.

Shibutani, Tamotsu. 1966. *Improvised News: A Sociological Study of Rumor*. Indianapolis: Bobs-Merrill.

Simmel, Georg. 1965. "The Ruin." In *Essays on Sociology, Philosophy and Aesthetics*, edited by Kurt H. Wolff, 259–266. New York: Harper and Row.

Simpson, Audra. 2016. *Mohawk Interruptus: Political Life across the Borders of Settler States*. Durham, NC: Duke University Press.

Slavishak, Edward. 2008. *Bodies of Work: Civic Display and Labor in Industrial Pittsburgh*. Durham, NC: Duke University Press.

Sloterdijk, Peter. 1988. *Critique of Cynical Reason*. Translated by Michael Eldred. Minneapolis: University of Minneapolis Press.

Sloterdijk, Peter. 2011. *Bubbles: Spheres*. Vol. 1, *Microspherology*. Translated by Wieland Hoban. Los Angeles: Semiotext(e).

Smith, Neil. 1996. *The New Urban Frontier: Gentrification and the Revanchist City*. London: Routledge.

Smith, Neil. 2002. "New Globalism, New Urbanism: Gentrification as Global Urban Strategy." *Antipode: A Radical Journal of Geography* 34 (3): 427–450.

Smith, Neil. 2008. *Uneven Development: Nature, Capital, and the Production of Space*. 3rd ed. Athens: University of Georgia Press.

Smith, Neil, and Peter Williams. 1986. *Gentrification of the City*. Boston: Allen and Unwin.

Soja, Edward. 1996. *Thirdspace: Journeys to Los Angelos and Other Real and Imagined Places*. Oxford: Blackwell.

Sokolovsky, Jay. 2009. *The Cultural Context of Aging: Worldwide Perspectives*. Westport, CT: Praeger.

Solnit, Rebecca. 2005. *A Field Guide to Getting Lost*. New York: Penguin Books.

Solomon, Harris. 2016. *Metabolic Living: Food, Fat, and the Absorption of Illness in India*. Durham, NC: Duke University Press.

Stanton, Cathy. 2006. *The Lowell Experiment: Public History in the Post-industrial City*. Amherst: University of Massachusetts Press.

Steedman, Carolyn. 1987. *Landscape for a Good Woman: A Story of Two Lives*. New Brunswick, NJ: Rutgers University Press.

Steedman, Carolyn. 2001. *Dust*. Manchester: Manchester University Press.

Stevenson Lisa. 2014. *Life beside Itself: Imagining Care in the Canadian Arctic*. Berkeley: University of California Press.

Stewart, Kathleen. 1996. *A Space on the Side of the Road: Cultural Poetics in an "Other" America*. Princeton, NJ: Princeton University Press.

Stewart, Kathleen. 2007. *Ordinary Affects*. Durham, NC: Duke University Press.

Stoler, Ann Laura. 2008. "Imperial Debris: Reflections on Ruin and Ruination." *Cultural Anthropology* 23 (2): 191–219.

Stoler, Ann Laura. 2009. *Along the Archival Grain: Epistemic Anxieties and Colonial Common Sense*. Princeton, NJ: Princeton University Press.

Stoller, Paul. 1995. *Embodying Colonial Memories: Spirit Possession, Power, and the Hauka in West Africa*. New York: Routledge.

Stoller, Paul. 1997. *Sensuous Scholarship*. Philadelphia: University of Pennsylvania Press.

Surve, Vinay. 2011. "Revitalizing Mumbai Textile Mill Lands for the City." Master's thesis, University of Massachusetts, Amherst.

Taussig, Michael. 1993. *Mimesis and Alterity: A Particular History of the Senses*. New York: Routledge.

Taussig, Michael. 2004. *My Cocaine Museum*. Chicago: University of Chicago Press.

Taylor, Diana. 2003. *The Archive and the Repertoire: Performing Cultural Memory in the Americas*. Durham, NC: Duke University Press.

Thackeray, Bal. 1967. "Shiv Sena Speaks." *Marmik Cartoon Weekly* (Bombay).

Thiranagama, Sharika. 2011. *In My Mother's House: Civil War in Sri Lanka*. Philadelphia: University of Pennsylvania Press.

Thrift, Nigel. 2000. "Performing Cultures in the New Economy." *Annals of the Association of American Geographers* 4: 674–692.

Tindall, Gillian. 1982. *City of Gold: The Biography of Bombay*. London: Temple Smith.

Trentmann, F. 2009. "Materiality in the Future of History: Things, Practices and Politics." *Journal of British Studies* 48 (2): 283–307.

Tuan, Y. F. 1979. "Space and Place: Humanistic Perspective." In *Philosophy in Geography*, edited by S. Gale and G. Olsson, 387–427. Dordrecht: Springer.

Upadhyay, Shashi Bhushan. 2004. *Existence, Identity, and Mobilization: The Cotton Millworkers of Bombay, 1890–1919*. New Delhi: Manohar.

van Wersch, Hugo. 1992. *The Bombay Textile Strike 1982–1983*. Bombay: Oxford University Press.

van Wersch, Hugo. 1995. "Flying a Kite and Losing the String: Communication during the Bombay Textile Strikes." In *Bombay: Metaphor for Modern India*, edited by S. Patel and A. Thorner, 64–88. Bombay: Oxford University Press.

Varma, Rashmi. 2004. "Provincializing the Global City: From Bombay to Mumbai." *Social Text* 22: 65–89.

Voss, Barbara. 2007. "Image, Text, Object: Interpreting Documents and Artifacts as 'Labors of Representation.'" *Historical Archaeology* 41 (4): 144–168.

Voss, Barbara. 2008. *The Archaeology of Ethnogenesis: Race and Sexuality in Colonial San Francisco*. Berkeley: University of California Press.

Voss, Barbara. 2010. "Matter Out of Time: The Paradox of the 'Contemporary Past.'" *Archaeologies: Journal of the World Archaeological* Congress 6 (1): 181–192.

Voss, Barbara. 2012. "Curation as Research: A Case Study in Orphaned and Under-reported Archaeological Collections." *Archaeological Dialogues* 19 (2): 145–169.

Voss, Paul J., and Marta L. Werner. 1999. *The Poetics of the Archive: Studies in the Literary Imagination*. Atlanta: Georgia State University Press.

Wacquant, Loïc. 2003. *Body and Soul: Notebooks of an Apprentice Boxer*. New York: Oxford University Press.

Walcott, Derek. 1962. *In a Green Night: Poems 1948–1960*. London: Jonathan Cape.

Walley, Christine. 2013. *Exit Zero: Family and Class in Postindustrial Chicago*. Chicago: University of Chicago Press.

Watkins, Claire Vaye. 2015. *Gold Fame Citrus*. New York: Riverhead Books.

Weber, Max. 1978. *Economy and Society: An Outline of Interpretive Sociology*. 2 vols. Translated by C. Wittich. Berkeley: University of California Press.

Wendling, Amy E. 2009. *Karl Marx on Technology and Alienation*. New York: Palgrave.

White, Luise. 2000. *Speaking with Vampires: Rumor and History in East and Central Africa*. Berkeley: University of California Press.

Whitehead, Colson. 1999. *The Intuitionist*. New York: Anchor Books.

Whitehead, Judy, and Nitin More. 2007. "Revanchism in Mumbai? Political Economy of Rent Gaps and Urban Restructuring in a Global City." *Economic and Political Weekly* 42 (25): 2428–2434.

Williams, Raymond. 1977. *Marxism and Literature*. Oxford: Oxford University Press.

Wolkowitz, Carol. 2006. *Bodies at Work*. London: Sage.

Yablon, N. 2009. *Untimely Ruins: An Archaeology of American Urban Modernity, 1819–1919*. Chicago: University of Chicago Press.

Yanagisako, Sylvia. 2002. *Producing Culture and Capital: Family Firms in Italy*. Princeton, NJ: Princeton University Press.

Yanagisako, Sylvia. 2012. "Immaterial and Industrial Labor: On False Binaries in Hardt and Negri's Trilogy." *Focaal: Journal of Global and Historical Anthropology*, no. 64: 16–23. Special section edited by Ara Wilson.

Yuen, Wong Kin. 2010. "On the Edge of Spaces: 'Blade Runner,' 'Ghost in the Shell,' and Hong Kong's Cityscape." *Science Fiction Studies* 27: 1–21.

Yuknavitch, Lidia. 2011. *The Chronology of Water*. Portland, OR: Hawthorne Books.

Zaher, Maged. 2016. *The Consequence of My Body*. New York: Nightboat Books.

Zeiderman, Austin. 2016. *Endangered City: The Politics of Security and Risk in Bogotá*. Durham, NC: Duke University Press.

Žižek, Slavoj. 2008. *The Sublime Object of Ideology*. London: Verso.

Index

Note: page numbers in italics indicate illustrations

Buchli, Victor, 211–212n23
Burton, Antoinette, 6, 208n4
Butler, Judith, 202nn10–11
Byler, Darren, 115

Calvino, Italo, 29, 115
Canetti, Elias, 156
Carney, Judith A., 65
Chandavarkar, Rajnarayan, 131, 214n30
chawls: as allochronous space, 88; archive
  of, 87–88, 97–108, 115–116; BDD, 90, 112–
  114; chronotope of, 108–111; communal
  kitchens in, 90–91; defined, 89; domestic
  decay in, 89–91; domestic/public space,
  110; dwellers as anachronisms, 110; fear of
  development in, 111–114; flooding in, 113–
  115; gallas, 90; habitation, 22, 30; palimpsest, 113; as sites of memory, 87–88, 95,
  115–116; spatial ruptures in, 97–108; time, as
  queer time, 25–26, 87, 92–96, 108, 110–111,
  114–115, 116; vibrancy of, 91
citizenship, 44, 136
City and the City, The (Miéville), 44–45
City of Gold / Lalbaug, Parel (film), 149–151
Closed Mills Committee, 46
Congress Party, 46, 136, 142, 218n30
Cornish, Mary, 138
curation, use of term, 194n7
"Cyborg Manifesto, A" (Haraway), 66
cyborg workers, 25, 62, 63–67, 73–76, 80,
  83–84

Dawdy, Shannon Lee, 97, 209n5
Derrida, Jacques, 181, 208n1
Development Control Rules (DCRs), 11, 46;
  one-third plan (DCR-58), 10–12
Dhanraj Spinning and Weaving, Ltd. (pseud.),
  1–5, 2, 3, 36, 37, 59, 62, 78–79, 82, 173, 178,
  183–185; as archive of lively ruination,
  13–16, 20, 25, 31–32, 49, 52, 56, 61, 155,
  191–192; as archive of shifting developments, 173–177; as archive of unvisible
  workers, 34–40; deindustrialization of,
  188; extralegal activities in, 42–43; financial
  distress of, 153; gossip in, 158–159; growth
  of ruins, 181–188; as industrial/postindus-

trial, 45–46, 53–54; infrastructure of, 41;
  as landfill, 159, 160; land sales by, 39; legal
  battles, 12–13, 176–178; mill fires, 151, 152,
  152–164, 163, 165, 166; owners, 12, 34–35, 38,
  42–43, 80, 142–143, 152–153, 166–168, 172,
  174, 189; reputation, 34; as rumor mill, 158–
  161, 169, 170–172, 176, 179–180; as space of
  disruption, 7; as uncanny ruin, 13, 58, 157,
  196–197n19; as unregulated, 34–35; walking
  through ruins of, 29–33. See also mill lands;
  mill workers
Dick, Phillip K., 63
Dinshaw, Carolyn, 92, 208n2
disidentification, 117, 125–126
D'Monte, Daryl, 220n39
Dr. Bhau Daji Lad City Museum, 3, 4, 23,
  190

Easterling, Keller, 22
Ebron, Paulla, 70
Eiland, Howard, 206n16
Ellison, Ralph, 40
enslavement, 65
Erfahrung (long experience), 70–73
Erlebnis (isolated experience), 70
Event Factory (Gladman), 16–18, 58, 60, 83
exclusion, 41, 94, 117, 127, 146
expectation, 92–93, 173, 180
experience, archive of, 70–73

Facebook, 55
failure of fluency, 16
Fenves, Peter, 222n1
Ferguson, James, 92, 93
fieldwork methodology, 16–24
food riots (1919), 90
Freeman, Elizabeth, 95
Fresh Kills Landfill (NY), 159
Fujii, Lee Ann, 122

Gandhi, Indira, 136, 142
Gandhi, Rajiv, 136
general textile strike (1918), 90
Ghati, 131–132
Ghosh, Amitav, 7
ghostly matter, 19–20

Maharashtrians (*continued*)
    reservation for workers, 119; xenophobia toward North Indians, 118–119, 122, 123–124, 130–132, 137
Mahindra Lifespaces, 12–13, 39, 82, 153, 170–171
Marmik (cartoon weekly), 137
Matulya Mills fire, 151
Mazzarella, William, 24, 199–200n37
McCarthy, Tom, 89
Mehta, Kaiwan, 91
memory: archive of, 24, 61, 73; chawls as sites of, 87–88, 95, 115–116; defined, 1; embedded in ruins, 16–17; embodied, 63–64, 72, 73; identity formation and, 129; production, 23; public, 31, 70–71
Menon, Meena, 55
metadata, defined, 122
MGKU. *See* Maharashtra Girni Kamghar Union
MHADA. *See* Maharashtra Housing and Area Development Authority
Miéville, China, 29, 44–46
mill fires, *152*, 152–164, *163*, *165*, *166*; archive of, 152–157; arson in, 152–153, 155, 162; film about, 149–151; interpretation of, 151; owners and, 152–153, 166–168, 172, 174, 178–179; retrenchment from, 153, 158, 162, 164, 165, 195n14; rumor of, 156–164
mill industry, *32*; decline of, 9–10; dependence on, 9; effect of strike on, 135, 138–141, 143; functional mills, 52; lively ruination of, 51; one-third plan, 10–12
mill lands: development rules, 46, 173; as industrial/postindustrial, 41; legal battles, 12–13, 176–177; lively ruins of, 7, 15, 31–32, *34*; as locked, 10; museum space of, 188–189; as mythological creations, 25; mythologies of, 32; neighborhoods, 4–5; sale of, 10–11; as temporal ruptures, 25; turning into malls, 155; walking through ruins of, 29–33. *See also* chawls
mill workers: accumulated exhaustion of, 72; as anachronistic subjects, 25, 174, 187; *badli* (temporary), 49, 67–68, 103; bodily archives of, 25, 57–67, 73–76, 83–84; call-and-response among, 72–73; as chimeric, 63–67; dependence on industry, 9; desire

of, 41–43; employment for, 46–49; existence of, 5; experience of, 23; friendships of, 145; housing for, 46, 47, 48, 54, 55; independence movement by, 30; as industrial cyborgs, 25, 62, 63–67, 73–76, 80, 83–84; nonrecognition of, 43–44; percentage of Maharashtrians, 119, 136, 139–140, 143–144; percentage of North Indians, 130, 139–140, 143–144; precarity of, 54–55; respectability of, 50–51; retirement concerns, 80–81; retrenchment of, 54, 153, 158, 162, 164, 165, 195n14; storytelling by, 5, 32, 63, 68, 70–71, 73–74, 103, 110, 144, 155, 158, 206n13; unvisible, archive of, 34–40; visible vs. unvisible, 33, 38, 44, 46, 49, 53–56; working conditions, 68–69
Mimesis and Alterity (Taussig), 17
mimetic archive, 24
misrecognition, 16–17, 19, 33
MNS. *See* Maharashtra Navnirman Sena
modernity, 14
Moon Mills fire, 150–151
Moraraji Mills fire, 151
Morgan, Jennifer L., 65
Mukesh Mills fire, 151
Mumbai: affectsphere of, 21–23; cityscape of, 20–21, *21*; fieldwork methodology, 16–24; housing policy, 89–90; as industrial and postindustrial cities, 45–49, 53, 174–175; infrastructure, 20–24, 41, 52; lively ruins of, 13–16; obsolete economies in, 48, 192; photographic perspective of, 17–19, *18*; redevelopment in, 4, 52; remapping, 8; as soot-stained, 153–155, *154*; trade unions in, 30; as unvisible, 50–52; urban gentrification, 155–156, 174
Muñoz, José Esteban, 117, 126

Nagarkar, Kiran, 129
National Textile Corporation (NTC), 52, 151
Navaratri festival, 76–77
negative affects, theory of, 148
Negative Dialectics (Adorno), 127
nonidentity, 26, 117, 126–129, 141, 148. *See also* identity
nonrecognition: archive of, 33, 40–44; unvisibility and, 44; use of term, 25, 41

North Indians: gender roles, 133–135; identity, 26, 126, 129–135, 141, 146; as other, 126–128, 129, 146; percentage of workforce, 130, 139–140, 143–144; on textile strike, 138, 144; xenophobia toward, 118–119, 122, 123–124, 130–132, 137

nostalgia, 93, 110, 191, 195n14

Oswin, Natalie, 94
Ozeki, Ruth, 57

Parry, Jonathan P., 158
Partners for Urban Knowledge, Action and Research (PUKAR), 3–4, 23–24, 31, 41, 54, 190
Peninsula Developers/Development, 39, 182
Phoenix Mills, 103, 106; fire, 149, 151
Pine, Jason, 198n26
prognostic time, 94
Proust, Marcel, 16, 128
puja (ritual), 77, 78
PUKAR. *See* Partners for Urban Knowledge, Action and Research

queerness: archives of, 91; of chawl time, 25–26, 87, 92–96, 108, 110–111, 114–115, 116; exclusion and, 211n19; theory, 94, 211n20; time, studies on, 208n2

Rani Baug gardens, 117–118, *118*, 144
Rashtriya Mill Mazdoor Sangh (RMMS), 40, 46, 49, 68, 103, 130, 135–136, 142, 175, 191
Ray, Sharmistha, *8, 9, 124, 125*
Republic of Exit 43, The (Scappettone), 159
RMMS. *See* Rashtriya Mill Mazdoor Sangh
ruins: defined, 1; disappearance of, 188–192; growth of, 181–188, *190*; lively, 13–16, 31–32, 48, 61, 155, 188, 191–192; studies, field of, 15; temporality of, 6; uncanny, 13, 58, 157, 196–197n19
rumor mill, 156–164, 169, 170–172, 176, 179–180

Said, Edward, 110
Samant, Datta, 129, 135–143

Scappettone, Jennifer, 159
Scheper-Hughes, Nancy, 19
Schwalm, Leslie A., 65
Scott, Joan, 70
Sedgwick, Eve Kosofsky, 148
Shivaraj Bhavan, 97–103, *99, 100, 102*, 213n25
Shiv Sena, 124, 129, 132, 136–137, 139, 218–219n34
Shri Nagji Chawl, 103–107, *104, 105*
shrug, as response, 114–115
Sitaram Mills fire, 151
Sloterdijk, Peter, 57, 64
Smith, Neil, 222n4
Solnit, Rebecca, 1
Solomon, Harris, 65
South Indians, 137
Steedman, Carolyn Kay, 67, 153
Stewart, Kathleen, 13, 58
Stoler, Ann Laura, 201n5
storage godowns, 36–39, 48, 79, 126, 153, 166–167, 168, 171–172, 196n16
"Storyteller, The" (Benjamin), 58
storytelling, 5, 32, 63, 68, 70–71, 73–74, 103, 110, 144, 155, 158, 206n13, 207n21
sweatshops: female workers in, 37–38; unregulated, 34–35, 45, 48, 196n16; unvisibility of, 38, 45

Taussig, Michael, 17
taxi driving, 50–51
Taylor, Diana, 194n8, 199n34
textile mills. *See* mill industry
Thackeray, Bal, 136–138
Tindall, Gillian, 23
truth in ethnographic fieldwork, 118–123
26 July flood (2005), 114

untruths: archive of, 26, 121–123; as ethnographic material, 122, 125, 147–148, 216n13; about great textile strike, 26, 121, 125, 128, 129; about identity, 26, 126–129, 146, 216n11, 216–217n15, 217n18; as theory of negative effects, 148
unvisibility: archive of, 34–40; vs. invisibility, 45; of mill workers, 33, 38, 44, 46, 49, 53–56; nonrecognition and, 44; of sweat

unvisibility (*continued*)
    shops, 38, 45; use of term, 25, 33; viewing, 50–52
urban gentrification, 155–156, 174

Voss, Barbara, 209n6

Walcott, Derek, 149
Walley, Christine, 204n4
Watkins, Claire Vaye, 177

White, Luise, 159
Whitehead, Colson, 111–112, 198n28
writing as magic, 18

Xu Lizhi, 76

Yuknavitch, Lidia, 188

Zaher, Maged, 44

www.ingramcontent.com/pod-product-compliance
Lightning Source LLC
Chambersburg PA
CBHW050346270326
41926CB00016B/3619